D1565758

This book may be kept

FOURTEEN DAYS

A fine will be charged for each day the book is kept overtime.

GAYLORD 142			PRINTED IN U.S.A.

Historical Problems:
Studies and Documents

Edited by
PROFESSOR G. R. ELTON
University of Cambridge

6
AGRARIAN PROBLEMS IN THE SIXTEENTH CENTURY AND AFTER

In the same series

Further volumes in preparation

AGRARIAN PROBLEMS IN THE SIXTEENTH CENTURY AND AFTER

Eric Kerridge
University College of North Wales
Author of The Agricultural Revolution

LONDON · GEORGE ALLEN AND UNWIN LTD
NEW YORK · BARNES AND NOBLE, INC

PRINTED IN GREAT BRITAIN
in 10 on 11 point Plantin type
BY WILLMER BROTHERS LIMITED
BIRKENHEAD

37, 021

TO FRANK

GENERAL INTRODUCTION

The reader and the teacher of history might be forgiven for thinking that there are now too many series of historical documents in existence, all claiming to offer light on particular problems and all able to fulfil their claims. At any rate, the general editor of yet another series feels obliged to explain why he is helping one more collection of such volumes into existence.

One purpose of this series is to put at the disposal of the student original material illustrating historical problems, but this is no longer anything out of the way. A little less usual is the decision to admit every sort of historical question: there are no barriers of time or place or theme. However, what really distinguishes this enterprise is the fact that it combines generous collections of documents with introductory essays long enough to explore the theme widely and deeply. In the doctrine of educationalists, it is the original documents that should be given to the student; in the experience of teachers, documents thrown naked before the untrained mind turn from pearls to paste. The study of history cannot be confined either to the learning up of results without a consideration of the foundations, or to a review of those foundations without the assistance of the expert mind. The task of teaching involves explanation and instruction, and these volumes recognize this possibly unfashionable fact. Beyond that, they enable the writers to say new and important things about their subject matter: to write history of an exploratory kind, which is the only important historical writing there is.

As a result, each volume will be a historical monograph worth the attention which all such monographs deserve, and each volume will stand on its own. While the format of the series is uniform, the contents will vary according to need. Some problems require the reconsideration which makes the known enlighteningly new; others need the attention of original research; yet others will have to enter controversy because the prevailing notions on many historical questions are demonstrably wrong. The authors of this series are free to treat their subject in whatever manner it seems to them to require. They will present some of their evidence for inspection and help the learner to see how history is written, but they will themselves also write history.

G.R.E.

PREFACE

This book treats of problems which have been consistently and tendentiously misinterpreted because the technicalities governing their reality have not been understood. The setting within which the rural society of the sixteenth century faced and solved its difficulties was created by the law, and I have therefore had to explain this law at length, and technically, in order to remove legends and restore the historical truth.

Thanks for kind assistance are due to Professors G. R. Elton, F. E. Hyde, J. U. Nef, Sir J. Neale, Duncan Black, H. R. Trevor-Roper and S. B. Saul; to Drs D. Oschinsky and J. R. Harris; to Miss Helen Miller; to Mr P. I. King; to my father and brother; to Steven and Jeffrey; and above all to my wife, but for whom nothing would have come of this study.

I am grateful to Messrs Sweet and Maxwell Ltd. for kind permission to reproduce an extract from Mr J. Ritchie's *Reports of Cases decided by Francis Bacon in the High Court of Chancery,* published by them in 1932. Translations and transcriptions of Crown-copyright records in the Public Record Office appear by kind permission of the Controller of Her Majesty's Stationery Office.

E.K.

NOTES ON ABBREVIATIONS

not among standard forms in C. C. Matthews, A DICTIONARY OF ABBREVIATIONS

Because this book argues an unfamiliar case, I have provided references to the materials on which my conclusions are based; but in order to save space I have presented them in a highly condensed form which yet makes tracking them possible.

Acc.	Accession	M.,m.	Membrane
Add.	Additional	MB	Miscellaneous Books
AO	Augmentation Office	Mont.	Montagu
BA	Bulk Accession	P. & M.	Philip & Mary
Bpl.	Birthplace	R.	Roll
Ch.	Chamber, Charter	R. & S.	Rentals & Surveys
Compl.	Complaint	Recog.	Recognition
Dep.	Deposition	Req.	Court of Requests Proceedings
DL	Duchy of Lancaster		
ECP	Early Chancery Proceedings	R.H.	Rider, Heaton, Meredith & Mills
EHR	English Historical Review	RO	Record (Archives) Office
F-H	Finch-Hatton	Rot.	Rotulet
F(M)	Fitzwilliam (Milton)	Sp.	Special
G'bury	Gorhambury	SPD	State Papers, Domestic
GS	General Series	Throckmorton	Coughton (Throckmorton)
I(L)	Isham (Lamport)		
KR	King's Remembrancer		
Lans.	Lansdowne		
Leigh	Stoneleigh (Leigh)	TR	Treasury of Receipt
LR	Land Revenue	W. de B.	Willoughby de Broke

CONTENTS

PART I: AGRARIAN PROBLEMS

Introduction

What are usually regarded as the agrarian problems of the sixteenth century and after are the eviction of copyholders, the depopulation of the countryside, the enclosure movement, and the conversion of tillage to pasture. These problems, it is generally agreed, were interlocked. Conversion to pasture is envisaged as taking place in enclosed fields and entailing depopulation largely by the eviction of unprotected copyholders.

The late Professor R. H. Tawney conjured up a picture of the career of a relentless and remorseless agrarian capitalism, which impiously rode down a wretched peasantry without any let or hindrance from the common law, as though there were one law for the rich and another for the poor. His denunciation of capitalism sought to convince us that we were face to face with giant manifestations of the exploitation of man by man. This may well be what he intended in *The Agrarian Problem in the Sixteenth Century* in 1912 and no less what he meant to convey in later life, for, despite his whimsical disparagement of it, this was always his most cherished work.

In Tawney, however, a harmful prejudice was all too evident. Tawney the politician barred the way to Tawney the scholar. Time which he might have given to studying history was devoted instead to the Fabian Society and the Labour Party, and he tended to see the world past and present in terms of socialist dogma. Hence his wholly untrue picture of early capitalism as cruel and greedy, destructive alike of social welfare and true spiritual values. No one would wish to deny that Tawney was a great man, but this greatness caused him to lead whole generations of history students into grievous error.

I

The Manor

IN law and in practice, the life of the countryside clustered around the manor. Lawyers and surveyors leave its definition clear and precise:[1]

'From whencesoever derived, a mannor is now that which hath therunto belonging messuages, lands, tenements, rents, services and heriditaments; wherof part are demeasnes, being those which anciently and time out of minde, the lorde himselfe ever used, occupied and manured with the mannor house; the residue are freeholds, farmes and customarie or coppihold tenements; and these have commonly divers services besides their rents properly belonging thereunto ... There is, moreover, belonging to a manor a court baron ... Neither do those parts formerly named properly of themselves make a mannor; for should any man at this day alott and appoint out any competent quantitie of land, and divide the same into demeasnes and tenement lands, infeoffing tenants in fee of some parts and granting others by copie of court roll, and perfecting the rest which before is said to belong unto a mannor, yet all this will not make a mannor, for that it is the office of time by long continuance to make and create the same.'

Although not primarily a territorial unit, 'a manor in substance is of lands, wood, meddow, pasture and arable: it is compounded of demeisns and services of long continuance.'[2]

The institution of new manors in the kingdom of England could not receive legal sanction; the power of creating them had been lost by the end of the thirteenth century.[3] Individuals, endeavouring to evade their own tenurial obligations to legally constituted manors might try illegally to set up their own.[4] Christopher Potticary's attempts

[1] A. Rathborne, *The Surveyor*, London 1616, pp. 176–7; and see J. Norden, *The Surveiors Dialogue*, London 1618, p. 42.
[2] Norden, p. 39.
[3] F. Pollock & F. W. Maitland, *The History of English Law*, Cambridge 1895, i. 596.
[4] PRO, Exch. TR, MB 157, pp. 72–3; Leics. RO, DE 40/22/1, f. 3; Dors. RO, Mus. 10762, m. 1.

B

to do this at Stockton in 1627 were foiled by his tenants' refusal to attend court and by searches which the true lord made in Domesday Book and elsewhere.[5] In 1616 John Norden finds at Helmswell that[6]

'Richard Bushop, an atturney . . . hath longe strugled to make himselfe lorde of the manor and much and longe trowbled the tenantes to drawe them into a usurped court of his own establishynge, depriving the prince of all wayves, estrays, and all other royalties, and hath been twice overthrowne by the lawe and comitted to the Fleete for his contemptyous arrogance.'

In short, he who tries to set up a new manor 'may have thereby a kind of seignory, a lordship or government in grosse over his tennants by contract or covenant, but no mannor.'[7]

Although new manors could not be created, old ones could be destroyed both in name and nature, by escheating the freeholds and copyholds, for without these there could be no suitors, and therefore no court and no manor, but only a seigniory, which could have no court baron at all.[8] Many manors were thus dismembered[9] in the early modern period, especially in the Midland Plain, the Cheese Country, and other farming countries undergoing enclosure.[10] In many places, too, even when manors were not dismembered, their courts were neglected.[11]

[5] BM, Add. R. 24745.
[6] Jn Rylands Lib. Eng. 216, f. 26.
[7] Norden, p. 42 (recte 44).
[8] Rathborne, p. 177; Brook's New Cs 55–6.
[9] A. W. Boyd, *A Country Parish*, London 1951, p. 18; W. M. Palmer, *John Layer of Shepreth*, Camb. Ant. S. 8vo ser. 1935, liii. 102–3; J. Aubrey, *Wilts. Topographical Collections*, ed. J. E. Jackson, Devizes 1862, pp. 9, 236; W. P. W. Phillimore & G. S. Fry, *Abstracts of Glos. Inquisitiones Post Mortem in Reign of Charles I*, Index Lib. 1893, i. 98–9, ii. 61; iii. 59–60; G. S. & E. A. Fry, *Abstracts of Wilts. Inquisitiones Post Mortem temp. Car. I*, *ibid.* 1901, pp. 109–10, 133–7, 158 sqq., 190–1, 195–9, 247 sqq., 273, 343–4; J. P. Rylands, *Lancs. Inquisitions returned into Chancery of Duchy of Lancaster, Stuart Period*, Rec. Soc. Lancs. and Ches. 1880–8, i. 271–3; *Wilts. N. & Q.* 1895, i. 487–8, 532; 1905, iv. 350; F. H. Manley, 'Customs of Manor of Purton', *Wilts. Archaeol. Mag.* 1917–9, xl. 111; 'The Society's MSS.', *ibid.* 1909–10, xxxvi. 217; PRO, Req. 102/45; Chanc. Proc. ser. i, B41/42, S39/64; Exch. LR., MB 207, f. 8(6); 229, f. 98; KR, Sp. Commn 1239; Wds, Feodaries' Svys bdl. 23 Jn Quarles; nos. 263, 273, 659; bdl. 46: Jn Bryan 1620 S. Marston, Ric. Morse 1611 Badbury, Hy Lee E. Marlboro' 1638; Ed. Baylie 17 Jac. Smallbrook, Robt Bayly 1628 Etchilhampton; vol. 40, ff. 48v.–9.
[10] For farming countries and background, see my *Agricultural Revolution*, London 1967.
[11] F. H. Hinton, 'N. on Ct Bks Manors Lacock &c.', *Wilts. Archaeol. Mag.* 1944, l. 474; PRO, Exch. AO, Parl. Svys Berks. 23, f. 3; 17, f. 6; Devon 14, f. 1; TR, MB 157, f. 59 (p. 111).

As long as copyholds continued, however, the discontinuance of courts was prejudicial to the customary tenants and, on their petition for a subpoena, might be countermanded by Chancery order. Francis Bacon, for instance, ordered the lords of Whitchurch manor to go on keeping courts.[12] As long as common fields persisted, too, township governments needed the sanction of manor courts for their bye-laws. In the Chalk Country, the dismemberment of Shrewton manor and the discontinuance of its courts threw the whole township into confusion until its government found some other way to enforce bye-laws. Similar results followed the dismemberment of other manors where common fields continued.[13] Generally speaking, therefore, manors were dismembered only where husbandry bye-laws were no longer needed and the land could readily be sold to non-customary proprietors. Elsewhere manors were as strong as ever. Many, if not most, continued to function in the eighteenth century, and not a few in the nineteenth, in both common-field and severalty districts.[14] So vital and beneficial an institution was the manor and so much reliance did the English place upon it, that after the final conquest of Ireland in 1650 and of Scotland in 1654, manorial courts were set up there under Acts of Parliament and exactly on the model of those in England.[15]

Manors could divide and unite. If a manor came into the hands of co-heirs, for instance, two courts could be held in place of one. The manor would then be divided, not by lands but by tenants, each lord taking half as his own. Two manors could become one, if one formerly held of the other and then escheated, or if the inferior manor decayed into a mere lordship, provided the lord wanted his tenants to do suit and service at the superior court, the tenants gave their consent, and long usage perfected the union.[16] In earlier times the division of manors had been common, but was now far rarer than their union. Sub-manors were so numerous that mergers could hardly be avoided in the course of consolidating estates. By various changes of property in successive ages in Westbury, the manorial rights were subdivided into many portions. Then the Earl of Marlborough bought up both the great or hundredal manor of Westbury and its seven sub-manors,

[12] Cary 3; J. Ritchie, *Reports of Cases decided by F. Bacon in the High Court of Chancery*, London 1932, p. 71.
[13] Bennett, 'Orders of Shrewton', *Wilts. Archaeol. Mag.* 1887 xxiii. 36–7; Bristol Univ. Lib. Shrewton 11–2, 36/1.
[14] W. Marshall, *The Rural Economy of Yorkshire*, London 1788, i. 28–9; Northants. RO, Mont. old box 36 Ct Bk Boughton & Pitsford; E. Sfk RO, S1/1/3.1.
[15] C. H. Firth and R. S. Rait, *Acts & Ordinances of the Interregnum*, London 1911, ii. 883–4; Stat. 16 Chas. I c. 33.
[16] Norden, p. 46; Rathborne, p. 177; R. C. Hoare, *The History of Modern Wiltshire*, London 1822–44, Hund. Branch & Dole p. 20.

and all these merged again into the great manor from which they had sprung.[17] Similar reunifications were made in Corsley, Amesbury, and Blythburgh. Wherever there were several manors to a single township, the tendency was now for them to be united.[18]

Sub-manors, however, remained extremely numerous. One manor might have as many as six or more sub-manors, some at some distance from the head.[19] A sub-manor had sometimes formed around the lands of a distinct hamlet, but frequently had resulted from a division of the tenants of a single township, and these tenants might still have all their lands in the same common fields. Thus Corton 'is no intyer lordshippe of ytselfe, but within the lordship of therle of Arundel' and its lands are 'intermedeled in the common feildes with the londes of the tenauntes of the erle ... And all paynes for good order in the common feilds and common meadowes have been alwaies assessed and levyed by the officers of the said erle and not in the lordes courte of this said mannor.'[20] For the head manor to sanction the bye-laws of the whole township was the usual arrangement.[21] It is partly this that explains why not all manor court rolls record bye-laws (Doc. 4).

No map could ever plot the bounds of a manor, strictly speaking, though in common parlance the precinct of a manor was the boundary of its lands, or of the main block of them. Land that was part and parcel of the manor was sometimes described as being outside the manor bounds, which it could not have been, when what was meant was that it was separated from the main body.[22] In any event, the lands of some manors were so dispersed that they could hardly be bounded. In upland districts, like the West Country, the lands of a single manor might be scattered over a radius of fifteen miles; and in great towns, like Worcester, they might be almost inextricably confused with those of other manors.[23] A manor's lands were not always

[17] *Ibid.* Hund. Westbury, p. 44; Fry, pp. 232 sqq.
[18] M. F. Davies, *Life in an English Village*, London 1909, pp. 10, 15; J. Spratt, 'Agrarian Conditions in Nfk & Sfk 1600–50', ts. thesis M.A. Ldn 1935, pp. 19, 68; R. B. Pugh, *Calendar of Antrobus Deeds before 1625*, Wilts. Archaeol. & Nat. Hist. Soc. Rec. Brch 1947 iii, p. xv.
[19] W. Cooper, *Wootton Wawen*, Leeds 1936, App. p. 27; Lancs. RO, DD. K1460/1, m. 2; PRO, Exch. AO, Parl. Svys Berks. 17, f. 4; LR, MB 207, f. 8 (6); Sp. Coll. Ct R.GS 195/78, m. 2.
[20] BM, Harl. MS. 71, f. 54(43).
[21] Leics. RO, DE. 40/22/1, f. 3.
[22] Rathborne, p. 200; Fitzherbert, *The Boke of Surveyinge & Improvementes*, London 1535, f. 12; PRO, DL, MB 115, ff. 18, 20, 31v.–32, 37v.–8, 44v., 48v.–9, 52v., 58, 62v., 69, 80.
[23] T. Cave & R. A. Wilson, *The Parliamentary Survey of Lands & Possessions of Dean & Chapter of Worcester*, Worcs. Hist. Soc. 1924, p. 215; BM, Harl. MS. 702, f. 111; PRO, Exch. AO, Parl. Svys Corn. 7, f. 5; 16, f. 7, 22, f. 1; 25, f. 47; 27, f. 14; 32, f. 7; 36, f. 23; 47, f. 12; 51, f. 27; 52, f. 5; Devon 17, f. 9; DL, MB 116, f. 79.

solely in the township or townships from which its name derived. A copyholder in Sevenhampton manor could have his holding in Marston township. Sometimes the lands of one manor were dispersed in several townships amongst lands pertaining to manors in those townships. Thus those of Bulbridge lay also in Chalke, Stoke Farthing, Knighton, Wilton, Avon and South Ugford, each of which had also its own local manor. Amesbury Earls manor comprehended freeholds in Whiteparish, Durnford, Netton, Salterton and Dean, and a farm near Maiden Bradley. Some lands in Clench and Wick were parcels of the manor of Bromham, nearly twenty miles away.[24] There were also hundredal manors, like Bishop's Cannings, Bromfield and Yale, and Cartmel, that might embrace as many as sixteen sub-manors and sixty townships, while the manor of Taunton Deane covered four hundreds. In these, however, although the sub-manors were held of the lord paramount as of his head manor, the lands belonging to them could not be considered as part of the head manor. 'Lands may be holden of a mannor by certain services, the service may be parcell of the mannor and yet the lands not.'[25] Much the same may be said of some other great manors, of which freeholds were held, often in townships at some distance from the head. Great manors were especially common in the Northdown Country, where many of them had foreign appurtenances in the Wealden Vales and Romney Marsh. Wye Royal was an outstanding example of such a great manor, for it had a huge rental of foreign freeholds. The most highly exaggerated of these great manors was that of East Greenwich, for freeholds all over the kingdom, and even lordships in North America, came to be held as of it.[26] Manors like these had more services than lands, but it should not be thought that these services were meaningless, for in the absence of an heir the freeholding itself might escheat to the lord of the manor. 'Most mannors', indeed, 'consist of divers towneships or particular parts.'[27] Coincidence between township and manor was no more common than the lack of it. Townships were often divided between

[24] C. R. Straton, *Survey of Lands of William, first earl of Pembroke*, Roxburghe Club 1909, i. 237 sqq.; Wilton ho. Svys of Manors 1631 i Svy Bulbridge &c.; Wilts. RO, acc. 40, Sevenhampton Ct Bk 1541–1624, 18 Sept. 33 Hy VIII; acc. 283, Liber Supervisus Amisburie Erles & Amesbury Pryorye, f. 16; Svy Amesbury 1635, ff. 1–3; Amesbury Misc. Papers & Docs. Billet Land c. aliis; BM, Add. MS. 37270, f. 311.

[25] Norden, p. 43; BM, Add. R. 37571; PRO, Exch. AO. Parl. Svys Denbighs 1A, f. 1; Lancs. 7, f. 9.

[26] J. Hurstfield, *The Queen's Wards*, London 1958, pp. 19 sqq.; N. S. B. Gras, *A History of Agriculture in Europe & America*, London n.d. p. 259; G. Markham, *The Inrichment of the Weald of Kent*, London 1625, pp. 3–4; Northants. RO, F-H 301, 3642; PRO, Exch. LR, MB 218, ff. 157 sqq.; 219, f. 214; AO, Parl. Svys Kent 26, ff. 1–2.

[27] Rathborne, p. 210.

more than one manor, an especially frequent circumstance in High Suffolk, East Norfolk, and the Fen and West Countries.[28] Manors frequently embraced more than one township or parts of more than one. This, indeed, is evident from their very names, such as Chilmark and Ridge, Bootle with Linacre, and so on. Nor were these townships always contiguous.[29] Moreover, the combination of two or more townships under one manor is frequently concealed by the simple nomenclature of the latter. The manor of Idmiston contained the two tithings or members of Idmiston and Gomeldon. Bremhill manor consisted of the three tithings of Bremhill, Charlcote and Foxham.[30] If the manor extended to more than one township, the same court dealt with their bye-laws separately, and the courts themselves were sometimes held in one township and another by rotation.[31] If there were two manors to a township, bye-laws could be promulgated in both courts or, more commonly, as at Corton, the sub-manor left the promulgation and enforcement of bye-laws to the other. This mean that the tenants of the two manors had to confer together to frame bye-laws, as they did at Wootton Wawen. When Nassington manor was divided into two, the tenants of both used to meet together to agree about husbandry regulations and stints.[32] When formed by the union of manors, a single hall might have likewise two separate tenurial customs.[33] If two manors were formed of one, each had the same customary tenures and the same body of precedents to refer to. Under such circumstances, the tenants of the two manors might confer together about these matters.[34] The manor was thus something quite distinct from the township, and coincidence of the two was only partial.

As has been seen, manors could lose their courts baron and decline into mere lordships or seigniories in gross. Even such a lordship, however, might still have a customary court where the steward was judge and took surrenders and made admissions just the same. The distinction between lordship and manor was thus of less practical

[28] Spratt, p. 17; W. Marshall, *The Rural Economy of the West of England*, London 1796, i. 21; W. M. & F. Marcham, *Court Rolls of Bishop of London's Manor of Hornsey, 1603–71*, London 1929, p. xv.; M. W. Barley, *Lincolnshire & the Fens*, London 1952, p. 98.

[29] F. S. Colman, *A History of Barwick-in-Elmet*, Leeds 1908, p. 100; BM, Harl. MS. 702, f. III; PRO, Exch. AO, Parl. Svys Lincs. 41A.

[30] Bowood ho. Svy Bremhill 1629; Hoare, Hund. Alderbury, pp. 67 sqq.

[31] Norden, p. 103; W. H. Godfrey, *The Booke of John Rowe*, Suss. Rec. Soc. 1928 xxxiv. 106; W. G. Hoskins, *The Midland Peasant*, London, 1957, p. 97; Wilton ho. Ct Bk Bemerton & Quidhampton; PRO, St. Ch. Jas, 55/29, mm. 2, 4.

[32] Cooper, App. pp. 27, 35; BM, Harl. MS. 71, f. 54(43) v.; PRO, Ct R. GS 195/78, m. 2, Northants. RO, Wmld 4. xvi. 5.

[33] Wilts. RO, Savernake: Svy Burbages 1574–5, f. 32.

[34] G. H. Rendall, *Dedham in History*, Colchester 1937, p. 33; PRO, Req. 80/47.

consequence than might appear. A mere lordship 'in the eye of the world is a manor, though in the judgement of the law it cometh far short of it' (Doc. 4).[35] In practice the terms were used loosely or combined in order to avoid the niceties of the law. A formula commonly employed was 'all that manor or lordship, reputed manor or lordship'. Nevertheless, the distinction between manor and lordship was never wholly lost and was not without significance. Huntingford was 'of old noe manor; after a manor; nowe only a manor in reputation'.[36] Cranbrook 'is nowe onely a mannor in reputation, for the tennancyes are all lost except one, soe that there be noe casuall profitts in the said mannor for want of a court'.[37]

Even in the strictly legal meaning, manors were far from being of a simple or uniform pattern. In common parlance the term was still more vague and compendious. Although manors and lordships were composed of demesnes, tenancies and services, these parts were of widely varying proportions. Some had little or no demesne and consisted mainly or wholly of free rents and royalties, or of a few customary tenants. Rectory manors had often only tithes, and a few small parcels of land in lieu, besides the rectory and its own farm.[38] Other manors were huge. But size was little guide to value or even to the superficial area owned by the lord himself. The lordship of some manors put thousands of acres of land at the lord's disposal, in others next to nothing. Wakefield manor was one of the largest, with some 1,400 copyholders, but had no demesnes apart from the moot-hall, the common bakehouse and a few intakes from the waste. The lord of a single small manor might derive from it an income larger than that enjoyed by the lord of a dozen larger ones with richer soil.[39]

It was no longer true that there was no land without a lord or that all land was part of a manor or lordship. Many manors were dismembered and the outlying freeholds were not necessarily sold with the manors they formerly held of. Special instructions governed royal sales of quillets that were 'no manors nor parcell of anie mannors'. At Bressingham, both Irlandes Farm and Boyland Hall were properties of this kind,[40] and their number was swollen by disforesting as well as

---

[35] E. Coke, *The Compleate Copyholder*, London 1641, sect. 31; Norden, p. 42,

[36] J. Smyth, *A Description of the Hundred of Berkeley* Berkeley MSS. iii. ed. J. Maclean, Gloucester 1885, p. 234.

[37] Northants. RO, F-H 119.

[38] Godfrey, pp. 93, 117–8; E. J. Bodington, 'Church Svys in Wilts. 1649–50', *Wilts. Archaeol. Mag.* 1917–9 xl. 308–10; 1920–2 xli. 14–6, 105 sqq.; E. Sfk RO, HA. 12/C9/9, p. 38; PRO, Exch. Parl. Svys Berks. 23, ff. 1, 5; Bucks. 15, 17; Ches. 14A; Corn. 42; Devon 12; Lincs. 29; Oxon. 10.

[39] J. P. Collier, *The Egerton Papers*, Camd. Soc. 1840, pp. 285, 302–3; BM, Harl. MS. 607, ff. 70 (63) v., 156 (138), 163 (145) v.

[40] PRO, Exch. LR, MB 220, f. 237.

dismemberment. But the overwhelming proportion of land remained manorial.

The heart of a manor lay in its courts. These did not include the view of the frankpledge, law-day or court leet, where the lord or his steward was judge in all personal actions under £2. This was simply the delegation to some lords, for local convenience, of royal jurisdiction. Where the lord had the right to a law-day, he commonly held it in the usual courthouse, often on the same day as the manor court, and the proceedings of the two were frequently recorded on the same roll, though separately, for they were quite different and distinct. The manorial court or hall-moot consisted of a court baron and usually a court customary also, and was concerned solely with its own customary law. In the court baron and customary (or court baron for short), cases were presented by a grand jury, investigated if need be by a jury of inquest, and tried before a steward by a trial jury chosen from, or including all, the suitors or homage, according to the custom. In respect of the court baron the steward was a registrar, and of the court customary a judge. In the latter, lord, steward and jury stood in the same relation to each other as did king, judge and jury in a court of common law. All trial was by jury and the lord was no more above the custom than the king was above the law. The manor court served as a registry for all conveyances of manorial land and promulgated and enforced bye-laws or customs. But the lord was party to all the conveyances registered and was bound by all the bye-laws. He might be fined for infringing them, or for committing trespass, in his own manor court. Moreover, the lord himself had equity jurisdiction in all customary cases and within the manor the last appeal was to him. Thus in the manorial court, the lord of a manor was in the nature of a constitutionally limited monarch (Doc. 4).[41]

Proceedings in manorial courts were noted at the time by the clerk of the court, in Latin. He then used his notes and the other documents in the court files, such as orders, grants and draft presentments, to compile a court book, which was a record of all such court business as the steward decided to have recorded, chiefly conveyances, bye-laws, orders and decrees. Afterwards the court book, which was

[41] T. E. Scrutton, *Commons & Common Fields*, Cambridge 1887, p. 21; G. Goodman, *The Court of King James I*, ed. J. S. Brewer, London 1839, i. 294, 342; G. P. Scrope, *History of the Manor & Ancient Barony of Castle Combe*, s. l. 1852, p. 337; Coke, sect. 31; H. Hall, *Society in the Elizabethan Age*, London 1887, p. 156; W. O. Ault, *Private Jurisdiction in England*, New Haven 1923, pp. 166–7, 169–71, 176, 344; W. B. Willcox, *Gloucestershire*, New Haven 1940, pp. 296–7; 1 Leon. 227–8; Cartwright Hall, Swinton: ct files W. Tanfield 1652; BM, Add. MSS. 23151, f. 44 v.; 37270, f. 54; 36920, f. 83 v.; PRO, Chanc. Decrees, 2nd Div. 1st pt, pt 358, no 8.

usually of bound paper folios, was engrossed on parchment as a court roll.[42]

In addition to the ordinary courts, special ones were held on particular occasions for specific purposes. Such was the court of recognition, the first court after the entry of a new lord, which was a court of attornment, where the lord became seised of the services of the manorial tenants. He received the recognition or acknowledgement of the tenants, who attorned or 'turned tenant' to him and in witness paid him a small sum, which was called a 'certain knowledge' or some such. The court of recognition also enabled the new lord to review the state of the manor and record the various deeds by which lands were held of him. Each tenant in turn came before the lord or his steward, showed his deeds, took his oath of fealty and was admitted tenant. The deeds were scrutinized by the steward to ensure authenticity and copied by the clerk of the court. When these proceedings and copies of writings were brought together by the clerk in a formal record of the court, what resulted was something in the nature of a survey of the manor, though what this record contained depended on the contents of the writings copied and recorded.[43]

Courts of recognition thus displayed many of the features of manorial surveys or extents, as they were earlier called. An Henrician extent of the manor of Candelent and Capel with Newton in Trimley, for example, was made 'by inspection and by information from the tenants'.[44] Some courts of recognition, indeed, were all but courts of survey, and occasionally courts of recognition and of survey were combined.[45] Then, again, some courts of survey followed the form of courts of recognition: the tenant came to court to acknowledge his lord.[46] The usual form for entering deeds in a court of recognition was, 'To this court came A.B. and acknowledged himself to hold of the same lord by copy dated ... and made fealty and was admitted tenant there', sometimes containing also 'showed copy as followeth'. A survey of Crimplesham has at the start of each entry just such a formula, commencing 'To this court came', as in a court of recognition.[47] In a survey of Burghlion Fee in Gedney each entry begins, 'To this court

[42] Cartwright Hall, Swinton: Ct Bk Tornock & Lympsham.
[43] E.g. Bristol Univ. Lib. Dauntsey Trowbridge Ct Bk, ff. 54 sqq.
[44] Straton ii. 501; E. Sfk RO, V. 11/3/3; BM, Add. MS. 21043, f. 2.
[45] Wimbledon Common Committee, *Extracts from Court Rolls of Manor of Wimbledon*, London 1866, p. 156; Oxon. RO, DIL. II/a/2; Staffs. RO, D. 260: box iii, bdl. (b) Ct Recog. & Svy Walsall 3 May 15 Jas; PRO, DL, MB 112, f. 5; R. & S. GS 10/7; Exch. LR, MB 187, f. 10.
[46] Staffs. RO, D. 260: box 16 bdl. (b).
[47] PRO, Exch. LR, MB 201, ff. 62 sqq.

came J.B. and exhibited a certain copy and begged the same to be enrolled, which followeth in these words'.[48]

When landed estates were about to be sold, on the succession of a
new lord, or otherwise when business demanded, a court of survey
was held. The lord commissioned one or two surveyors, or occasionally
more, to hold an inquisition or series of inquisitions. The surveyor
called upon the steward of the manor to summon a special sitting
for a court of survey. Sometimes steward and surveyor were one and
the same gentleman, but more usually separate persons who held
court jointly. Sometimes again the surveyor was commissioned to hold
the courts of survey by himself and had only to issue a warrant to the
bailiff of the manor 'to summon and warn twenty four of the ablest
tennants of the said manor to appear before us at a court of survey . . .
at the usual court house'. The bailiff, in his turn, then summoned all
the tenants of the manor to bring in their deeds, charters, evidences,
letters patent, leases, copies of court roll, court rolls, rentals, custom-
aries and all other writings to the court of survey. When the surveyor,
or the steward on his behalf, had opened the court, when the tenants,
'both feudatories and fermors', had entered, and when the jury had
been impanelled and sworn in, the work of the court of survey could
begin.[49]

Surveyor's commissions had various terms of reference. The Earl of
Pembroke's commission to Vaughan and Grove was

'To viewe, survey, lett and sett all my landes, tenementes and
hereditaments whatsoever which I have in myne owne right, my wives
right or by lease, within the counties of Deven, Dorset, Somerset, Wiltes
and Southampton, for term of lief or lives, after the severall custoumes
of my manours in the sayd counties, for such fines as shal be for my
moost advantage and profytte, according to their discrecions and
wisedom . . .'

On crown estates, however, the surveyor was usually commissioned
merely to survey and not to set and let. Interrogatories were drawn
up for the surveyor to present to the jury and he had only enquire
under those heads.[50]

'The lords records and the tennants informations are the pillars of

[48] BM, Harl. MS. 702, ff. 2 sqq.
[49] Rathborne, pp. 205, 208; W. Folkingham, *Feudigraphia*, London 1610,
p. 86; T. H. Baker, 'Notes on History of Mere', *Wilts. Archaeol. Mag.* 1896–7
xxix. 331; E. Straker, *The Buckhurst Terrier 1597–8*, Suss. Rec. Soc. 1933
xxxix. 1; Straton ii. 501; Sy RO, 34/3 Svy Gt Bookham 1614; *Sy Archaeol.
Colls.* 1926 xxxvii pt i. 104–5; E. Sfk RO, 312/422, Westleton arts. for svy
manor; Northants. RO, R.H. 45 Winwick svy 1652; PRO, DL, Sp. Commn
1040; R. & S. 9/6, m. 2; 9/13; Exch. LR, MB 221, f. 3.
[50] Rathborne, p. 200; Straton i. 1.

a survey.'[51] The surveyor went to court armed with previous surveys
of the manor and properties and with the court rolls, and court, field
and lease books from the estate office, all of which he endorsed before
returning.[52] The tenants came to court with the deeds and writings
by which they held their lands and possessions, with indentures of
lease or enfeoffment, with copies of court rolls and other title deeds.
The task of the surveyor was to scrutinize each writing in turn as it
was shown by the tenant, to compare it with the estate office record
of the same, in case of discrepancy to obtain a sworn statement as to the
true circumstances from the jury, to note their findings, and to record
all the deeds and evidences, either in person or with the assistance of
a clerk or recorder. Sometimes copies of court roll could not be produced, because lost or destroyed or because the tenant was in London
on business, or at sea, or out of the kingdom. Sometimes copies of
court roll were found to be fraudulent and forged or invalid because
not signed by the steward. In all such cases, the jury had to make a
sworn statement by reference to the court rolls or other records. It
paid the surveyor to be utterly meticulous in these proceedings, because he was usually allowed the tenancy of all concealed holdings he
could recover for the lord, but was legally responsible for any error
to the lord's detriment. The surveyor usually made his records, in
English mostly, on loose sheets of paper that were filed immediately,
then reorganized at leisure and brought together into a survey book,
which might later be engrossed and translated into Latin.[53] The
survey was thus made 'as well by the viewe of the indentures,
wrightinges and copies, as by the examination of the customary tenantes'. Under the supervision of the jury, the surveyor enrolled the
copies, leases and deeds.[54] The manorial survey was not a survey of
the lands of the manor in a general sense, not a field survey, but a
survey of the deeds of the manorial tenants. The particulars in the
finished survey, therefore, depend directly on those provided by the
deeds and writings. The survey is thus not a cross-section of the state
of the manor on any particular day or even in any one year. If the
freeholder proved his title by an ancient deed, then the information
provided by the survey would be as old as the deed itself. Leases and

---

[51] Norden, p. 22.
[52] PRO, DL, Ct R. 105/1501; Exch. LR, MB 201, f. 65.
[53] Rathborne, pp. 208–10, 218; Folkingham, p. 86; Norden, pp. 23 (recte 32),
88; T. I. J. Jones, Exchequer Proceedings concerning Wales in tempore James I,
Cardiff 1955, pp. 296–7; H. King & A. Harris, A Survey of the Manor of
Settrington, Yks. Archaeol. Soc. Rec. Ser. 1962, cxxvi. 7; PRO, Exch. LR, MB
185, f. 172.
[54] Norden, p. 23 (recte 32); Wilton ho. Svys Manors 1631 i Svy Bulbridge
&c. f. 1(2).

copies were most likely to be up-to-date, but even some of these might be a score of years or more old at the time of survey, which was thus a description of copyholds and leaseholds when last granted or renewed and of freeholds when last conveyed.

Enrolment completed, the surveyor presented the survey, thus far made, to the jury for signature and certification.[55] This was not merely a formality, for occasionally some of the jury refused to agree to one or more of the presentments, alleging partiality.[56] In addition, the surveyor was usually commissioned to estimate and record the values of each holding, i.e., the yearly value over and above the reserved rent. This he could do merely from his knowledge of local farm rents, by conference with the steward of the manor who knew the farmers' ability to pay, by enquiring into the upper rents paid to the holders by their undertenants,[57] by ascertaining the average value of a certain unit of farmland and making calculations on this basis for all the farms,[58] or best of all by reference to the book of rates for taxes levied by the township, state or church.[59] The valuations, however, were solely for the eyes of the lord and his estate officers and were not shown to the jury.[60]

The surveyor might also have a stroll about the premises and even walk some of the farms, but he was not usually commissioned to do either. When, however, manors were being surveyed in preparation for sale, the surveyor was sometimes instructed to make short descriptions of the general nature of the farmland and the amenities of the manor house.[61] Otherwise, particulars of housing contained in surveys, though apparently the result of first-hand inspection, are based on the descriptions contained in deeds, presentments of the court of survey and records of repairs ordered at previous courts.[62] The surveyor was sometimes commissioned to perambulate the bounds of the manorial lands with the jury of the court of survey, chiefly to prevent encroachments and to facilitate the drawing up of conveyances

[55] Norden, p. 145; Folkingham, p. 87; Rathborne, p. 217; e.g. N.R. RO, ZQ. 1, Marske Svy 1655, m. 1.

[56] J. Smyth, *The Lives of the Berkeleys*, Berkeley MSS. ed. J. Maclean, London 1883, ii. 295.

[57] Salop. RO, Bridgwater: Jn Charlton's Bk 1637, f. 1v.; PRO, Exch. LR, MB 229, f. 222.

[58] *Ibid.* 206, f. 3.

[59] Worcs. RO, 2636/9 (ii) p. 92; E. Bateson & al. *A History of Northumberland*, London 1893–1940, viii. 241; Wilts. RO, acc. 212B: BH. 8.

[60] Norden, p. 189.

[61] PRO, DL, MB 115, 117.

[62] PRO, DL, Sp. Commn 1040; Exch. LR, MB 221, ff. 177–9; BM, Egerton MSS. 3002, f. 58; 3007, ff. 69 sqq.; Add. R. 5063; Northants. RO, Mont. old box 7 no 66/4 ct files Weekley 4 & 5 P. & M.

when the manor was to be sold.[63] Finally, the survey might contain a presentment of the customs of the manor.[64]

The surveyor was thus not usually a 'land-meter'. He did not measure the lands or even count parcels in the common fields. He had only to transcribe the numbers of acres attributed to the holding in the tenant's deeds. For the surveyor the badge of truth was in antiquity. Nevertheless, in some surveys there were entries of parcels measured out at some previous time for the purposes of division or enclosure, and these measurements were recorded from the deeds.[65] There were other surveys, too, in which all acreages were recorded as measured by the surveyor at the time of the court of survey. This practice appeared on the royal estates in the early seventeenth century as part and parcel of administrative reforms in the nature of a feudal reaction, and for the purposes of sale and disforestment.[66] Surveys by admeasurement, too, were required in preparation for general division and enclosure,[67] for the demarcation of lands whose bounds were confused,[68] and where the nature of the estate itself put it in great danger of concealments and encroachments arising from laxity of supervision, as on college estates[69] and crown lands.[70] The chief exponents of this kind of surveying where Ralph Agas, John Norden and Aaron Rathborne. They worked with chains, plain-tables and theodolites by methods evolved already by 1577 and simplified by the use of logarithms after 1614.[71] One of these 'land-meters' aptly described himself as a 'practitioner in the mathematic'.[72] Such methods, however, were not usually required and did not become general in the

[63] PRO, DL, MB 115, ff. 18, 20, 31v.–2, 37v.–8, 44v., 48v.–9, 52v., 58, 62v., 69, 80.

[64] Wilts. RO, Savernake: Svy Burbage, ff. 32–4; G. F. Farnham, *Quorndon Records*, s. l. 1912, p. 14.

[65] Wilton ho. Svys Manors 1631, i, Dinton & Teffont.

[66] See below, pp. 30, 55–7.

[67] Vent Farm, Forest Hill, Oxon. penes Mr W. Pinchin, fd maps; E. Sfk RO, V5/22/1; Northants. RO, F(M) Misc. Vol. 99; BM, Egerton MS. 3003, ff. 97 sqq.

[68] PRO, Exch. KR, Deps. by Commn. 10 Chas Mich. 61; BM, Add. R. 24745; Deene ho. Brudenell H. vii. 6; Wilts. RO, acc. 153 fd map Stockton 1640.

[69] R. H. Tawney, *The Agrarian Problem in the 16th cent*. London 1912, pp. 30, 235–6, 410–1; G. N. Clark, *Open Fields & Inclosure at Marston*, Oxford 1924, p. 9; J. L. G. Mowat, *16 Old Maps of Properties in Oxfordshire*, Oxford 1888.

[70] My 'Movement of Rent, 1540–1640', *Econ. Hist. Rev.*, 2nd ser. 1953 vi, 29 sqq.; PRO, Exch. LR, MB 230, ff. 202v., 204v.

[71] Rathborne, pp. 123 sqq.; Norden, pp. 130–1; R. Agas, *A Preparative to Platting of Landes & Tenements for Surveigh*, London 1596, pp. 4 sqq.; V. Leigh, *The Most Profitable & Commendable Science of Surveying*, London 1577.

[72] Shak. Bpl. Leigh: Stoneleigh Svy 1597.

early modern period. They were not adopted, except in unusual circumstances, even in the great series of parliamentary surveys made in the time of the Commonwealth.[73]

Generally, the surveyor met with compliance or willing co-operation from the tenants of the manor. Attendance at the court was one of the services they gave as a matter of course. Nevertheless, occasions might arise when he encountered opposition from the suitors, who might even refuse to attend. This happened in many courts of survey on crown estates in Jacobean times, when feudal reaction was at its height and the surveyors came to be regarded as instruments of an oppressive power. In one place Norden has to report, 'We coulde not procede in the survey of this manor for that of nere 100 tenantes not 30 appeared, yet had almoste 6 dayes warning by a messenger sent of purpose'.[74] At another court of survey, the tenants appeared, but were very obstinate. In some, they refused to show their rentals and evidences. One surveyor reports that 'Stephen Blashall, in the name of the rest of the tenants, denyed to show anie rentall or anie evidence; neither could I have anie workemen to lead the chaine, but was forced to use my clerks in that business'. Elsewhere, a royal surveyor met with 'verie badd and uncivill speeches'.[75] The difficulty of persuading freeholders to attend the courts of survey was met almost everywhere and attempts were sometimes made to overcome this by assuring them that they could show their deeds to the surveyor in private and not in open court.[76] Ordinarily it mattered little whether the freeholders attended or not, for their rents and services were known, and on most estates little attempt was made at enforcement.

When the court of survey was over, the surveyor prepared his book of survey, 'made authentically by evidence, recordes, and the oath and subscription of the jury'. This survey book was to be 'delivered to the steward, thereby to direct him to call the tenants to their suite and service att the lords courte and leet and also to dirrect, by vallue of the lands, how to assess fynes upon copyholders etc'. From this survey book also a rent roll was made and copies of this were delivered to the bailiff and the auditor, to help the former in the collection of rents and the latter in making his view of ministers' accounts. After this, the survey book was returned to the surveyor for safe custody and the use of the lord and his estate officers.[77] The survey thus

[73] Except PRO, Exch. AO, Parl. Svys War 12, f. 7; 21, f. 7; 32, ff. 11, 14, 21.
[74] BM, Add. MS. 6027, f. 134 (124)v.
[75] PRO, Exch. LR, MB 207, f. 53 (51); 230, ff.202v., 204v., 210v.; Jn Rylands Lib. Eng. MS. 216, f. 56.
[76] Sy RO, acc. 344 svy Dorking 1649; Sy Archaeol. Colls. 1926 xxxvii pt i. 105; BM, Add. MS. 6027, f. 86 (85).
[77] BM, Add. MS. 28529, f. 4.

remained in the estate office. Here it was in everyday use and amendments and additions were made to it as occasion demanded. Most office copies of survey books left an ample allowance of space for this purpose, not only in wide margins, but also in deep spaces between the various entries. As long as it remained in use, which might be for half a century or more, the book of survey maintained its intimate connection with the courts baron. Amendments and additions made to the book were taken from the court books and rolls as well as from the lease book and counterparts of leases. At every court baron and at the next court of survey, the survey book would rest at the steward's or surveyor's elbow. Indeed, the survey book was kept up-to-date and revised so that it always amounted to a new or revised survey, until it was easier to start afresh than to continue with the old book. Thus one survey was begun at a court held in 1575 and then amended at every court until 1579, when it was used instead of holding another court of survey.[78]

Thus the manor, with its various courts, its registration of conveyances, its promulgation and enforcement of bye-laws, and its administration of customary law, was an essential institution in the life of most of the countryside and in some sense a microcosm of English society itself, for 'is not every mannor a little commonwealth, wherof the tenants are the members, the land the body and the lord the head?'[79]

[78] Wilts. RO, Savernake: Svy Shalbourne Westcourt 1574–5.
[79] Norden, p. 27; Ault, p. 344.

Tenures and Estates

THE manor was the basic unit of feudal landownership. Although this was not susceptible of exclusive rights, it would be both paradoxical and false to regard it as any less than ownership. In early modern times, the tenant of demesne in fee was considered, and often called, the owner of the land.[1]

Land tenures, that is the manners and conditions of service by which lands were held of their lords, were extremely various and mostly of great antiquity; but what was more significant was the system of estates, that is, of the properties or interests in land that could be enjoyed under any of the ancient tenures. Tenures belonged to the province either of common law, these being the frank tenures, or of local customary laws, these being the base or bond tenures subordinated to courts customary. The doctrine or system of estates, however, applied with equal force to both frank and base tenures and to both common and customary law. There were three pillars in the legal system—local customary laws, common law, and statute law—each of which was concerned in one way or another with estates and tenures.

Unlike estates, tenures fell into two main groups according to branches of the law. All base tenures held at the will of lords according to the customs of manors were termed customary. Since, however, most customary tenants in the early modern period held as title deeds certified copies of entries of their holdings and grants in the rolls of manor courts, they were commonly termed copyholders, even though, as will be seen, some customary tenants were not copyholders and some copyholders not customary tenants. In this loose sense the terms copyhold and copyholder were in contradistinction to the ambiguous words freehold and freeholder, which were used generically to embrace all tenures and tenants that were not customary but under the common law. These distinctions were held to derive from Anglo-Saxon times, it being generally believed that 'copyhold lands are very auncient, before the Conquest, in the Saxons time, who called this

[1] Pollock and Maitland, ii. 5.

kinde of land Folkeland and their charter lands were called Bokeland'.[2] With reference to estates, however, the word freehold meant an estate with a term of not less than one life. In this sense most copyholds were freeholds. As Coke explains (Doc. 11),

'A freehold is taken in a double sense: either 'tis named a freehold in respect of the state of the land or in respect of the state of the law ... In respect of the state of the land, so copyholders may be freeholders; for any that hath any estate for his life, or any greater estate in any land whatsoever, may in this sense be termed a freeholder ... In respect of the state of the law, and so it is opposed to copyholders, what land soever is not copyhold is freehold.'

It was this double sense of the word 'freehold' that Tawney, right up until his death, refused to admit, even when confronted with Coke. He merely expressed disbelief without looking further into the evidence. He could not see that not all copyholders were customary tenants. Of modern writers, Leadam, whom Tawney[3] cavalierly ruled out of court, is the only one to have crossed this bridge of asses.

First, then, for the freehold tenures as distinct from copyhold and customary tenures. The most honourable and most burdensome of the freehold tenures was knight service. Military service in the field, or the scutage money into which it was commuted, was more or less out of use in the sixteenth century, but not the other burdens on knights' fees. It was still useful to maintain scutage rolls and to remember that 'Escuage drawith unto him homage and homage drawyth unto him fealtie, for fealtie is incydent to every manner of service; and so homage, fealtie and escuage draweth unto them warde, maryage and relieff'. These last three incidents were by no means neglected. At every succession, the heir owed a relief to his overlord and if the heir were below age, 21 years for a man and 14 for a girl, then the fee, multiple or fractional, was subject to wardship and marriage at the disposition of the overlord. Castle-guard service carried similar burdens.[4]

'Every tenure which is not tenure in chivalry is a tenure in socage.'[5] Thus were lumped together all other freehold tenures. Chief socage was held immediately of the king as of his crown, but the more usual type was common socage, held as a lord as of a manor. Common socage was usually free, and then called free and common socage. It rendered only suit of court, homage, fealty and a fixed rent, either in

[2] Norden, p. 103.
[3] p. 289.
[4] Norden, pp. 57–8; Straton i. 3–6; J. H. Round, 'Castle Guard', *Archaeol. Jnl*, 1902 lix (ix) 144–5; PRO, Exch. LR, MB 191, ff. 163v.–4; Co. Litt. 68b sqq., 87.
[5] *Ibid*. 85b–6.

money or in kind.[6] For the most part, these rents were nominal or symbolic: if in kind, perhaps a red rose, a peppercorn, a pound of cumin, a pair of gloves or spurs; if in money, no more than a few pence or shillings. In addition, some socagers owed a few boon works or light labour services.[7] On taking up a socage holding, the tenant had to do his services of submission, i.e. homage and fealty, thus (Docs. 3, 4):[8]

'When the tenante shall make homage to his lord, he shall descende, and his hedde uncoveryd, and his lord shall sitt; and the tenante shall kneele before hym on both his knees, and holde his hands joyntelye togethere bytwene the handes of his lorde and shall say thus: "I become your man from this daye forwarde of life and limb..."'

In doing fealty, he said: 'Hear you this my lord, that I unto you shall be faithful and true...'. These ancient feudal ceremonies could not be neglected, for the lord might distrain 'for homage and fealty beyng behynde'.[9] The new socage tenant had also to pay a relief, usually fixed at one year's rent. Some socagers, too, at decease, owed heriot-service.[10] Wardship and marriage, however, were no burden. The guardian appointed by the deceased had the wardship for the heir's sole profit and until he came of age at 14 years.[11] Some other tenures amounted to socage, notably holding by castle-guard rent and free burgage.[12]

Under socage tenure, descent was usually to the eldest son, by course of common law, but in some places by gavelkind, i.e. equally to all the sons or, in default, to all the daughters. Gavelkind was not confined to socagers, for it also attached to some customary tenures, and it was by no means peculiar to Kent, for it occurred in such widely separated places as Wales, East Norfolk, the Isle of Portland,

[6] Folkingham, p. 75.
[7] Straton i. 61 sqq.; Wilton ho. Svy Chalk 1595, ff. 1 sqq.
[8] W. Beaumont, 'Homage R. of Manor of Warrington', *Miscellanies relating to Lancs. & Ches.*, Rec. Soc. Lancs. & Ches. xii, 1885 i. 12.
[9] R. Stewart-Brown, *Lancs. & Ches. Cases in Court of Star Chamber*, pt i, Rec. Soc. Lancs. & Ches. 1916 lxxi. 50-1; J. E. Jackson, 'Chas Lord Stourton & the Murder of the Hartgills', *Wilts. Archaeol. Mag.* 1862 vii. 267.
[10] Co. Litt. 89b–91; R. Carew, *The Survey of Cornwall*. London, 1769, f. 30 (recte 38)v.; W. Hooper, *Reigate*, Guildford 1945, p. 199; Godfrey, p. 199; R. L. Kenyon, 'Manor of Ruyton of the 11 Towns', *Salop. Archaeol. Soc.* 1901 i. 98; 'Rowley Regis Rent R. 1556', *Colls. Hist. Staffs.* 1936, pp. 210 sqq.; R. Dymond, 'Customs of Manors of Braunton', *Devon Assoc.* 1888 xx. 284; B'ham Lib. 430213, ff. 1–2; Northants. RO, Wmld 5. ix; BM, Add. MS. 37270, ff. 41, 50; PRO, Exch. LR, MB 185, ff. 111v., 117v., 122v.; Parl. Svys Berks. 11, f. 6; Kent 14, f. 2; 15, f. 3; War. 25, f. 10.
[11] Co. Litt. 87b–8.
[12] *Ibid.* 87, 108b–9.

the Vale of London, the Midland Plain and the North Country.[13] It had been usual in Wales but was abandoned on some estates even before being generally abolished by the statute of 34 Henry VIII c. 26. Another disgavelling statute (31 Henry VIII c. 3) abolished this custom on many estates in Kent; but in 1601 a bill to take away all gavelkind in Kent failed on the ground that its incidental custom of 'the father to the bough, the son to the plough' was worthy of preservation, since it defeated escheat on account of the deliction of the tenant.[14]

Generally speaking, socage tenants were more common in eastern than in western England, if the kingdom be divided by an imaginary line along the Pennine watershed, to the north-eastern extremity of the Cotswold Country and the south-westerly of the Chiltern, and so to the south coast. In East Anglia about half the manorial tenants held some land in socage, but this distribution was uneven. Some eastern manors had only socage tenants and no customers, while in others the latter outnumbered the former. There were, in various places, some lordships without any socagers, but even in the west, where freeholders were generally less frequent, some manors had great numbers of them, a hundred or more, or even consisted exclusively of them.[15] In Kent there was little copyhold and much socage.[16] Even this picture is too sharp, for not only did many people hold by both freehold and copyhold tenures,[17] but where both common-law and customary tenures were of inheritance, the lands of the two were often inextricably confused.[18] The difference between the two tenures was so slight that the trouble and expense were rarely warranted, but, if necessary, such confused lands could be disentangled with rough justice under a writ of partition.[19]

The majority of manorial tenants held by customary law. Customary tenures were extremely diverse, but most were copyholds. Great diversity, however, was found even amongst copyhold tenures.

In the west generally, with the exception of the Vale of Taunton

[13] E.g. S. Taylor, *The History of Gavelkind*, London 1663, pp. 151–2.
[14] T. Blount, *Tenures of Lands*, ed. W. C. Hazlitt, London 1874, p. 179; *VCH Kent*, iii. 325–7; W. Lambard, *A Perambulation of Kent*, London 1576, p. 11; W. Marshall, *The Rural Economy of the Southern Counties*, London 1798, i. 26; C. A. J. Skeel, 'Wales under Henry VII', in *Tudor Studies*, ed. R. W. Seton-Watson, London 1924, pp. 11–2; F. Hull, 'The Custumal of Kent', *Arch. Cant.* 1959, lxxii. 152; BM, Add. MS. 28530, ff. 3, 18 (p. 23) (24).
[15] Space forbids refs. rel. to tenurial geography.
[16] Lambard, p. 11.
[17] Spratt, pp. 108, 127–30.
[18] *Ibid.* 108, 111; BM, Add. MS. 14850, f. 148; Jn Rylands Lib. Eng. 216; PRO, DL, MB 117, ff. 173, 208; Exch. LR, MB 203, f. 180; AO, Parl. Svys Ess. 17, f. 18; Herts. 7, f. 17; Lincs. 10A, f. 12.
[19] 3 Dyer 265b, 266a; PRO, Exch. KR, Deps. by Commn 10 Chas Mich 61.

Deane, the commonest customary tenure was copyhold for life or lives, with fines arbitrable at the will of the lord. Occasionally four or five lives might be granted on the one copy, in some places only one or two; but usually the lord might by custom grant three lives to a copy, the three persons named holding successively. Generally speaking, only persons named in the copy were customary tenants, but a few manors had a custom of allowing grants to one person on the understanding that other names could be added later, the habendum (the part of the grant starting 'to have and to hold'), being not to three named persons but to one person, 'to him and his'. This form of habendum was open to abuse and led to many disputes,[20] one of which serves to illustrate the custom. The customers of Preston manor claimed to have copyhold of inheritance with the habendum 'to him and his' for which they were beginning to substitute 'to him and his heirs'. Norden[21] discovered this and remarked:

'Although the wordes *sibi et suis* and *sibi et heredibus* in some mens construction be all one, I holde the difference great, for the first extendes but unto a man and his issue at the moste, wher the seconde is infinite. In Watlington wher they holde onlie for 3 lives, whereof 2 to be named by the taker, not named in the copie, the habendum is *sibi et suis* and so the estate determines upon the death of the laste. And so no dowbte the intention of *sibi et suis* was that the estate shoulde determyne upon the death of the takers laste childe and reverte into the lordes handes.'

In most lifehold manors reversions for one, two or three lives were allowed, and often even reversions on reversions. Like all copyholds, those for lives rendered a heriot to the lord at decease or surrender, usually the best beast or good, but occasionally a commuted money payment. This due was called a 'farlieu', 'farelife', 'farewell' or 'farefree' in parts of the West Country and Wales.[22] Almost invariably

[20] Moore (KB) 677; Northants. RO, Wmld 5.v. 1; Berks. RO, D/EBy. M. 1, pp. 12, 31; M. 13; Oxon. RO, DIL/IIA/2; Shak. Bpl. Throckmorton: Sambourn Ct R. 28 Sept. 1580, 1684, abs. customs 1708; Leigh: Ct R. id. Mich. 1545; BM, Add. R. 5068, 27987–8; PRO, Ct R. GS 207/82; DL, Ct R. 81/1119, m. 17; MB 116, ff. 64–6, 68; Exch. LR, MB 188, f. 23; 207, ff. 71 (68), 96 (93); 210, ff. 439 sqq.; 217, ff. 210 sqq.; TR, MB 157, f. 8 (p. 17); AO, MB 379, ff. 27 sqq., 49 sqq., 59 sqq., 66 sqq.; Parl. Svys Herefs. 16, f. 6; 19, f. 14; B'ham Lib. 381201, pp. 37, 119, 140; A. T. Bannister, 'Manorial Customs on Hereford Bishopric Estes', *EHR*, 1928 xliii. 219; Rec. Commn, *Calendars of Proceedings in Chancery in the Reign of Queen Elizabeth*, London 1827–32, i. 157, 239, 320; ii. 274; iii. 266.

[21] BM, Add. MS. 6027, f. 119 (118).

[22] Rathborne, p. 178; Norden, p. 53; BM, Harl. MS. 6006, f. 158; PRO, Exch. AO, Parl. Svys Corn. 22, f. 12; 46, ff. 4 sqq., 12; 54, f. 12; LR, MB 260, f. 18v.

the copyholder for lives paid for his holding an entry fine that was arbitrary at the will of the lord and unrestricted by customary law. That the next in line of descent were sometimes allowed first option on the holding made little difference for they had to pay as much as the next man.

Copyhold for years was rare, even in the Midlands, where its incidence was highest. These grants were usually for 21 years, but sometimes for as many as 40 or 61 or as few as 9, the term frequently being variable in one and the same manor. With copyholds for years, the fines were also arbitrary at the will of the lord.

In eastern England, where the highest general incidence of socage tenures was to be found, the usual customary tenure was copyhold of inheritance, as it was also in Taunton Deane,[23] the Cheshire Cheese Country and the Lancashire Plain. In this form of copyhold the habendum was 'to him and his heirs'; or, occasionally, to the tenant himself and his heirs for a fixed number of years only, yet with a certain right of renewal to the tenant or his heirs on expiry of the term, so amounting to a right of inheritance. Assimilated to copyhold of inheritance likewise was the burgage tenure of some manorial boroughs, where the burgesses held of the lord of the borough, according to the custom of the borough 'by copye of court roll of this manor under the graunt and lettinge of the lorde of this manor'.[24]

For the most part, copyholds of inheritance descended, by the provisions of customary law, according to the course of common law, i.e. to the eldest son or, in defect, to the daughters as co-heiresses. In a considerable minority of the manors, however, descent was by borough English or 'cradle-hold', to the youngest son of the last wife, unless a former wife had a jointure in the tenement or a feoffment to her own use, in which case her youngest son inherited. Yet in a few manors, the issue of the first wife had precedence over all others. In defect of sons, the youngest daughter was usually sole heiress. Borough English was widely distributed but concentrated in Taunton Deane, the north Midlands, East Anglia and the more southerly of the Wealden Vales. Elsewhere again, copyholds of inheritance descended by a combination of borough English and the course of common law. In Cheltenham the eldest son inherited tenements in the borough and the youngest those outside it. In Wadhurst, sokeland descended as by common law and bondland by borough English, the eldest or the youngest son inheriting both according to whether the deceased had made his first entry into the sokeland or the bondland, while if both had been entered simultaneously, the sokeland drew the bond-

[23] W. Marshall, *A Review . . . of Reports to the Board of Agriculture from Southern and Peninsular Departments of England*, London 1817, p. 602.
[24] Straton ii. 383–5.

land with it to the eldest. There were several other variations on the same theme. From these intermixtures of the common-law course and borough English, partible inheritance resulted. In a few places, partibility was carried to the extreme, and inheritance was to all sons and daughters equally, as in Wareham. In addition, some copyholds of inheritance descended in gavelkind proper.[25] Sometimes, too, partible inheritance existed in an attenuated form, the heir's brothers and sisters being allowed monetary compensation or some rights of pasturage in the holding in their capacity of 'bedreapers'.[26]

Nearly half the copyholds of inheritance paid no more than fixed and certain entry fines. One or two years' customary rent was the usual rate, though sometimes this was assessed by the yardland, oxgang or acre, in such a way that the sum amounted to much the same as one or two years' rent, which was only a nominal payment. Not uncommonly the fine on alienation was two years rent and on descent only one. In a few places, too, where the lands were charged with the repair of waterworks, entry fines were not taken at all. In other and increasingly numerous places, the fines were certain, perhaps recently ascertained, and assessed at about one or two years' improved annual value of the holding. This was considerably and increasingly in excess of the customary rent, but still much less than would have been paid for an arbitrary fine at the will of the lord.

In many manors, however, especially in the Vale of London and the Chiltern Country, and to a lesser extent in the Fen and Southdown countries, the Wealden Vales, High Weald and East Anglia, as well as elsewhere, in copyhold of inheritance, while fines were certain on descent, they were arbitrary at the will of the lord on alienation. Occasionally, too, was found a custom whereby the fine was certain if the holding passed to a native or someone already a tenant of the manor and arbitrary if sold to a stranger.

Nearly half, but a somewhat dwindling proportion, of the copyholds of inheritance were subject to arbitrary fines at both descent and alienation or surrender, this custom being widespread, especially in the Southdown, South Sea-coast, Fen and Northwold countries, the Midland Plain and East Anglia. All told, then, about half the fines under copyhold of inheritance were arbitrary.

None of these arbitrary fines on copyholds of inheritance, however, was merely at the will of the lord. They all had to be 'reasonable', i.e., had to be compatible and consistent with the custom of inheritance and

[25] 1 Leon. 56; Marcham, p. 153; J. Bradney, *A History of Monmouthshire*, London 1904–34, iv/ii. 111; Bannister, p. 218; *Sy Archaeol. Colls.* xxix. 159–61; H. M. Doughty, *Chronicles of Theberton*, London 1910, p. 134; W. Sfk RO, E. 7/10/9; BM, Add. MS. 28530, f. 3; PRO, Exch. AO, Parl. Svys Dors. 12, f. 4.
[26] PRO, DL, MB 116, f. 73.

not so large that they defeated the heir of his inheritance. If the lord and the heir failed to agree on what was a reasonable fine, the sum had to be assessed in the manor court by the jury. Even if the heir or purchaser had reached agreement with the lord on what they considered a reasonable fine, this had still to be 'affeered' (scrutinized and approved or rejected) by jurymen to ensure that it was not so great as to set an evil precedent. The fine, in short, had to be reasonable and agreed by both contracting parties and by all tenants of the manor. Three, or more usually two, years' annual improved value of the holding was commonly regarded as the maximum reasonable fine. For example, a copyholder was asked for what he considered an unreasonable fine. The jury affeered the fine and concurred with him, so the tenant was admitted on payment of a reduced sum.[27] Were such a decision disputed, it could be taken for review to a higher court. Coke tells us that such a fine, 'though it be incertain, yet it must be reasonable. And that reasonablenesse shall be discussed by the justices upon the true circumstances of the case appearing unto them'; and 'where a fine be reasonable, or not, shall be determined by the justices either upon demurrer, or upon evidence to a jury, or confession or proof of the yearly value' (Doc. 4). This is precisely what happened. Common-law courts allowed only one and a half years' value, and, upon a demurrer in the Common Pleas, two years' profit of the land was adjudged an unreasonably high fine for copyhold of inheritance. Chancery followed suit. From at least 1586 onwards, cases concerning arbitrary but reasonable fines were being brought to Chancery and reasonable maxima being decided variously as two years' and a half of rent, two years' value, one year's value, or most commonly, one year's value and a half if the holding were not heriotable, one year's value otherwise. Two and a half years' value was deemed inordinate. Similar judgments were made also in the court of Requests. Since the arbitrary fine had to be reasonable with inheritance, its non-payment entailed no forfeiture if it was judged unreasonable by the copyholder, by the affeerers, or by a superior court. Thus the court baron and of survey of Tardebigge in 1630 advised the customers to offer reasonable fines, and if these were not accepted, to hold the land

[27] Rathborne, p. 178; Spratt, p. 145; Willcox, p. 271; 2 Brownl. & Golds. 85; Godfrey, pp. 82-3, 118, 224; I. S. Leadam, 'Security of Copyholders in 15th & 16th cents.', *EHR* 1893 viii. 695; J. C. K. Cornwall, 'The Agrarian History of Sussex 1560-1640', ts. thesis M.A. Ldn Univ. 1953, p. 281; Leconfield, *Petworth Manor in the 17th Century*, London 1954, pp. 20-1; M. Campbell, *The English Yeoman*, New Haven 1942, pp. 135-6; W. Marshall, *A Review of Reports to Board of Agriculture from Eastern Department of England*, London 1811, p. 315; Herts. RO, G'bury X.D. 4e; BM, Add. MS. 6027, f. 4(8); PRO, R. & S. GS 8/47; Exch. AO, Parl. Svys Cams. 1, f. 10; Hunts. 7, f. 37; Lincs. 15, f. 33; Sy 38, f. 15; TR, MB 157, f. 4 (p. 9).

against the lord. Gedney Burghlion Fee's custom is that 'a coppihold tennaunt ought not to forfeit his customarye land for non-payment of his fyne' and no precedent for such a forfeiture can be found. Various manorial customs in the same sense were adjudged reasonable and good in law by both Chancery and common-law courts, and Coke was only following precedent when he said such a copyholder of inheritance was not obliged to pay an unreasonable fine (Doc. 4).[28] Hence, even when the fine was arbitrary at the will of the lord, the copyhold was of inheritance in nature as well as in name. Although a few unlikely claims were made for fines certain on copyhold for lives, they could be reasonable, though arbitrary, only in copyhold of inheritance, for any fine, however high, would have been reasonable with holding for term of life, provided only that a taker could be found; and

'the law has fixed what shall be a reasonable fine for a copyholder in fee to pay; but it has nowhere fixed what shall be a reasonable fine for a copyholder for life to pay; therefore, if a copyholder for life would set up a tenant-right of renewal, he must set forth the fine in certain.'

Thus even when both are called arbitrary, the fines on copyhold of inheritance and copyhold for lives were quite different, and Tawney's statement that 'the ability of the lord to demand what fine he pleased could be used as a means of excluding a successor even when the copy was ... from father to son' is sheer fabrication.[29]

Copyhold of inheritance was, then, much the same as socage tenure, though the former was under the customary and not the common law, and though fines were paid instead of reliefs.

One kind of copyhold tenure, indeed, was also a freehold tenure just as socage was, even though still customary. All the forms of copyhold reviewed so far were bond copyholds, that is to say, whether of inheritance or for lives or years, they all originated in the will of the lord, who retained the fee or the freehold of the land. There were also a few free copyholds held solely by copy of court roll according to the custom of the manor and yet not at the will of the lord. They had the

[28] Co. Litt. 60a; 4 Co. Rep. 27b; Coke, *Copyholder*, sect. 57; Moore (KB) 622–3; Tothill 100–3; 1 Eq. Ca. Abr. 120; Ritchie, pp. 16–7; D. E. C. Yale, *Lord Nottingham's Chancery Cases*, Selden Soc. lxxiii, lxxix, 1957–61 ii. 562, 726–7; Godfrey, p. 83; W. Notestein, F. H. Relf and H. Simpson, *Commons Debates 1621*, New Haven 1935, v. 178; R. C. Gaut, *A History of Worcs. Agriculture & Rural Evolution*, Worcester 1939, p. 83; A. Savine, 'Eng. Customary Tenures in Tudor Period', *Q. Jnl Econ.* 1905, xix. 72–3; BM, Harl. MS. 702, f. 70v.; Glos. RO, D. 45, L. Slaughter Ct R. April 14, 1651, January 19, 1652, April 6, 1659.
[29] Tawney, pp. 297–8; 4 Co. Rep. 27b; 1 Eq. Ca. Abr. 120; PRO, Exch. AO, Parl. Svys Northants. 40. f. 21.

frank tenure in themselves and were themselves freehold tenures, being quite distinct from base copyholds held at the will of the lord. These free copyholds were generally found only on ancient demesne, that is the ancient Saxon royal demesne as it was taken over and augmented by William the Conqueror. Free copyholds were protected and secured by the king's writ of right close, or little writ of right. In some instances, too, both free and bond copyholds were found in the self-same manor.[30]

Finally, there were some customary tenants of inheritance who did not hold by copy but were otherwise the same as copyholders of inheritance. These tenants by the verge, as they were often called, were given seisin by the handing over of a verge, rod, staff, straw or glove; but their admittances, surrenders and conveyances were recorded in the court rolls and in all essentials they were copyholders of inheritance. (Docs. 3, 4). [31]

This analysis of copyhold tenures has so far been confined to grants and admittances in the first instance and has thus exaggerated the relative importance of copyhold of inheritance, for though the custom of copies for lives or years excluded the custom of inheritance, copyhold of inheritance was not exclusive of copyholds for lives or years. On the contrary, custom nearly always permitted the copyholder of inheritance to surrender his holding to the use of another party for a term of years or for the term of the life of this second party, the copyholder of inheritance reserving the remainder to himself and his heirs. The fines paid on these limited surrenders were usually purely nominal, much less than those on infinite surrenders. Limited surrenders were therefore convenient instruments for copyholders of inheritance who wished to provide for a widow or a ward or simply to lease out their lands. In this way were created myriads of copyholds for years and for lives.[32]

Three regions had their own peculiar customary tenures. In the country of Wales, a confusion of common-law and customary tenures had resulted in a mongrel of the two; in the north, border tenure or tenant-right prevailed; and on the manors of the Ancient Duchy of Cornwall, there were many tenants in free conventionary.

In Wales many so-called freehold tenants owed not only heriots and suit of mill as most customary tenants did, but also leyrwite, a due paid on the marriage of their daughters and a casualty unknown in England after the passing of villeinage. In North Wales, indeed, many 'freeholders' were the former bondmen on royal and ecclesiastical

[30] Folkingham, p. 76; A. Fitzherbert, *Natura Brevium* [1534], f. 10(G); Coke, *Copyholder*, sect. 32.
[31] *Ibid.* sect. 39; Norden, p. 47; Fitzherbert, *Svying*, ff. 16v.–7.
[32] Moore (KB) 753.

estates manumitted by Henry VII's charter in 1507. Side by side with these, especially in the Englishry parts, there were many holders in so-called free socage, who owed heriots and some of whom were avowedly customary tenants. To both these groups the names of 'free customary tenure' or 'husbandry hold' were commonly applied, and they were both originally customary, although the tenants were more and more avoiding conveyance in manor courts and using instead common-law deeds, so concealing their true tenures. Norden says of these tenants: 'Though they be in name freeholders, they be in nature customary, and were in times past the most of them bondmen.' This confusion of tenures and systems of law was finally cleared up in 1603 when the Exchequer Court decreed that the 1507 charter conveyed merely personal manumission and not the enfranchisement of the land. Thereupon these bogus freeholders were compelled to compound for common-law leases, sometimes with a right of renewal, since their ancient tenures were now compromised and forfeited by their own infringement of the customs they had held under.[33]

In Cornwall, in addition to many copyholders for lives, there were, in seventeen manors of the Ancient Duchy, though in none of those of the Annexed Duchy, conventionary tenants or tenants 'in free conventionary'. Conventionary lands were customary and no one could be a conventionary tenant except by descent or by the lord's demise. The tenants held to themselves and their heirs for ever, descent being to the eldest son or, in defect, to the eldest daughter. Conventionary tenants owed suit of court and mill, customary rents, heriots, due capons, harvest journeys, the discharge of the offices of reeve and tithingman, and, in some instances, merchet. They held not by copy, but by septennial leases renewed of right every seven years at a special court of assession or assessionary court. At each renewal there

[33] G. Owen, *The Description of Penbrokshire*, ed. H. Owen, H.S.C. Rec. Ser. i 1892–1936, pt i. 61; B. E. Howells, 'Pembroke Farming c. 1580–1620', *NLW Jnl* 1955–6, ix. 414–6; E. Evans, 'Manor of Uwchmynydd . . . 1618', *ibid.* 1949–50, vi. 388–90; E. A. Lewis & J. C. Davies, 'Man. Docs. rel. to Manor of Broniarth 1536–1773', *Montgom. Colls.* 1946, xlix. 225–7; R. Lewis, 'A Breviat of Glam. 1596–1600', in *S. Wales & Mon. Rec. Soc.* iii. 97 sqq.; 'Man. Customs in co. Carm.', *W. Wales Hist. Rec.* 1921, viii. 147 sqq.; J. Lloyd, 'Svys of Manors of Rads.', *Arch. Camb.* 1900 xvii. 1–4, 7, 9–11, 15–8, 22–3, 110–1, 113–4, 116, 118 sqq., 125–8; *ibid.* 1847 ii. 215–7; *Cal. Pat. R.* 1494–1509, p. 534; T. Jones-Pierce, 'Some Tendencies in Agrarian Hist. Caerns. . . .', *Trans. Caerns. Hist. Soc.* 1939, pp. 20, 27; 'N. on Hist. Rural Caerns. . . .', *ibid.* 1940, pp. 35 sqq.; W. Rees, *A Survey of Duchy of Lancaster Lordships in Wales, 1609–13*, Cardiff 1953, pp. 5, 29–30, 73–4, 113 sqq., 177, 206, 210, 217 sqq., 237–8; W. Davies, *A General View of the Agriculture & Domestic Economy of N. Wales*, London 1810, p. 78; id. *S. Wales*, London 1814, i. 120; D. R. Phillips, *The History of the Vale of Neath*, Swansea 1925, p. 33; W. J. Slack, *The Lordship of Oswestry*, Shrewsbury 1951, p. 59; PRO, Exch. AO, Parl. Svys Mon. 2; 3, f. 1; 7, f. 1; 9, f. 1.

was payable to the lord a fixed and certain fine, sometimes called 'old knowledge', which might be up to £6 or so. Payment was not in a lump sum, but spread over the first six years of the septennium, the tenant paying every year his customary rent and one sixth of his fine; it was in the nature of recognition money tendered as a running fine, but due irrespective of any change of lord. In addition, after surrenders, a 'new knowledge' of two years' rent was due within three years following the assessionary court. Provided he himself was in possession at the time of the assessionary court, the tenant could make subtenancies from seven years to seven years without licence. Holdings could be surrendered or transmitted to heirs out of court at any time during the septennium, provided only that presentments of these transactions were made at the next assessionary court and recorded in the court rolls. Free bench (holding by widow's right) was allowed to the widow, as in most customary tenures, and rents or fines might be distrained, but there was no forfeiture for non-payment. The right of renewal was certain, but it did not confer a right of inheritance in law, for renewal was subject to the assessionary court. In practice, however, conventionary tenure amounted to a customary tenure of inheritance.[34]

In the North-western and North-eastern Lowlands and in the North Country, the prevailing tenure was tenant-right. Holders by tenant-right properly so called held 'after the manner and custom in the country of tenant-right', 'according to the custom of husbandry', 'according to the custom of the manor'. Customers by tenant-right were bound to do military service on the border by horse and on foot at their own expense in their own persons and in those of all able-bodied men over sixteen years of age, by day or night immediately upon a signal from the warden of the marches. They had to repel the Scots, rescue cattle taken in border raids, and keep themselves in horse and gear against all emergencies. All forms of border tenure were burdened with these services, but otherwise varied greatly. Some tenant-right was of inheritance without any entry fines or with small fixed fines or 'gressoms'. Elsewhere the fines were arbitrary, but reasonable and modest, perhaps four or five years rent, and were often accompanied by a 'knowing' or recognition payment made every two, three or five years in the form of a running 'gressom'. Sometimes strangers taking

[34] Carew, ff. 30 (recte 38)v., 36v.; Norden, p. 47; M. Coate, *Cornwall in the Great Civil War*, Oxford 1933, pp. 10–2; 'Du. of Corn', *Trans. R. Hist. S.* 1927, x. 137–9, 143–6; PRO, Exch. AO, Parl. Svys Corn. 6, ff. 7 sqq., 22; 7, ff. 1, 3–4; 9, f. 17; 17, ff. 7 sqq., 22–5; 18, ff. 7 sqq., 23; 25, ff. 13 sqq., 47–9; 27, ff. 6 sqq.; 29, ff. 3–4; 30, ff. 3–6; 31, ff. 3–5, 7; 35, ff. 7–10; 37, ff. 11–2; 40, ff. 9 sqq., 35–6; 42, ff. 1–4; 43, ff. 7 sqq., 18–20; 44, ff. 7, 18; 45, ff. 5 sqq.; 47, ff. 4 sqq., 12–3; 51, ff. 14 sqq., 27–8.

up a tenant-right holding paid a fine at the will of the lord, while an heir only owed a fixed and certain one. There was, indeed, a whole range of local customs not unlike those found with customary tenures in other parts of England. Other border tenants, however, held merely at will or by lease and did not enjoy tenant-right properly so-called even though they were liable for military service and sat at similarly modest rents and fines.[35] The border district was notoriously lawless, and tenant-right may have been a feeble tenure compared with socage, but the customary holders by tenant-right were not mere tenants at will; they were tenants at the will of the lord according to the custom of the manor or country. Coke did not say, as Tawney, without chapter or verse, wrongly alleged, 'The customary tenants upon the borders of Scotland ... are mere tenants at will, and though they keep their customs inviolate, yet the lord might, sans controll, evict them.' What Coke did say was:[36]

'I need not stand to discourse at large the antiquity of the *copy-holders* ... Immediately upon the conquest they were known by the name of villains ... wholly depending upon the will of the lord, and outstable at his pleasure ...; having shaken off the fetters of their bondage, they were presently freed of their opprobious name, and had other new gentle stiles and titles conferred upon them: they were everywhere then called *tenants by copy of court-roll*, or *tenants at will* according to the custom of the manor: which stile imports unto us three things: 1. *Name*, 2. *Origin*, 3. *Title*. 1. His name is *tenant by copy of court-roll* ... 2. His commencement is at the will of the lord. For these tenants in their birth, as well as the customary tenants upon the borders of *Scotland,* who have the name of tenants, were meer tenants at will: and though they keep the customs inviolate, yet the lord might, *sans* controll, eject them. Neither was their estate hereditary in the beginning, as appeareth by *Britton*: for if they died, their

[35] A. Bagot, 'Mr Gilpin & Man. customs', *Trans. Cumb. & Wmld Antiq. & Archaeol. Soc.* 1962, lxii, 224–6, 228–9; Bateson, iii. 87, 100, 104; v. 256–7; viii. 237–8; ix. 197, 322; x. 275; xiv. 230, 575; xv. 248; Campbell, pp. 148–9; C. L. M. Bouch & G. P. Jones, *A Short Economic & Social History of the Lake Counties,* Manchester 1961, pp. 65 sqq.; 'Humberstone's Svy', *Yks. Archaeol. Jnl* 1903, xvii. 136–7; Stewart-Brown, *St. Ch.* i. 69; H. Fishwick, *Pleadings & Depositions in Duchy Court of Lancaster in time of Henry VII & VIII,* Rec. Soc. Lancs. & Ches. 1896, xxxii. 99, 192–4; id. *Edward VI & Mary, ibid.* 1899, xl. 145, 147; *Cals. Proc. Chanc. R. Eliz.* i, 65; Man. Lib. Lancs. Deeds L. 4; PRO, R. & S. GS roll 986; Exch. KR, MB 42, pp. 5–7, 30, 85, 89; 47, ff. 90, 93–4; LR, MB 212, ff. 160 sqq. 261v., 279, 301v.–2, 308, 489, 513; 220, ff. 1, 2; AO, Parl. Svys Cumb. 6, ff. 1, 3 sqq., 51; 8, f. 2; Lancs. 14, f. 12; Wmld 5, ff. 1, 4–6; 6, ff. 1, 5–6; R. H. Tawney & E. Power, *Tudor Economic Documents,* London 1924, i. 77–80.
[36] Lambard, p. 11; Coke, *Copyholder,* sect. 32. Cf. Tawney, p. 299.

estate was presently determined; as in case of a tenant at will at common law; and in some points, to this present hour, the law regardeth them no more than a meer tenant at will; for the freehold at the common law resteth not in them, but in their lords, unless it be in copyholds of frank-tenure, which are most usual in ancient demesne.'

Coke's 'keep' is not in the present tense but the old form of the past conditional, which can hardly be appreciated if his 'were' be changed into 'are'. As Coke well knew, the common law protected tenant-right according to the custom of the manor or country. Whenever a custom of inheritance could be proved, even upon the borders of Scotland, the law countenanced and confirmed it.[37]

Tenant-right completes this conspectus of tenures. Apart from limited surrenders of copyholds of inheritance and copyholds for lives and years, no provision was made for agricultural leases, for tenures had been evolved at a time when farming for profit was hardly conceived of. It was to repair these deficiencies, as well as to codify the bewildering variety of local tenures, that there had been evolved, in the later middle ages, the system and doctrine of estates. In the early modern period, it may fairly be said, tenures themselves were of only secondary consequence, and the whole business of both farming and landownership depended not on tenures but on real estates and present interests in land.

The least interest that anyone could have in land was a tenancy at will. Tenancies at will by the common law were frequent in the early modern period, in cottages built on the waste and similar encroachments, and on demesne lands in common-field townships, notably in the Midland Plain.[38] These were not freehold estates but chattels. Where demesne lands were let at will they could still be properly described as 'in hand', or 'in possession', for the lord could resume their occupation whenever he wished, only allowing the tenant to harvest his own growing crops.[39] Such tenancy at will was usually confined to cottagers, paupers or poor tenant-farmers, and was much the same as the villein tenancy after the conquest that Coke (Doc. 11)

---

[37] Bateson, ii. 427; iv. 137; viii. 237–8; ix. 322; Campbell, pp. 150–2; Bouch & Jones, pp. 75–6; Bagot, p. 232; Notestein et al. iv. 142; v. 258, 287; vii. 65 sqq., 75–7; G. P. Jones, 'Decline of Yeomanry of Lake Cos.', *Trans. Cumb. & Wmld Antiq. & Archaeol. Soc.* 1962, lxii. 200; 'Manor of Cotherstone w. Hunderthwaite', *Yks. Archaeol. Jnl* 1943, xxxv. 330–3; PRO, Exch. LR, MB 214, ff. 152 sqq.; AO, Parl. Svys Lancs. 18, ff. 2, 32; 14, f. 11; Wmld 5, f. 1; 6, f. 1; Chanc. Decree R. 2nd Div. 1st pt, pt 362 nos. 8, 10; pt 363, nos. 10–2.

[38] See below, p. 87.

[39] Co. Litt. 55a; Glos. RO, D. 184, M. 11, pp. 2,3; PRO, Exch. AO, Parl. Svys Corn. 15, f. 5.

speaks of, examples of which survived, in the North-eastern Lowlands chiefly, under the name of customary tenancy at will.[40]

Similar in form, though quite different in content, was the lease-parol from year to year (annual tenancy), with a rack-rent proper, that developed on many enclosed farms in the Midland Plain, the Wealden Vales, the Vale of Pickering, the Fen, West, Butter and Cheese countries and elsewhere after 1560 and by the eighteenth century had largely displaced all other tenancies. Lease-parol had no savour of inferior status, and gentlemen farmers and the like had no objection to annual tenancy because they dealt on equal terms with their landlords and had nothing to fear from them, especially in view of the advanced rack-rents they paid. The lease-parol was also a real chattel, for the estate was agreed only by word of mouth and usually ran from year to year, depending solely on the mutual trust and interest of landlord and tenant, which lent it ample security. Concurrently, there was a similar rise of leases by indenture for short terms of three, five or seven years, or from three years to three years for a period of nine. These likewise carried rack-rents and were found chiefly in enclosed farms. Rack-rents were on an adjustable scale. The notion that rack-renting meant screwing up rents to the impoverishment of the farmer is mistaken. Rack-rents moved up or down according to such things as price movements, good and bad harvests and the state of the land. Both rack-renting and leases-parol or for short terms admirably suited landlords and farmers with enclosed and improved farms, especially where up-and-down husbandry was practised. Rents could be varied according to the acreage ploughed and landlords could let out single 'pastures' to be corned by farmers or woaded by woadmen under leases whose terms coincided with the period of tillage or of tillage and ley formation.[41]

[40] Straton i. 307-8; PRO, Exch. LR. MB 260, f. 22.

[41] Cary 51; W. Marshall, The Rural Economy of the Midland Counties, London 1790, i. 16-7; Yks. i, 26, 32; Cave & Wilson, pp. 59, 77; Willcox, p. 279; Cals. Proc. Chanc. R. Eliz. i. 200; ii. 262; iii. 304; M. E. Finch, The Wealth of 5 Northants. Families 1540-1640, Northants. Rec. Soc. 1956, xix, 159; Stat. 29 Chas II c. 3; D. Gardiner, The Oxinden & Peyton Letters 1642-70, London 1937, p. 278; Bateson, i. 275; ii. 407-8; Glouc. Lib. 16062, p. 55; Northants. RO, F(M) Misc. 77, 200, 202, 205, 207, 211, 453, 459, 1033; Misc. Vol. 433, pp. 14 sqq; Wmld 7/16; F-H 119; 298, p. 57; Shak. Bpl. Throckmorton: Ct R. Spernall October 9, 1662; W. de B. 1080; Deene ho. Brudenell A. iv. 1; Leic. Mus. 35/29/478; City Recs. BR2 p 8a/1963; Leics. RO, DE. 10, Wm Herrick's A/c Bk 1610-36, pp. 51 sqq.; BM, Egerton MS. 3003, ff. 91-3; Add. MSS. 21608, ff. 130-1, 192, 195, 276v.-8; 36582, f. 77; Longleat ho. Misc. Papers Sir Jn Thynne sen. 1561-76, II/xlix, f. 282; Wilts. RO, acc. 84 Clayton 3, 9; B'ham Lib. Winnington 52; PRO, Sp. Coll. Shaftesbury Papers 2/33; St. Ch. Jas 54/10; SPD Jas, vol. 48 no 26, f. 398; Interregnum vol. G58A, f. 338; Exch. LR, MB 185, ff. 101(2)-102(3); KR, Deps. by Commn 10 Chas Mich. 61; 15-6 Chas Hil. 8.

In the early sixteenth century, farm leases for years usually had long
terms, often forty years and sometimes even sixty or even ninety-nine.
From about 1540 onwards, however, they generally became shorter:
in the east for terms of seven, fourteen or twenty-one years, renewable
(and usually renewed) every seven years; in the west, where copyholds for lives prevailed, for one, two or three lives, usually for three
and renewable at the fall of each life. These lives were nearly always
those of the takers: very few leases were for *terme d'auter vie* (for
the life of another person). Many of these leases by indenture, however, were not simply for three lives but for ninety nine years determinable on three lives. This habendum was especially common in the
south-west, as in the Chalk and West countries, but simple lifeholds
were usual in the Cheshire Cheese Country and the Lancashire Plain.
In the midlands and north, leases by indenture were generally for
twenty-one years, three lives or years determinable upon lives. Twenty-
one years and three lives were regarded as equivalents and were of
much the same length in practice; and renewals at every seven years
and at the fall of each life were likewise similar, so there was little
difference between the terms and conditions of all these leases. There
is thus no truth in Miss Mildred Campbell's suggestion that leases
were generally longer in the west and away from London than in the
east and near the metropolis.[42] The chief difference between these
leases by indenture was in the estates they conferred. Leases for years
were mere chattel interests, while those for lives were freehold estates.
Leases for years determinable upon lives were real chattels and the
freehold estate was not conveyed to the tenant by livery of seisin as
with an indenture for lives; yet the tenant had all the other advantages of a lifehold estate.[43]

Lease terms by indentures did not differ generally and essentially
from place to place, but they did between estates, particularly between
those of the crown, the Church and lay mesne lords. On ecclesiastical
and college estates, after 1540, leases were mostly either for twenty-
one years or for three lives; but in the early sixteenth century many
longer terms had been granted, especially by monastic houses. The
monasteries wrung the last drop out of their estates just before the
Dissolution and prolonged their interests in the lands as long as they
could, by granting leases for exaggerated terms such as ninety-nine
years or four lives. Lease terms on royal estates generally conformed
to local practice, but there were everywhere some royal leases for
terms of unusual length, 31, 41 or even 61 years and in the midlands
and the north 31 years became an increasingly common term on
crown estates. Generally speaking, then, the usual terms of leases by

[42] Campbell, pp. 82–3; Bateson, ix. 197–8, 200.
[43] Shak. Bpl. W. de B. 1162.

indenture were three lives or twenty-one years. These were long leases, long enough to encourage farming improvements and ensure improvements of rent. Leases longer than this were granted only with ulterior motives and were disallowed by the common law on the ground that such leases were never without suspicion of fraud. Finally, in farms where no more major improvements remained to be undertaken, short terms and lease-parol were introduced.[44]

Misinterpretation of the evidence of manorial surveys has created a tenurial illusion that must be shattered. In commissioning a survey of his manors, the lord was solely concerned with tenants who held of him and not with their subtenants. Yet in most farming countries these undertenants were an important and numerous body.

Many manorial freeholds belonged to landowners whose concern was not with farming but with the receipt of rents. There are innumerable instances of substantial landowners whose property was largely composed of socage holdings in many different manors and sometimes in a score of townships. Even when it is not explicitly stated, as it often is, that these properties were mostly occupied by undertenants, such an inference is reasonable.[45] Of these undertenants the manorial surveys disclose little or nothing. The only circumstances under which a survey would record an undertenant was when the socager had made the undertenant responsible for the payment of rent to the lord of the manor and when the subtenancy had been noted for the convenience of the rent-collector.[46] To take an example, in consideration of a lump sum of £145, Francis Goddard esquire of Standen Hussey leased to Thomas Collins yeoman of Aldbourne, in reversion, for ninety-nine years determinable on three lives, a yardland in the common fields and a tenement in the High Street at Aldbourne. It was a condition of the lease that the lessee discharged all duties and payments to the lord of the manor. He had to pay the quit-rent and reliefs and perform suit of court on Goddard's behalf. When the manor was later surveyed, Thomas Collins claimed to hold this freehold by virtue of a deed from Francis Goddard, who claimed to hold by socage also seventeen other tenements, ranging in size from one sixteenth of an acre to 178 acres, of which probably all, and certainly most, were in the hands of some half dozen undertenants.[47] At Upton-on-Severn in 1664, of the 88 manorial freeholders, one had

[44] D. E. C. Yale, *Lord Nottingham's 'Manual of Chancery Practice' & 'Prolegomena of Chancery and Equity'*, Cambridge 1965, pp. 221–2.

[45] E.g. Spratt, pp. 79–80.

[46] C. W. Sutton, 'Svy of Manor of Penwortham 1570', *Chetham Miscellanies iii*, Chetham Soc. 1915, lxxiii. 1 sqq., 6 sqq.

[47] PRO, Exch. TR, MB 157, ff. 40–1, 43–4 (pp. 74, 76–7); BM, Add. Ch. 40095.

5 undertenants, one 3, one 2, and fourteen 1 each.[48] At Walkeringham, 16 of the 23 manorial freeholders may have been owner-occupiers, but one had 24 subtenants, one 15, another 9, one 2, and three more one apiece, so that seven socagers had 53 undertenants between them.[49] Market Bosworth, at the end of the sixteenth century, had nine socage tenants, of whom three were owner-occupiers and six had 14 undertenants between them, while the parson sublet parts of his glebe to several other persons who were neither tenants nor undertenants to anyone else.[50] At Bedfont, out of 140 freehold parcels in the sixteenth century, 47 were occupied by their tenants and 93 by undertenants (Doc. 14). Henry Mayhew, a socage tenant of Dinton and Teffont, 'held the landes belonginge to the same house in his own occupacion . . ., saving that he did let sometimes most part thereof from yeare to yeare'.[51]

Similar subletting was also practised by many lessees by indenture. Lessees of farms, as might be expected, often sublet their cottages.[52] Lessees are found subletting half their farms and taking bonds from undertenants for the payment of reserved rents to the lord of the manor. Landlords impose lease covenants against subletting without licence. Undertenants dispute the titles of the lessees from whom they hold.[53] John Ernle esquire leased Wedhampton Farm in Urchfont from the Earl of Hertford, sublet it to John Toucker and sold the reversion of the undertenancy. Edward Ernle was lessee of Urchfont Manor Farm, which had over a thousand acres, but he sublet all the arable to a number of cultivators.[54] The leasing of demesne farms to single tenants by no means shows that they were farmed as large units; where small farms were the general rule, the lessees of demesnes frequently sublet them to a number of undertenants.[55]

Customary tenants also engaged in subletting. As has been seen already, copyholders of inheritance often made limited surrenders that were effective subtenancies; but, in addition to this, all kinds of

[48] Worcs. RO, BA 104, parcel 37 freeholders' roll 1664.
[49] PRO, R. & S. GS 13/87.
[50] Leics. RO, DE. 40/22/2–3.
[51] PRO, Exch. KR, Sp. Commn 2445.
[52] Leics. RO, DE. 40/22/2.
[53] PRO, Req. 23/78, 24/2, 53/38; St. Ch. Hy VIII vol. 6, ff. 74, 255; Wilts. RO, acc. 283 Svy Amesbury 1635, ff. 47–8.
[54] Ibid. Svy Urchfont c. 1640, ff. 71, 91–2; W. H. Jones, 'Hist. Par. All Cannings', Wilts. Archaeol. Mag. 1869, xi. 191–2.
[55] T. S. Willan, 'Parl. Svys N.R. Yks.', Yks. Archaeol. Jnl 1934, xxxi. 239; L. J. U. Way, '1625 Svy smaller Manor Clifton', Bristol & Glos. Archaeol. Soc. Trans. 1913, xxxvi. 223; PRO, DL, MB 117, f. 96v.; 119, f. 255; 123; Exch. LR, MB 230, f. 52; AO, Parl. Svys Lincs. 13A, f. 5; Notts. 17, f. 1; War. 9, 26–8.

D

copyholders sublet land. According to the customs of most manors with copyhold for lives, the copyholder could let his holding for a year and a day without licence. In manors where the copyholds were of inheritance, subletting without licence was usually allowed without licence for terms of three years, and sometimes even longer, as befitted customary tenants who were in the nature of landed proprietors. Before subletting for periods longer than these, the copyholder was obliged to obtain his lord's licence, under payment of a small fine, and to take out a copy of licence, i.e. a copy of the licence as recorded in the court rolls. Hence the statement sometimes found that 'there are two kinds of copy', copies of grants or leases and copies of licences. As the object was simply to ensure that the holdings were not wasted by irresponsible persons, licences were never or rarely refused, provided the undertenant was 'of honest conversation'. Thanks to these licences recorded in court rolls, it is possible to form an impression of the degree to which copyholders underlet their tenements. Licences granted do not prove that part of the holding was sublet, far less that all of it was, but it is a reasonable inference that most licences were accompanied by some subletting for terms longer than the customary limit. The absence of a licence does not disprove subtenancy for such a term, however, for frequent presentments for subletting without the required licence suggest that failure to comply with this custom was a common offence.

Nearly all records of manor courts in the early modern period abound with entries of subtenancy licences, presentments for not obtaining licences and references to undertenants, 'undersettles' and inmates. Altogether these constitute impressive evidence of a profusion of copyhold undertenancies. From this abundance of evidence, a few examples may be displayed. Between June 1555 and October 1557, when there were about fifty copyholders, seventeen new copies of licence were issued in Bremhill manor. In Bremhill and other manors on the same estate, where there were between one and two hundred copyholders, sixty-three copies of licence were made between 1565 and 1594. Durrington cum Knighton manor between 1610 and 1618 had a score of copyholders. During this time only one copy of licence was issued, but reference is made to seven other copyhold subtenancies.[56] An early Elizabethan rental of tithe-hay at Mere, the tail of which has been torn off, discloses twenty-eight subtenancies of meadowland alone. There were 58 copyholders in this manor in 1617 and between 1566 and 1627 22 copies of licence were issued, 4 unlicensed tenancies presented, 5 cases opened against copyholders for unlicensed non-residence, and references made to 16 other under-

[56] BM, Add. MS. 37270; Wilts. RO, acc. 84 Ct Bk Andr. Baynton 1545–57, ff. 57 sqq.; Ct Bk Durrington & Knighton 1609–17, ff. 2. sqq.

tenancies.[57] At Keevil in 1623, of a total of 35 copyholders, 29 had each one undertenant, one had 4, two 3 and three 3, while 17 other undertenants had recently been installed in newly-erected cottages. In Great Wishford court in 1685, the homage moved that all undertenants might be displaced, because nobody was bound for their orderly behaviour, and it was decided that all copyholders with unruly undertenants should be amerced £2. In the next court, presentments showed that eight copyholders had between them nine unruly undertenants. Less than two years later eight additional unlicensed undertenancies were presented.[58] Year after year ten or a dozen undertenancies were presented in Deverill Longbridge court.[59] The lord of a manor could distrain on a copyholder or his undertenant for amercements, but the latter might be a man of straw, and the best safeguard against disorder was to disallow undertenants for whom the tenant concerned had not undertaken to be responsible.[60]

Records of copies of licence reveal only a fraction of the subtenancies under copyhold, for they take no account of subletting for no more than a year and a day. The significance of these short-term subtenancies was grasped by John Norden when he surveyed Mere in 1617. The copyholders, he says, have usurped the freedom 'to lett and sett theire tenements for manie yeares under colour of one yeare and then a second, third etc., pretendinge the same all but for a yeare if it continewe 20 yeares'.[61] As long as he nominally took the holding into his own hands for one day a year, the copyholder was not obliged to seek a copy of licence. Moreover, subtenants could let out their lands to still further undertenants below them and such double undertenancy was not, apparently, rare, for in Bremhill manor it was the custom that 'he that holdeth by coppy of licence may make tenants and undertenants as he shall think good, by virtue of the same coppy'.[62]

In addition to limited surrenders, then, all kinds of copyholds opened the door to undertenancies by leases indented for terms of twenty-one years or three lives or similar periods and by short leases and annual tenancies.[63] It turns out that much of the copyhold land

[57] PRO, R. & S. GS rolls 712, 874; Ct R. GS 209/19–41.
[58] Wilts. RO, Heytesbury Hosp. Keevil c. Bulkington Ct Bk 44 Eliz.–2 Chas, September 29, 21 Jas; BM, Add. MS. 23152, ff. 13–4, 20.
[59] Longleat ho. Thynne Papers, Ct Bks Manors Sir Jn Thynne sen. 1567–77, box liv, bk 2, f. 44v.; 3, ff. 51–2; 4, ff. 95, 121; box lv., bk 5, ff. 3(5), 28–9.
[60] Ibid. box liv, bk 3, f. 47; Smyth, Hund. Berk. pp. 21–2; Wilts. RO, acc. 84 Ct Bk Andr. Baynton 1545–57, ff. 42v., 53.
[61] PRO, Exch. LR, MB 207, ff. 24v.–5.
[62] E. of Kerry, 'King's Bowood Pk', Wilts. Archaeol. Mag. 1920–1, xli. 203.
[63] Moore (KB) 123, 184–5; Savile 70–1; PRO, Chanc. Proc. ser. ii 291/25; Exch. AO, Parl. Svys Worcs. 1, f. 7; R. & S. GS 13/33; BM, Lans. 758, p. 6 (f. 4v.).

was occupied on precisely the same terms and conditions as the demesnes.

To say this only begins to plumb the depths of subtenancy, for share-tenancy and share-cropping have still to be considered. These were excluded from the consideration of manorial customs, implicitly, because they did not constitute real chattels or any kind of estate in land, and sometimes also explicitly. A customal attested by Chisbury homage in 1639 forbids the underletting of copyholds for more than a year and a day without licence, '(excepte it bee to thirds and halfes)', this being the English expression for what in the United States are called share-tenancy and share-cropping. Similarly, at Farcet no copyhold tenements were to be sublet to foreigners from other townships, unless to halves.[64] As manor courts disregarded letting to thirds and halves, what evidence there is of such tenancies is necessarily fragmentary. Nevertheless, in the Chalk Country, substantial socage holdings were sometimes let to thirds and halves,[65] and so were demesnes. Edward Ernle put out all the 541 acres of Urchfont Manor Farm to thirds and halves. At one time Robert Loder used to let out Harwell demesne farm to halves.[66] Similar letting and sowing to thirds and halves was practised in the Cotswold, Chiltern, Oxford Heights, Fen and Cheshire Cheese countries, the Vale of Evesham, the Wealden Vales, the Vales of Hereford, the Midland and Lancashire plains—in a word, wherever much cultivation was undertaken; and dairy herds and pastures were sometimes let out in much the same fashion.[67] Agreements for sowing to thirds and to halves were usually only by word of mouth and records of them are purely fortuitous. Copyholders frequently let their lands to thirds and halves, but just how often remains an enigma.

It is, then, impossible to trace more than a fraction of the subtenancies and sublettings of demesne, socage and customary lands. That these were at one time occupied largely by subtenants was none the less generally recognized, and it was known that many undertenants paid rack-rents. Leases by indenture rather than by copy were advocated by some writers on estate management on the ground that they facilitated the control of subtenancies.[68] The surveyor of Broad

---

[64] Wilts. RO, Savernake: svy Chisbury 1639; Northants. RO, Wmld 5. v.1 Ct R. Farcet September 19, 10 Jas.

[65] E.g. PRO, Req. 62/85.

[66] Wilts. RO, acc. 283 svy Urchfont c. 1640, f. 92; PRO, Chanc. Proc. ser. ii. 250/9; Exch. KR, Deps. By Commn 42 Eliz. Trin. 9; St. Ch. Jas 273/8; G. E. Fussell, *Robert Loder's Farm Accounts*, R. Hist. S. Camd. 3rd ser. 1936, liii. 1, 19, 34, 72, 90, 122.

[67] E.g. Folkingham, p. 32.

[68] E. Laurence, *The Duty of a Steward to his Lord*, London 1727, p. 34; *A Dissertation on Estates upon Lives or Years*, London 1730, p. 25.

Hinton notes in 1636 that 'the copyholders and leaseholders dwelling away from their tenementes and letting them out to others at racked rentes is the maine cause of the decay of the tenementes'.[69]

Complex as tenures and estates were, they were further complicated by the changes to which they were subject. The dismemberment of manors and the selling of their lands and fees, often to the sitting tenants, that occurred in the Vale of London, the Cheese and Cheshire Cheese countries, the Midland and Lancashire plains and elsewhere, was necessarily accompanied by a fall in the numbers of customary tenants and the creation of new freehold or common-law tenures. The lands were sold off in fee simple or fee tail, or in the form of perpetual leases with terms of a thousand or more years, or in fee-farm, where the fee was sold subject to a new reserved or chief rent.[70] In one royal manor, Elizabeth's sales in fee simple were voided by Prince Henry, who restored copyhold tenure;[71] but this was an exceptional circumstance and almost all the new freehold tenures created became permanent. Disforesting and the sale of assarts in fee-farm still further increased the numbers of freehold tenants.[72]

In one instance, at Wrexham and thereabouts, Queen Elizabeth replaced a merely pretended custom of inheritance by leases for forty years at common law. The tenants were given an assured right of renewal and descent to heirs was allowed according to the course of common law; yet considerable recognition money was due at a change of lord, so that this new tenure was not unlike fee-farm or free conventionary.[73] There were also a few instances of copyholds being leased over the heads of their tenants to persons who drew the customary rent and compounded with the customers for further estates; but, though some moot points remained in law, it was generally held that such leasing could not determine the customary estate. Finally, in some manors copyholders who had falsely claimed estates of inheritance by virtue of the habendum, 'to him and his', were nevertheless allowed to compound with their lords in large sums for the grant of such estates.[74]

More important than such extraordinary changes was the slow but perceptible replacement of lifehold leases by copy of court roll by similar leases by indenture. Some of these instances relate to copyholds on demesne lands, which were only tenancies at will; but others

[69] Wilts. RO, acc. 212B, BH. 8.
[70] Noy 136; 2 Brownl. & Golds. 134, 208; and see above, p. 18.
[71] PRO, Exch. LR, MB 207, f. 22(20).
[72] E.g. PRO, SPD Jas vol. 71 no 107; Exch. KR, Sp. Commn 4577.
[73] BM, Harl. MS. 3696, ff. 4, 7v., 47, 131; Stat. 3 Chas I c. 6; A. N. Palmer and E. Owen, *A History of Ancient Tenures of Land in N. Wales & the Marches,* s. 1. 1910, pp. 208–9; T. I. J. Jones, pp. xvi, 151.
[74] Gouldsborough 34; B'ham Lib. 381201.

concerned customary copyholds and involved putting the leases under a different code of law.[75]

The most frequent and general tenurial change in the late sixteenth and early seventeenth centuries was the minor one of substituting a certain fine for the arbitrary but reasonable fine paid by many copyholders of inheritance. This ascertainment of fines was usually agreed by landlords and tenants and was to their mutual benefit. The landlord abandoned his claims to fines that no more than kept pace with the general inflation of prices, in return for a lump sum. The copyholder rid his tenure of an anomaly and in return for ready payment ensured that future fines were paid at nominally stable, and really often diminishing, rates. The opportunity was often taken, also, of setting out and confirming all the manorial customs. In 1582, controversies over the customary law of Ivinghoe were settled by an agreement between the lord and his tenants for which the latter paid a consideration of £300. In return for this, fines were ascertained at one year's rent and the total recognition money at £10 13s 4d, while fines for copies of licence were fixed at purely nominal sums. Usually the copyholders and their lord concerted to bring a fictitious action in Chancery to sanction the ascertainment of fines and the other customs new or unrevised. Thus in the agreement for customs between St John's College and the Charlbury copyholders in 1592, the twelfth article provided for a bill of complaint to be entered in Chancery by the customers. In this bill they were to claim the customs set out in the other articles, one of which ascertained the fine at two years' rent, while the college agreed to enter an answer confessing that the customs were justly claimed, this being done in order that the customs should 'for the better corroboration of the same ... by order and decree ... be confirmed and established'.[76] Similar ascertainment agreements were made for so many manors and between so many individual copyholders and their lords, that Francis Bacon could regard the fictitious actions by which they were ratified as part of the ancient practice and course of proceedings in Chancery. Some six or eight persons usually acted for all the copyholders, which they could not have done in common-law courts. Only those copyholders who contributed to the expenses of the Chancery suit, however, could be bound by the decree that resulted from it, so that any copyholder who wished

[75] 4 Co. Rep. 31a; Willcox, p. 278; Cornwall, p. 278; Bateson viii. 264; H. Fishwick, *The Survey of the Manor of Rochdale 1626*, Chetham Soc. 1913, lxxi, p. viii; A. Ballard, 'Tackley in 16th & 17th cents.', Oxon. Archaeol. Soc. *Rep.* 1911 (1912), p. 40; PRO, Exch. LR, MB 207, f. 13 (11); TR, MB 157, f. 5v. (p. 12); KR, Deps. by Commn 5–6 Chas I Hil. 17; Glouc. Lib. 28899 (4) Ct Bk Wortley April 11, 24 Chas; Wilts. RO, acc. 88, Sfk & Berks.: Charlton Este Papers, 'A Bk of Svy of the E. of Sfk's Time'.
[76] Oxon. RO, DIL. IV/b/6b; Bucks. Mus. Ivinghoe 137/49.

could exclude himself from the agreement and continue to pay reasonable arbitrary fines.[77] Some of these ratified agreements were further confirmed by private Act of Parliament. This was an intention expressed in the most famous of all ascertainment agreements, the Isleworth-Syons Peace, a treaty between the Earl of Northumberland and his copyholders in that manor. The articles were to be confirmed by Act of Parliament or by decree in Chancery, as counsel advised. In 1656 a fictitious bill in Chancery recited the agreement and accused the earl of refusing his consent and 'intending and devising' to break it, which he denied.[78]

In the early seventeenth century the ascertainment of arbitrary but reasonable fines on copyholds of inheritance on the royal estates assumed the dimensions of a campaign. A surveyor was commissioned for no other purpose than to sell off holdings to the sitting tenants or to compound with them for the ascertainment of their fines. By no means all the copyholders concerned were willing either to buy their fees or to pay a lump sum for ascertainment; but many agreements were made, ratified in Chancery, the Duchy Court or the Exchequer Chamber, and then sometimes confirmed by private Act of Parliament. The copyholders at Newcastle-under-Lyme paid a composition of £626 12s 6d, at Wirksworth of over £1,193, at Wakefield of over £458, and at Irchester of £723. Tenants of 'new copyholds' in Clitheroe paid £6,906 odd for an ascertainment ratified in Parliament. Copyholders were thus made to pay dearly for ascertainment, sometimes as much as thirty or forty years' purchase of the customary rents, and it is understandable that some preferred arbitrary fines.[79]

Since the lord could expect a substantial consideration for the ascertainment of arbitrary fines on copyholds of inheritance, it was to his advantage if they were arbitrary and to that of the tenants if certain. Hence there arose on the crown estates a series of disputes as to

---

[77] Ritchie, pp. 14–6, 71; Campbell, pp. 140–1, 143–4; Notestein et al., v. 178–80, vii. 20–3; *Cals. Proc. Chanc. R. Eliz.* i. 161; ii. 214; Stat. 7 Jas I c. 21; Priv. Act 29 & 30 Chas II no 3; F. J. Baigent, *The Crondal Records*, Hants. Rec. Soc. 1891, iii. 177; R. J. Whiteman, *Hexton*, s. l. 1936, pp. 106–8; *Acts of Privy Council 1591–2*, xxii. 379; Berks. RO, D/EEl/E.1; Glouc. Lib. RF. 30. 5; PRO, Chanc. Decree R. 2nd Div. 1st pt, pt 361 no 2.

[78] *Isleworth-Syons Peace*, London 1657; Priv. Acts 14 Chas II no 22, 29 and 30 Chas II no 3; Notestein et al., ii. 63, 133, 184–5; vii. 20–2.

[79] *Ibid.* ii. 135, 383, 482; J. Tomlinson, *The Level of Hatfield Chace*, Doncaster 1882, pp. 295–6; 'Aulicus Coquinarie', in *Secret History of the Court of James I*, Edinburgh 1811, ii. 152; R. V. Lennard, *Rural Northants. under Commonwealth* in *Oxf. Studs. Soc. & Legal Hist.* ed. P. Vinogradoff, 1916 v. 110; J. Charlesworth, *Wakefield Manor Book 1709*, Yks. Archaeol. Soc. Rec. Ser. 1939 ci. 16–7; Priv. Acts 7 Jas I nos. 2–3; L'pool RO, Moore Deed 1046; PRO, SPD, Chas I vol. 176 no 63; DL, Accts. (Var.) Rec. Gen. Acct 11/5, f. 6; Exch. LR, MB 230, ff. 195v., 202v.; AO, Parl. Svys Derbys. 25, ff. 1–3; 28, ff. 10–1; Ess. 14, f. 18; Staffs. 38, ff. 5–7.

whether the fines were arbitrary or certain, the crown wishing to precipitate, and the copyholders to escape, ascertainment. Whether a fine was certain or not could be decided in law only by reference to the manorial court rolls. If a search in these showed that fines had once been arbitrary and there had since been no express ascertainment, the entry of fines as certain in rolls of later date did not make them any less arbitrary.[80] In manor after manor, copyholders of inheritance claimed fines certain, while the royal surveyors delved far back into the court archives to prove the contrary.[81] As far as can be seen, many copyholders of inheritance were mistaken in their claims, and some may well have perjured themselves. At Easingwold they claimed fines certain, but could not say what was the rate of assessment.[82] At Leven they continued to claim certainty, but even the parliamentary surveyors, who were usually fair to copyholders almost to the point of indulgence, reported that the copies themselves proved the fines to be uncertain.[83] The copyholders of Pickering also pretended to fines certain, but could not say at what rate they were assessed and Norden declared that the records showed them 'manifestlie uncertaine'.[84] In the soke of Kirton, by connivance or corruption, the royal stewards had been taking fines as though they were certain, despite 'infinite . . . recordes provinge the uncertaintie of fines'. The Wakefield copyholders were said to have conspired to give out that the fines were certain when they were not.[85] The homage of Wem had to admit that their custumal had been erased and altered. Norden says of the stewards of Blewbury, 'where fynes have byn arbitrable they have not stickt to incerte in the coppies *"de fine certo"* ' (of fine certain). Sometimes the copyholders won their point, as at Knaresborough, where even Norden has to confess that the tenants 'stand upon it that their fynes are certain upon alienation and so they are for anything I could either see or learne'.[86] At Hemel Hempstead, the crown alleged fines arbitrary, but could produce nothing by way of proof, while the copyholders showed sixteenth-century evidence of certainty and triumphed in the suit.[87] About 1618 the attorney-general of the Duchy of Lancaster alleged that the fines of some copyholders of inheritance in Clitheroe who held 'new copyholds'

[80] 4 Co. Rep. 27b.

[81] PRO, DL, R. & S. 9/13; Exch. LR, MB 207, f. 37 (35); 230, ff. 195v., 198v., 214v.; AO, MB 390, f. 37v.; Parl. Svys Lincs. 16, f. 27.

[82] PRO, DL, MB 124, f. 94.

[83] PRO, Exch. AO, Parl. Svys Yks. 34, f. 8.

[84] R. B. Turton, *The Honor & Forest of Pickering*, N.R. Rec. Soc. 1894–5, i. 59–60; PRO, DL, MB 124, f. 81.

[85] Charlesworth, p. 19; Jn Rylands Lib. Eng. 216, pref. & f. 9.

[86] *Wills & Administrations from Knaresborough Court Rolls*, Surtees S. civ, cx, 1902–5, i.p. xi; Salop. RO, 167/43, f. 1; PRO, Exch. LR, MB 207, f. 78 (75).

[87] PRO, Exch. KR, Memoranda, Recorda, Trin. 7 Jas I, rots. 145, 163.

were uncertain. This they denied, 'but shortly after, upon some offers from the said attorney, the copiholders, to purchas their peace and quiett with so greate a man', compounded for ascertainment. As soon as the Long Parliament assembled, however, the copyholders made haste to petition that body for relief.[88] At Potterspury the copyholders of inheritance paid fines certain until about 1610, when, as they said, the royal stewards started to break the custom. When a man came to pay his fine, the 'steward would call him aside into a corner and there contract for the fine, whereas it should have bene in open court before the jury'. At Worplesden likewise the fines had been certain at one year's rent until about 1640, when the lord farmer of the royal manor, the Earl of Arundel, 'racked, raysed and sett farr above the rate, to the greate impoverishing of the poor tenants', the fines they had to pay.[89]

Similar situations arose on the manors of some mesne lords. Taverner's case in 1573 became justly famous in this regard. Taverner, a copyholder to Lord Cromwell in North Eltham, forged a customary of the manor, tending to the lord's disherison, and completed it with a dozen forged seals. On exposure, he was justly evicted, for he had broken his oath of fealty.[90] The Hanbury customers raised pretensions to fines certain with copyhold of inheritance, but when the court of Requests made a discovery of the court rolls, these proved the fines arbitrary and the copyhold for lives.[91] About 1563 the Bosham copyholders corrupted Lord Berkeley's stewards in order to obtain the confirmation of spurious customs by an indenture that 'the tenants, for the canonicalnes thereof, called the Bosham bible'. Over half a century later Chancery found that the copyholders had not obtained this alleged ascertainment of fines from Lord Berkeley on good composition, for he had been wronged by his officers therein, and by the ancient custom of the manor the fines were arbitrary at the will of the lord, though reasonable. After a suit that cost the copyholders £900, the Bosham bible was abrogated and the tenants were still ready to pay £2,000 for a valid ascertainment agreement 'to redeem their folly'.[92] Copyholders elsewhere alleged that their lord tried to break the custom of fines certain by making his servants secretly give high fines.[93] The bailiff of Yoxall was accused of seizing the court rolls with intent to erase and alter records of fines paid. Fines had been certain in Austenfield manor until shortly before 1570, when, allegedly, 'the lord troubling and vexing divers of the copy-

[88] L'pool RO, Moore Deed 1046.
[89] PRO, Exch. AO, Parl. Svys Northants. 39, f. 8; 40, f. 21; Sy 63, f. 5.
[90] 3 Dyer 322b, 323a.
[91] Savine, pp. 70–1.
[92] Ritchie, pp. 14–5; Smyth, *Lives* ii. 432–4.
[93] PRO, Chanc. Proc. ser. i Jas I, W. 1/35, compl. & answ.

holders, drove many of them for buying of their quietness to be at fines uncertain'.[94] In Tardebigge, it is said in 1630, the fines should have been reasonable, yet 'of late years the lord hath taken great fines contrary to our ancient custom'. In 1651 the lord of Lower Slaughter tried to change certain fines of one year's rent to arbitrary ones of one year's improved value, but the copyholders resisted and obtained a Chancery decree in their favour.[95]

In some of these disputes, copyholders or lords made false pretences. It was partly for this reason that such cases were decided in Chancery. The juries of law courts would hardly have been able to understand the precise significance of entries in manorial court rolls, and lords of manors ran the risk of being out-sworn by unscrupulous tenants. Hence the House of Commons rejected a bill to have such cases determined in law. The ascertainment of arbitrary fines depended on agreement between lords and copyholders, and this in turn was a matter of *quid pro quo*. In 1617 an ascertainment agreement gave a lord improved rents, but conferred no monetary advantage upon his copyholders. The chancellor held that he should either relinquish the agreement or moderate the fines. The lord chose the latter alternative and the fines were fixed at one year's improved value. It would have been no less inequitable had all arbitrary fines on copyholds of inheritance been ascertained at one year's value of the premises, for the copyholders might have been advantaged and the lords partially expropriated. Moreover, some copyholds were heriotable, some not, and their was usually an equitable differentiation between their fines. Hence in 1656 the Commons rejected a bill for compulsory ascertainment at one year's value.[96]

Another great tenurial change was witnessed in the north of England. The Tudor monarchs had always done all in their power to strengthen border tenure or 'tenant-right', i.e. tenure owing military service on the border. They had tried, sometimes successfully, to support the tenants against the oppressive exaction of gressoms by their lords. According to customary laws, as allowed by the common law, recognition money could only be demanded at a change of lord, if this were by an Act of God or natural contingency; but the northern tenants were so servile that their lords demanded this money almost whenever they chose, even by making conveyances especially for the purpose. By intervening to moderate gressoms, the crown hoped to kill two birds with one stone: to maintain a necessary mili-

---

[94] W. K. Boyd, 'Chanc. Proc. temp. Eliz. 1560–70', *Colls. Hist. Staffs.* 1906, ix, 97–8; 'Eliz. Chanc. Proc. ser. ii: 1558–79', *ibid.* 1938, pp. 65–6.

[95] Gaut, p. 83; Glos. RO, D. 45 Ct R. L. Slaughter April 14, 1651, January 19, 1652, April 6, 1659.

[96] Ritchie, p. 16; Notestein & al., v. 178–80; *Jnl H.C.* 1651–9, p. 433.

tary force, and to weaken the servile dependence of the tenants upon their great lords, so depriving the latter of the unquestioning support of their tenantry when they rode south against the English Government, as in the Pilgrimage of Grace and the Rebellion of the Earls.[97]

But royal policy could meet with only limited success, for the tenants themselves were so servile by nature that they were at the mercy of any lord or steward set over them. Even on the crown's own estates, although the crown itself exacted no arbitrary tallages under colour of fines and gressoms, its stewards filled this unnatural vacuum and took their private tribute from the peasants. In 1580 the Amble tenants are so 'extracted by the queen's officers, they are ready to give up their holdings', for 'the earle of Northumberland's deputy captaine was always deputy steward ther, who governed them, as they say, not accordinge to their customes but according to his own will'. At this time, too, one Haggarston, farmer of several royal manors, extorted 'great and uggsome' fines from their tenants. Shortly after the Benwell tenants complained of oppression at the hands of the crown's lord farmer, the Earl of Northumberland, who apparently tried to force them to exchange their copies for twenty-one year leases. At Kendal the fines were certain by custom, but some tenants paid more than the fixed amount, 'onely of their own good will and benevolence at the perswasion of their officers'. In Tudor times, then, oppression usually took the form of extortion rather than eviction, although in the North-eastern Lowlands there was some of each. These extortions resulted in progressive impoverishment, so that the tenants were, many of them, no longer able to keep horse and armour. Thus the whole basis of border service was undermined, while the long peace after 1569 encouraged lords to discount military services.[98]

With the accession of James I, border service became redundant overnight. Almost immediately the northern lords, on James's initiative, decided to abolish tenant-right in favour of other tenancies more

[97] R. R. Reid, *The King's Council in the North*, London 1921, pp. 300–1; Fishwick, *DL*, i. 99–101, 192–3; J. M. W. Bean, *The Estates of the Percy Family 1416–1537*, London 1958, pp. 65–6; Bateson, v. 256–7; my 'Rent', p. 16; Campbell, p. 149; T. S. Willan and E. W. Crossley, *Three 17th-century Yorks. Surveys*, Yks. Archaeol. Soc. Rec. Ser. 1941, civ. 147–8; Bouch & Jones, pp. 73–4; *VCH Durh.* ii. 230–1; E. Hughes, *North Country Life in the 18th Century: the N.E. 1700–50*, London 1952, pp. 419–21; Tawney & Power, i. 77–8; D. L. W. Tough, *The Last Years of a Frontier*, Oxford 1928, pp. 149–50; PRO, Exch. KR, MB 37, f. 3; LR, MB 212, ff. 308–9; SPD, Eliz. Add. vol. 20 no 28; Chanc. Decree R. 2nd Div. 1st pt, pt 362 no 10; A. E. Bland, P. A. Brown & R. H. Tawney, *English Economic History*, London 1914, pp. 232–4; 'Humberstone's Svy', p. 137.

[98] *Ibid.*; PRO, Exch. AO, Parl. Svys Wmld 5, f. 5; Scottish RO, *The Border Papers*, London 1894–6 i. 15–7, 19–22; ii. 337, 341; G. P. Jones, p. 200; Reid, p. 300; my *Ag. Rev.* pp. 171–3; Bateson v. 244, 278, 282, 489; xiii. 228.

beneficial to the commonwealth and more profitable to themselves. James set the example by abolishing tenant-right on his own estates, and then in 1620 issued a proclamation ordering others to follow suit and 'make leases or other estates upon reasonable compositions by indenture'. No entry in any court was to as much as mention border service. Judges were commanded to dismiss cases brought in defence of border tenure, though suits in equity against unreasonable landlords were to be allowed. Tenant-right was to be 'damned to perpetual oblivion'.[99]

After the labyrinthine complexity of tenures, the system of estates seems simple and rational. Tenures originated in custom to meet the necessities of past ages, estates in common reason formulated in common law. An estate was an interest, irrespective of the tenure by which it was held. The system of estates thus cut across the system of tenures. An estate was an interest, irrespective of the system of law under which it was held. Estates thus applied equally to both common-law and customary tenures.

All estates were either freeholds or chattels. Chattels, in turn, were either personal or real. Such things as corn, cattle, money, plate, and good and sperate (hopefull) debts constituted personal chattels. The lowest form of real estate was the real chattel, which was the least interest anyone could have in land. Real chattels consisted of leases for years, leases for term of a wardship, which could not last more than a certain number of years, and tenancies at will, which included both lease-parol and annual tenancy. In contradistinction to the real chattels, were the freehold estates, in which the interest was for one life at the least. Freehold estates were thus those terminable only by the will of the freeholder, by his demise, or by some similar casualty. Freehold estates could be in fee simple, either by descent or by purchase; or in fee tail, either general or special; or by term of life; or by the courtesy of England; or by dower; or by term of life of another; or after possibility of issue extinct. The owner of a freehold estate in fee simple may dispose of it as he wishes. In fee tail, descent is entailed to general or special heirs and the estate may not be granted out of this line of succession. The last of such a line cannot, by the nature of things, hold in fee tail, but only after possibility of issue extinct. The widow who holds one third of her former husband's land in dower has an estate in it for her own life, but cannot dispose of any interest in it after her death. The widower who holds, by the courtesy of England, half the land he formerly held in the right of his wife, is in the same position. The tenant for term of life of another holds the fee as long as someone else shall live. This estate was convenient to be held of a widow or widower who had no interest in the land beyond his or her life. Finally, the freehold estate for term of life was that created by a lease for life or lives.[100]

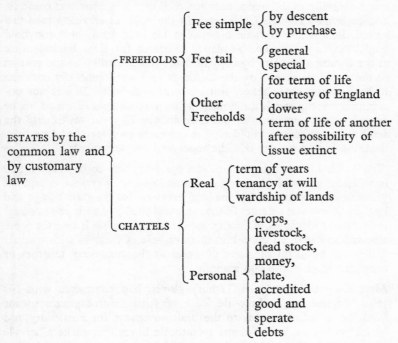

Each of these estates, it must be insisted, could be enjoyed by either the common or the customary law. 'In respect of the state of the land, so copyholders may be freeholders; for any that hath any estate for his life, or any greater estate, in any land whatsoever, may in this sense be termed a freeholder.' Whether leased by copy at the customary law or by indenture at the common law, the estate remained the same. Freeholders of inheritance and freeholders for life both had estates that were equally freehold, but it was nevertheless convenient for some purposes to distinguish between copyholders of inheritance, say, and lessees for lives. Thus, 'all the estates whatsoever may be reduced to one of these three heads: 1. inheritance, 2. franck-tenant, 3. chattells'. The broader division, however, was between freehold and chattel estates. This position has sometimes been concealed because the words 'freehold' and 'freeholder' are homonyms, but the

[100] Co. Litt. 17 sqq.; Rathborne, pp. 181, 190; Fitzherbert, *Svying*, f. 14; Leigh, op. cit.

importance of the distinction between freehold and chattel estates can hardly be exaggerated.[101]

The system of estates was founded in common sense and there was no significant difference between corresponding estates at common and customary law. As Coke says, 'In the point of service a man can scarce discern any difference between freehold lands and copyhold lands' (Doc. 11).[102] The similarity of leases for lives by indenture at the common law and by copy of court roll according to the custom of the manor is shown by the incidents that were generally common to both: entry fine, heriot, suit of court and fealty. It was not uncommon for the indenture-holder, as he was sometimes called, to be bound by the covenants of his lease to suit of court on exactly the same terms of the copyholder.[103] A covenant to a lease of Amesbury demesne farm stipulates that the lessee and the next takers

'shall suffer him and themselves and every of them to be ordered and justified for controversies and matters and questions rysinge upon the premisses by the steward of the said mannour for the time beinge and by the homage and tenantes of the same and shall pay such paines amercyamentes and somes of money as shalbe at anie such courtes there assessed and affeared upon him them or anie of them in such manner and forme to all intentes and purposes as the customary tenantes or coppiehoulders of the said mannor'.

After Robert Edwardes, a Tisbury glover, had contracted with Sir John Thynne for a three-life lease of Little Horningsham manor farm, he raised objections to the draft covenants for husbandry and heriot, saying he 'never mente to inthrale himself in suche a servyle manner'.[104] In point of fact, heriots, albeit suit-heriot and not heriot-service or heriot-custom, were standard form in lifehold indentures,[105] for without them the landlord could hardly know how many lives remained. Covenants for suit of court were not confined to lifeholds, but were found also in leases for years, even those with short terms,[106]

---

[101] Coke, *Copyholder*, sect. 7.

[102] *Ibid.* sect. 15–7.

[103] Phillips, p. 32; Marshall, *Yks.* i. 44; PRO, Chanc. Proc. ser. ii. 291/25.

[104] PRO, Req. 61/91; Wilts. RO, acc. 283 Lib. Sup. Amesbury, ff. 24–5.

[105] Rathborne, p. 179; my *Surveys of Manors of Philip earl of Pembroke & Montgomery 1631–2*, Wilts. Archaeol. & Nat. Hist. Soc. Rec. Brch, 1953, ix, 2 sqq., 11–2, 29, 63, 102–3, 109, 127; Phillips, p. 32: W. Marshall, *The Rural Economy of Glocestershire*, Gloucester 1789, ii. 13; Glouc. Lib. RF. 7. 1; Glos. RO, D. 326, E.1, f. 65v.; Shak. Bpl. W. de B. 1161–5; Leigh: partic. Stoneleigh c. 1540; Soms. RO, DD/WO, Bk Svys Nettlecombe &c. 1619, f. 32; BM, Add. R. 28283; Wilton ho. Ct R. of Manors 1689–1754, box 1, vol. 2, pp. 31, 56; PRO, Ct R. GS 207/82; Exch. AO, MB 380, f. 6; Parl. Svys Mon. 1, ff. 15 sqq.

[106] *Ibid.* Corn. 12, f. 3; A. L. Humphreys, *Materials for History of Town & Parish of Wellington*, London 1908–14, ii. 260; Lancs. RO, DD. K. 1456/1,

because the business of farming demanded a rustic court at which disputes between neighbours and petty misdemeanours might be settled out of hand. When the lifeholder by indenture at the common law owed suit of court and a heriot at decease, and when, after the death of a widow, who has held the farm, the next taker comes to the court baron to claim it by virtue of the counterpart of the indenture that he exhibits, is admitted tenant in open court and does his fealty, it is plain that only a point of law stood between him and the copyholder.[107]

As far as most legal processes were concerned, all estates were much the same whether they were by common or customary law. One has it on no less an authority than Coke's[108] that

'though the franke tenement be in the lord by the common law, yet by the custome the inheritance abideth in the copyholder; and it is not denied if a copyholder be impleaded in making tytle to his copyhold, he may justly plead that he is seised in his demesne, with this addition, according to the custom of the manor ... the lord having no power to resume his landes' (Doc. 11).

Copyholders of inheritance, then, plead that they are seised in their demesne as of fee according to the custom of the manor, 'seised in his demesne as of fee to him and his heirs for ever by copy of court roll according to the custom of the manor', 'seised in fee tail according to the custom of the manor', 'seised in their demesne as of fee tail, that is to say, to them and to the heirs of their bodies lawfully begotten, according to the custom of the manor', and so on and so forth.[109] To make an entail the copyholder of inheritance surrendered to the use of his heirs or of himself with remainder to his heir and tail.[110] To dock an entail the copyholder had only to surrender to the use of his last will and testament, which devised the holding out of tail and was produced in court at the admittance of the next holder; or to suffer a recovery in the manor court and bar issues in tail to cut off the remainder expectant; or to suffer a fictitious forfeiture after a

m. 2; Northants. RO, F(M) Misc. 77; Staffs. RO, D. 260, box 16, bdl. (b) Svy Penkridge 1660, f. 2; Wilton ho. Ct R. Manors 1689–1754, box i, vol. 2, pp. 5, 31, 56, 67; Ct Bks starting 1724: Chalk 1724, Burcombe 1740, Wylye 1733–4, Fugglestone, Quidhampton and Avon 1756; BM, Add. MS. 21608, ff. 192, 278v.; 33355, ff. 25v.–6.

[107] BM, Add. R. 13133.
[108] Coke, *Copyholder*, sect. 14; Co. Litt. 58; J. Kitchin, *Jurisdictions*, London 1653, p. 137.
[109] E.g. Bland, Brown & Tawney, pp. 232, 235, 241; Choyce Cs 115; Benloe (CP) 77; 2 Brownl. & Golds. 42–3, 826.
[110] Ritchie, pp. 221–2; Shak. Bpl. W. de B. 1217; Herts, RO, G'bury X.B. 3a; PRO, Exch. AO, Parl. Svys Sy 55, f. 10; Leconfield, p. 14.

prior agreement for a new grant.[111] In some few manors no entails were allowed, while in others they could not be cut off by a recovery,[112] but in most of them recoveries, as by the course of common law, largely for the purpose of cutting entails, were commonplace.[113] Even if entails were disallowed by the custom, the land could be virtually entailed by making feoffees in trust declared in a pair of indentures or in a last will and testament.[114] With these pleadings, with these customary instruments, with no forfeiture for non-payment of entry fines, not even for what, if committed by his own lessee, would have been a waste at common law, the copyholder of inheritance may truly be said to have enjoyed his estate 'as far forth as anie freeholder of like estate att common law';[115] and it is understandable that copyhold of inheritance was sometimes considered superior to socage, because conveyance was easier and the widow had surer provision for her widowhood.[116]

The copyholder for life under a limited surrender of copyhold of inheritance also had a freehold estate, but what is still more significant is that the copyholder for life on customary land in a manor with the custom of copyhold only for lives had a freehold estate and could plead in just the same form as did the lifeholder by indenture at the common law. Copyholders for lives in manors with lifehold customs plead to hold by the custom 'as of freehold for life' or that they are 'seised ... in their demesne as of freehold after the custom of the said manor ... for term of their lives and the longest liver of them and the same did hold of the said manor for the time being by copy of court roll of the manor ... according to the custom of the said manor'.[117]

In short, estates were no different by the customary than by the common law.

[111] Ibid.; Godfrey, p. 92; Coke, Copyholder, sect. 48; Moore (KB) 753; 4 Co. Rep. 23a; Dalison 76; 1 Brownl. & Golds. 147; 2 Brownl. & Golds. 121–2; Herts. RO, 12762; B'ham Lib. 381201, p. 124; Mx RO (G. Ldn RO) acc. 276, bdl. 9 Harrow Manor & Rectory Manor customs; PRO, Exch. AO, Parl. Svys War. 25, f. 10.

[112] Ibid.; 12, f. 43.

[113] E.g. Marcham, pp. 13–4.

[114] E.g. W. Farrer, Court Rolls of Honour of Clitheroe, Manchester, Edinburgh 1897–1913, i. 414–5, 480.

[115] Cary 63; Tawney, p. 127; Isleworth-Syons Peace, p. 14; VCH Ess. ii, 319; PRO, Exch. LR, MB 207, f. 29 (27) v.; AO, Parl. Svys War. 25, f. 10; Mx RO, 249/875, 479/1.

[116] N. Kent, A General View of the Agriculture of County of Norfolk, Norwich 1796, pp. 30–1.

[117] Dalison 62; Fishwick, DL, i. 25–6; Phillimore & Fry, i. 87–8; G. Bradford, Proceedings in Court of Star Chamber in Reigns of Henry VII & VIII, Soms. Rec. Soc. 1911, xxvii. 186; 'Proc. Ct St. Ch. temp. Hy VIII & Ed. VI', Colls. Hist. Staffs. 1910, p. 63; PRO, Req. 21/61.

3

Security of Tenure

WE now come to what Tawney[1] calls

'the most difficult problem which confronts the student of the sixteenth century agrarian changes—the degree of protection enjoyed
by the copyholders. . . . If all copyholders had complete security, and
were readily protected in their holdings by the courts, there would be
little sense in talking of an agrarian revolution.'

Security of tenure can only mean the legal security of the tenant
against wrongful eviction or ouster, not against all the hazards of this
fleshly world. One thing security of tenure cannot mean by any
stretch of the imagination is a perpetual and inalienable right to pos-
sess a certain property. He who has a lease for a year and is fully
protected in it has as ample a security of tenure as the man with an
undisturbed estate of inheritance.

The whole argument of Tawney's book turns on his conclusion[2]
that

'The problem centres in the question to what extent a copyholder who
was threatened with eviction could obtain protection from the courts.
It is not at all easy to extract a definite answer on this point from the
writers of the period, whose views as to the degree of security enjoyed
by copyhold are often inconsistent with each other, and sometimes
seem to be inconsistent with themselves . . . Fitzherbert . . . expressly
states that copyhold tenants cannot get protection from the courts:
"These manners of tennants shall not plede nor be impleded of their
tenements by the king's writte" . . . , while Coke, in a well-known
passage emphasizes the copyholder's security as long as he makes no
breach in the custom by failing in his services, and points out that
he can protect himself either by proceeding in Chancery or by a writ
of trespass. It is not surprising, in view of the variety of opinion as
to the copyholder's status which obtained in the sixteenth century,
that there should have been much disagreement about it among

[1] pp. 287–8.
[2] pp. 288–91.

historians. . . . The case of the year 1482 [*recte* 1481], which is quoted by Professor Ashley to show the hesitation which the judges felt as to whether a copyholder had any legal remedy, is really one of a long series in which the courts considered the claims of copyholders, and which Coke must have had in mind when he said, "Now copyholders stand upon a sure ground: now they weigh not their lord's displeasure, they shake not at every sudden blast of wind, they eat, drink, sleep securely . . . Let the lord frown, the copyholder cares not, knowing himself safe, and not within any danger." To overlook that series of cases is really to misread a change of the first importance, a change which almost amounted to a legal revolution.'

More recent writers have repeated Tawney's argument, and none more clearly than the latest, Dr Gray, who says of the 'copyholder'[3]

'The winning of his new position was probably a gradual process. The beginning of a shift in opinion is perhaps signalized by the insertion of Brian and Danby in Littleton in 1534 [*recte* 1530]; Edward VI's reign saw both a balancing of conflicting opinions and the first stages of resolution; in Elizabeth's, the last doubts vanished.'

But, let us note at the outset, neither Tawney nor Mr Gray ever succeeds in distinguishing between either customary and non-customary copyholds, or the two meanings of 'copyhold', or tenures and estates, or personal and real actions. Small wonder that new Gray is but old Tawney writ small.

The key to what is really not a hard problem is the relationship between customary law, statute law, and the common law. This was best explained by Sir Edward Coke[4] when

'he said that Fortescue and Littleton and all others agreed, that the law consists of three parts. Firstly, common law. Secondly, statute law, which corrects, abridges and explains the common law; the third, custom, which takes away the common law: but the common law corrects, allows and disallows both statute law and custom, for if there be repugnancy in statute, or unreasonableness in custom, the common law disallows and rejects it.'

Parliamentary statutes, moreover, applied with equal force to both customary and common-law estates, unless one were explicitly excluded, and provided the acts were not prejudicial to custom, lord or copyholder.[5]

As Coke explains, the common law corrects, allows and disallows

[3] C. M. Gray, *Copyhold, Equity & the Common Law*, Cambridge, Mass. 1963, pp. 64–5.
[4] 2 Brownl. & Golds. 197–8; & J. W. Gough, *Fundamental Law in English Constitutional History*, Oxford 1955, pp. 4–6, 10–1, 13–5, 17, 19 sqq., 29–32, 37.
[5] 1 Leon. 97–9; 2 Brownl. & Golds. 156; Savile 66–7.

customary laws, according to whether they are reasonable or not. Just as a party accused of infringing a penal statute was tried under the statute, even though the common law was without precedents in the case, so a party accused of infringing customary law was tried by reference to the custom. In all actions at law or equity that concerned the customary law, therefore, everything depended in the first instance on an examination of the custom in question. Either side might testify as to the custom, but the only proof of it was by record, usually by record of the manor court itself. For this reason, as Savine says, 'The court of Requests looks for truth, not in the *Rechtsbewusstsein* of the local population, but in the dust of the manorial records', and Requests, Chancery, Exchequer Chamber, Star Chamber, and the common-law courts can and do inspect, if necessary by action of discovery, the court rolls and surveys of manors, in order to establish the custom. To take an example of an issue often before the courts, a plaintiff claims to hold by copy of court roll according to the custom of the manor. He has to show that the tenement is customary, subject to the customary law. If it is part of the demesne, then it cannot be customary; it cannot be held according to the custom unless it has been demised and demisable according to the custom of the manor for as long as the memory of man is not to the contrary. Questions like these were usually put beyond dispute by the manorial archives.[6]

The common law could only allow and confirm customary laws that were reasonable, certain, on good consideration, compulsory, without prejudice to the king, and to the profit of the claimant. Tawney assumed that 'reasonable' in this context was used in a loose or general sense, and that the lord's interests were more likely to seem reasonable to the lawyers than were the customer's; but 'reasonable' and 'unreasonable' are legal terms of art and mean 'compatible', 'consonant', 'consistent', 'reconcilable', or their opposites.[7] A reasonable custom was one that could be reconciled with the other customary laws of that manor and with the common law. Thus to disallow unreasonable customs was, in almost every instance, to reject fraudulent ones. For instance, no good custom would allow a copyholder for life to prejudice the estate of the reversioner or remainderman. A pretended custom that the copyholder for life could waste his tenement and so defeat the next taker of the value of the estate, was judged unreasonable and disallowed in the lawcourts, for such waste constituted a forfeiture in the custom of lifehold manors, just as it did in

---

[6] 1 Leon. 55–6; Cave & Wilson, pp. xlvi–vii; A Savine, 'Copyhold Cs in early Chanc. Proc.', *EHR* 1902, xvii. 300.

[7] C. Calthrope, *The Relation betweene the Lord of a Mannor & the Coppyholder his Tenant*, London 1635, pp. 21–2; Tawney, pp. 293, 307–8.

common law for lifehold estates. A further illustration of the adjudgement of reasonableness of a custom is provided by the case of Rowles v. Mason in 1611. The pretended custom that a copyholder for life could fell trees at pleasure was pronounced void, for it was unreasonable and against the commonwealth, since every custom ought to include the preservation and maintenance of the holding. Were this unreasonable custom allowed, the succeeding copyholder might be deprived of loppings for fuel and timber for housebote and ploughbote, both of which the custom allowed him. Hence the pretended custom defeated another and unquestionable custom and could itself be regarded as none other than unreasonable. In the reign of Henry VII a custom supposedly permitting the distraint of all beasts doing damage by trespass was adjudged void, for where the damage was uncertain, the distraint ought not to be certain in value. A custom that all leases of copyholds to undertenants were null and void was itself voided, because contrary to common reason and against the liberty of the subject seised of an estate in fee simple. In Henry IV's reign a pretended custom that no tenant should have common until the lord had put in his beasts was adjudged void, because rights of common, by definition, could not depend on the will of a single individual. Customs had to be reasonable, and if they were generally inconvenient and incompatible with other customs, they were unreasonable. 'Custom may be against common right, but not against common reason, which is the common law.'[8] Perhaps the clearest instance of customary reasonableness was that concerning arbitrary fines payable on copyholds of inheritance. The arbitrary fine had to be compatible with the custom of inheritance.

The common law allowed customary estates, even though these were held at the will of the lord of the manor, for

'although such customary tenants are termed in law tenants at will, yet they are not simply so, nor meerly tenants at will, but only tenants at will, *according to the custom of the manor*, which custom warrants his possession here for his life, and therefore it is a more certain estate than an estate at will, for the copyholder may justifie against his lord, so cannot a tenant at will, whose estate is determined at the will and pleasure of the lessor: and although this estate is but by custom and by no conveyance, the estate is raised, it is as material, so as it be an estate: and this estate being supported by custom is known in law as an estate and so accounted in law; and the law hath notably distinguished copyhold tenancies by custom and tenancies at will by the common law; for a copyholder shall do fealty, shall have aid of his lord in an action of trespass, shall have and maintain an action of trespass against his lord.'

[8] 2 Brownl. & Golds. 85–90, 153–4, 197–8.

In other words, 'although in respect and in consideration of the estimation that the common law hath of a copyholder, he has but an estate at will, yet respecting the custom his interest is good and not defeasible'.[9]

Since the common law recognized copyhold by the custom as an estate, not by the common law, but in the eyes of the common law, the customer could take action at common law. Hence, in order to proceed in equity, he had to plead some matter other than mere holding by customary law. The court of Requests, for instance, dismissed to trial at the common law suits showing only customary holding as matter of equity.[10]

From 1500 the law reports contain abundant evidence that customary suits, in general, were determined and determinable by common law. Rather few such cases, it is true, appear in the Year Books in Henry VIII's time, but this is partly because the books themselves are scarce, partly because Wolsey and Wriothesley illegally commissioned ministers to act in their steads, so facilitating the uncontrolled growth of Chancery business, and party because Wolsey, by abuse of injunctions, deliberately diverted suits from the lawcourts to Chancery.[11]

But although the common law allowed customary estates, common and customary law still remained two distinct legal systems. Since, in one sense of the word, the freehold, that is the frank tenure, was in the lord and not in the customer, the common law could not permit the customer to start any real action, not to start any action directly concerned with the frank tenure. As Littleton says, 'Such tenants shall neither implead nor be impleaded *for their tenements* by the King's writ' (my italics): (Doc. 3). Again, says he, 'Nor writ of right shall he have either, for no franktenement is in him but the franktenement is in the lord &c.' (Doc. 5). This is what Fitzherbert means when he says, 'These maner of tenauntes shall not plede nor be impleded *of theyr tenementes* by the kynges writte' (my italics). Coke, then, makes no innovation when he writes,

'A copyholder cannot in any action real, or that savoureth of the realty, implead or be impleaded in any other court but the lord's court for and concerning his copyhold. . . . If a copyholder be ousted of his copyhold by a stranger, he cannot implead him by the king's

---

[9] 1 Leon. 4; Savile 66–7.

[10] PRO, Chanc. Proc. ser. ii 328/1.

[11] W. S. Holdsworth, *A History of English Law*, London 1903–26, iv. 253 sqq.; W. C. Richardson, *History of the Court of Augmentations 1536–54*, Baton Rouge 1961, pp. 379–81; Yale, *Manual*, p. 10; R. W. Chambers, *Thomas More*, London 1938, pp. 272–4; F. W. Maitland, *Selected Historical Essays*, ed. H. M. Cam, Cambridge 1957, p. 143; pace A. F. Pollard, *Wolsey*, London 1953, pp. 59 sqq.

writ, but by plaint in the lord's court. . . . If a copyholder be ousted by his lord, he cannot maintain an assize at the common law, because he wanteth a franktenement.'

All lawyers at all times agreed on this (Docs. 4, 9).[12]

But although the common law could never allow the customary tenant any real action, it was pleased to accommodate him with a personal one, with a writ of trespass against the lord or whomsoever wrongfully ousted him of his estate, for to deprive someone of a freehold estate, albeit the person trespassed against was not a frank tenant, was a tort. Whoever wrongfully ousted the customer from his estate was a trespasser in the eyes of the law. Ever since actions of trespass had been allowed, therefore, they had been allowed to customers in respect of their customary estates, even against their own lords. Numerous Tudor instances of such actions are to be found, and already in 1389–90 we have a clear instance of the lady of a manor proceeding against her customary tenant by writ of trespass upon the case; and what was sauce for the goose was sauce for the gander—the customer could maintain similar action against his lord (Docs. 8, 9).[13] Danby answering a query in 1467 as to whether a copyholder wrongfully ousted by his lord had any remedy in law, has no doubt on this score. He says, 'It seemeth that he hath, for if the lord oust him he doth to him a tort, for he is as well inheritor to have this land to him and his heirs according to the custom of the manor as any man is of lands at the common law, an he make fine when he enter &c.' (Doc. 5). As a tort is a breach of a duty imposed by law whereby the person wronged acquires a right of action for damages, to say a tort is done is to say a common-law action lies. Wrongful eviction was tortious and ground for action of trespass. Littleton says much the same in 1481: 'The custom of the manor in some case can aid him to bar his lord in an action of trespass' (Doc. 3). If he ignored Brian's famous pronouncement, this was not because he disagreed with it, but because it was not made until shortly after Littleton sent his manuscript to the press. Brian agreed with Littleton when he said, 'So long as the tenant pay the customs and services, if the lord put him out of possession, he shall have action of trespass against him,' and he indicates that this had always been his opinion (Doc. 6). When it is said in the mid-sixteenth century that the lord cannot oust his copyholder (customary tenant) so long as he does his services and pays his rent due according to the custom, this merely reiterates

---

[12] Coke, *Copyholder*, sect. 51; Co. Litt. 63a; Fitzherbert, *Svying*, f. 15.

[13] T. F. T. Plucknett, *Year Books of Richard II: 13 Ric. II 1389–90*, London 1929, xliii–iv, 108–9; 2 Brownl. & Golds. 146–9, 328–30; Bridgman, J. 81–3; Moore (KB) 350, 753; 1 Leon. 1; Noy 58; Gouldsborough 143; 4 Co. Rep. 23b; PRO, Req. 33/120.

Bracton, Britton, Brian and Littleton (Docs. 1, 2, 3, 5, 6), and when it is noted that 'there are divers precedents that the copyholder is to recover in trespass against his lord', this is as Brian and Danby said long before.[14] Coke, then, makes no innovation when he writes of the customer, 'In actions that are merely personal he may sue or be sued at the common law. . . . If a copyholder be ousted by his lord . . . he may have an action of trespass against him at the common law' (Docs. 4, 9).[15] All the lawyers agreed on this (Doc. 10).[16] Brian and Danby were usually cited, not because they gave the first precedents in point of time, but the ones first encountered when thumbing back in reverse chronological order, as one naturally does when looking for a precedent. Only Coke took the trouble to search further back and find fourteenth-century precedents. He cites a whole series of such precedents and then concludes, 'By which cases it appeareth, that the judges in all successions of ages have allowed copyhold estates to be established and sure by the custom of the manor, and descendible to their heirs as other inheritances are (Doc. 9).[17]

If we now put back together the two halves of Coke's statement, we have a perfect summary of the long-established legal position:

'A copyholder cannot in any action real, or that savoureth of the realty, implead or be impleaded in any other court but the lord's court for and concerning his copyhold; but in actions that are merely personal he may sue or be sued at the common law. If a copyholder be ousted of his copyhold by a stranger, he cannot implead him by the king's writ, but by plaint in the lord's court. . . . If a copyholder be ousted by his lord, he cannot maintain an assize at the common law, because he wanteth a franktenement; but he may have an action of trespass against him at the common law; for it is against reason, that the lord should be judge where he himself is the party.'[18]

Nevertheless, it is not to be denied that customers were originally at a slight disadvantage in having to rely on personal instead of real actions at the common law. By the action of trespass they could recover no more than money damages, and although these were enough to be likely to deter trespass, they might sometimes be less advantageous than actual recovery of possession. But although trespass was a personal action, it none the less settled the question of title. Possession was nine tenths of the law and the plaintiff had first to prove rightful

---

[14] Dalison 62; BM. Add. MS. 24845, pp. 40–1.
[15] Coke, *Copyholder*, sect. 51; Co. Litt. 63a.
[16] *Ibid.* 60a–61a; *Copyholder*, sect. 9; I. S. Leadam, 'Inquisition of 1517. Inclos. & Evictions', *Trans. R. Hist. S.* vi-viii, 1892–4 vi. 207; H. Cary (ed.) *A Commentary on the Tenures of Littleton*, London 1829, pp. 185, 187, 193–4.
[17] Cf. Benloe (CP) 187–91.
[18] As n. 15.

possession. The title having thus been settled in law, most trespassers
would have desisted. There is perhaps an instance of a lord of the
manor who did not, but generally the personal action obviated the
need for a real one, thus making trespass virtually as good as a writ
of right. Moreover, customers with a real, dummy or fictitious undertenant for years, could regain tenements from which they had been
ousted by an action of trespass *de ejectione firmae,* for, from at least
as early as 1425, the tenant for years under a copyhold could defend his estate by the same action that gave security to all other
leaseholders for years, it being held that 'an ejectione firmae lieth upon
a demise of copyhold land by the lease of the copyholder himself,
but not upon a demise by the lord of the copyhold'. Furthermore,
from 1468 or 1482 perhaps, from 1499 certainly, judgment on such
an action could be obtained with a specific recovery of the land.
Finally, from 1588, 1596 and 1599–1610, in the King's Bench, Exchequer, and Common Pleas respectively, this specific recovery could
be obtained irrespective of whether the custom of the manor explicitly
allowed subletting for one year or not.[19] Thus being debarred from
real actions in law was scarcely any practical disadvantage.

But any such possible disadvantage was that of personal as against
real action, not of customer as against frank tenant, for while
common-law action was the frank tenant's sole defence, it was only
the second line of defence for the customer. His first line was the
custom of the manor. He made a plaint in the manor court in the
nature of a writ of right and this normally sufficed for the recovery
of a rightful estate (Docs. 1, 2). Recourse to the common law was
necessary only in the event of some failure in the customary law or
if one wanted damages by common law in addition to recovery by
the custom. We do not know exactly how often customary law failed
of its purpose, nor how many customers took action of trespass solely
on that account, and not just to secure damages for trespass to land
already being, or to be, recovered in the manor courts; but the more
records one sees, the stronger grows the conviction that the first line
of defence nearly always held, and this being so, the customer with
his plaint in the nature of a writ of right and his actions of trespass
was no worse off than the frank tenant with his writ of right and his
actions of trespass. The proof positive of this is that both customers
and frank tenants came equally to prefer personal to real actions and
to discard writs of right or plaints of that nature in favour of trespass
de ejectione firmae giving specific recovery as well as damages. By

[19] Moore (KB) 109–13, 128, 188–9, 271–2, 569; 2 Dyer 192a; 1 Leon. 100,
289–90, 328; 4 Co. Rep. 26a; 1 Brownl. & Golds. 140–1; Hutton 102–3;
Winch 3; PRO, Req. 33/120; Boyd, 'Chanc. Proc.', pp. 226–7; Holdsworth,
iii. 216.

Coke's time all titles were for the greatest part tried in such actions of ejectment.[20]

In so far as writs and plaints of right were relied upon, frank and customary tenants were in much the same boat, except only in the event of judgment going against them. The frank tenant could then maintain an appeal by writ of error, but the customer could not. If he wished to appeal, he could only do so, in the first instance, by a petition to his lord, in the nature of a bill of right, for the lord was chancellor in his own court and the equity of the customary law was in him, as may be proved by a precedent in 1389–90 (Doc. 9). This is what Littleton meant when he said, 'Writ of false judgment ... shall he have [not], for no franktenement is in him' (Doc. 5). This is what Fitzherbert alluded to when he wrote, 'Tenant at will according to the custom of the manor, who is tenant by copy of court roll, shall not have a writ of false judgment there against him.'[21] He is following Littleton on this point, as is Calthrope when he says, 'If a false judgment be given against them in the lord's court, they shall have no remedy but to sue the lord by petition' (Doc. 10). All lawyers always agreed on this. If the customer's petition of error failed before his lord, he could then only resort to a petition in the nature of a writ of false judgment, in Chancery (or Requests, Exchequer, or Star Chamber under special circumstances), for a subpoena to his lord to appear there (Doc. 9).[22] As Chancery was the first and main royal court to provide the customary tenant with an action in the event of alleged false judgment in the manor court, the customer was not fully protected in equity until he could petition in Chancery for a subpoena against his lord. It was precisely such actions that Savine found in early Chancery proceedings. Commencing in the fourteenth century, these petitions became a stream in the fifteenth.[23]

Of course, not all these Chancery suits went in favour of the pretended customers, nor did they all, in fact, concern the security of tenure specifically; but they all concerned either this security or some other aspect of customary tenure whose security was thereby assumed; and it matters not whether the pretended custom actually existed, as long as the chancellor did not dismiss, and, on the contrary,

[20] 5 Co. Rep. 105a.

[21] Cary 3; Calthrope, p. 5; A. Fitzherbert, *Grand Abridgement of the Common Law*, London 1517, Faux Jugement 7; *La Novel Natura Brevium*, London 1598, f. 18b; Plucknett, pp. xxii–iii, xxxvii–ix, 122 sqq.

[22] *Ibid.* pp. xxxix, 128; Co. Litt. 60b; *Copyholder*, sect. 51; Yale, *Manual*, pp. 195–6; 1 Eq. Ca. Abr. 118; Moore (KB) 410–1; 3 Leon. 81–3; 2 Brownl. & Golds. 78; Cary 3.

[23] Fitzherbert, *La Graunde Abridgement*, London 1565, f. 116a; Savine, 'Copyhold Cs', p. 299.

accepted, a petition based on *prima facie* customary tenure; nor whether the pretended customer won or lost, for all the cases, in one way or another, show that the chancellor entertained suits regarding customary tenure and customary law, that this other law was recognized by Chancery. In order to prove equitable jurisdiction, we no more have to show that every customary complainant won his case than, in order to prove murder illegal, we have to show that all alleged murderers were convicted.[24] Anyway, we know from a clear report by Fitzherbert of a Chancery suit in 1453–54 that 'tenant at will by copy of court roll shall have a subpoena against his lord if he oust him'.[25] Littleton discusses exactly such a subpoena accepted by the chancellor in 1467 (Doc. 5). Coke goes further and shows this to be the practice as early as 1390 (Doc. 9).

However, the protection afforded the customer by equity suffered from a minor procedural flaw. Faced, for example, by an injunction from the court of Requests to quit the premises, a man might scorn the writ, declaring it 'a counterfeyte and made under a busshe.' Even Chancery decrees and processes, especially the service of subpoenas, were occasionally resisted violently, by fortifications, guns, long bows, pistols, great stones and scalding water. Although such contempts did not pass with impunity and were punishable by imprisonment for an indefinite period at the discretion of the court, they might occasionally delay restitution. But in respect of the enforcement of orders, Chancery removed this slight blemish when, at the beginning of the seventeenth century, it began to issue writs of assistance, which recited disobedience to the court order, 'in manifest contempt of us and our said court', and directed the sheriff to maintain the plaintiff in possession.[26]

The combination of plaint in the nature of a writ of right, petition to the lord, writs of trespass *quare clausum fregit* and *de ejectione firmae*, and petitions for subpoena—of custom, common law and equity—gave the customary tenant a security as ample as that enjoyed by any frank tenant. The customer's security was not agitated in the courts in the sixteenth and seventeenth centuries for the simple reason that the question had been settled long before. The supposed hesitations of lawyers to protect customary tenants in the late fifteenth century and after arise solely from the misreading of the law books in such a way that judgments on actions by writ of false judgment were ascribed to actions on writ of trespass, and vice versa. Leadam could

---

[24] Gray, pp. 24 sqq.
[25] *Graunde Abr.* f. 116a.
[26] Yale, *Manual*, p. 29; Hall, pp. 7–8; my 'Revolts in Wilts. agst Chas I', *Wilts. Archaeol. Mag.* 1958, lvii. 66–7.

have put Tawney right on this, but was contemptuously brushed aside.[27]

What did agitate the lawcourts in the sixteenth century was the security neither of customary tenants, nor, in general, that of their undertenants, but solely these two particular questions following. Copyholders for lives were usually punishable in waste, copyholders of inheritance often not; but what remedy had a copyholder against an undertenant who committed waste? This was settled by a judgment in Chancery in 1576–77, that even if a copyholder were not himself punishable in waste, he had such rights of forfeiture against his own lessee in respect of the same copyhold tenement.[28] Secondly, since the customer's executors could only enjoy his estate for a year and a day after decease, what was to become of the estate of an undertenant when its term was still unexpired? The common law sought to follow the custom, but customs varied. In some manors, where the copyhold was of inheritance, the lease by which a copyholder had let his lands was voided if the lessor died or surrendered up his holding. More usually, even where the copyhold was for lives, a licensed lease for years of copyhold was good at least against the widow's free bench; she was only to have the rent and not expel.[29] Popham reports a case in the year 4 James as follows:

'A copyholder made a lease for yeares by license, and the lessee dyed, that this lease shall not be accounted assets in the hands of the executors, neither shall it be extended. But the case was denied by Justice Hutton and others, and that an ejectione firmae lies of such a lease. But he said, that if a copyholder makes a lease for yeares by license of the lord, and dyes without heire, the years not expired, the lord notwithstanding this may enter, for the estate of which this lease was derived is determined. But Yelverton Justice was contra, because this license shall be taken of a confirmation of the lord, and therefore the lease shall be good against him, and there (as I heard) it was argued by all, that if a copyholder makes a lease for a yeare, this is a lease by the common law, and not customary, and shall be accounted assets in the hands of the executors of the lessee.'

Similarly, a copy of licence made the underletting stand, even if the copyhold were forfeited, since the lord's licence confirmed the grant, and the grant itself was paramount (Doc. 7).[30] Clearly, the security

---

[27] Tawney, pp. 289–90.
[28] Cary 63.
[29] Smyth, *Hund. Berk.* p. 20; PRO, Exch. LR., MB 187, f. 64v.
[30] Popham 188; Moore (KB) 8, 271; Owen 72–3; Noy 171; 1 Brownl. & Golds. 140–1, 147–8; 2 Brownl. & Golds. 40; Hutton 101–2; Cro. Eliz. 484; Co. Litt. 59a; Yale, *Chanc. Cs*, i. 12.

of customary tenure had been left far behind the front lines of legal dispute; the battlefield was far away.

The security of copyhold has been legally proved, but even if it had not been, it would be fair inference from the well-known fact that knights, esquires and other gentlemen took up copyholds both of inheritance and of lives; they would not have done so had these estates been indefensible. Even from a layman's viewpoint, therefore, it is inconceivable that Coke, when taking his supposedly rosy view of the copyholder's position in law, should have had under examination a long series of sixteenth-century cases, as Tawney avers. Had Tawney given this series the briefest glance he would have seen that it related to the fourteenth and fifteen centuries (Docs. 4, 9).

One point remains to be elucidated. What, then, did Coke mean by his words 'But now' in the following locus classicus?

'But now copyholders stand upon a sure ground; now they weigh not their lords displeasure; they shake not at every suddine blast of wind, they eate, drinke, and sleepe securely, onely having a speciall care of the mainechance, viz. to performe carefully what duties and services soever their tenure doth exact and custome doth require: then let lord frowne, the copyholder cares not, knowing himselfe safe and not within any danger, for if the lords anger grow to expulsion, the law hath provided severall weapons of remedy; for it is at his election either to sue a subpoena or an action of trespasse against the lord. Time hath dealt very favourably with copyholders in divers respects' (Doc. 11).

If the argument here presented be correct, the time that Coke said had dealt favourably with the copyholder must have been long before the sixteenth century to which Tawney assigns it. To clinch the argument, upon which turns the whole interpretation of early modern English agrarian history, we must discover what exactly Coke meant. All we need to do is to turn to Coke's text, which charity bids us assume Tawney never did. The merest glance suffices to show that Coke's 'now' of the early seventeenth century is opposed by him to a 'then' not of the sixteenth century, nor even of the fifteenth, but to a 'then' of Anglo-Saxon and Norman times, and that 'copyholder' is used to mean 'customer'. Starting at the previous paragraph, Coke says,

'For, as I conjecture, in the Saxons time, sure I am in the Normans time, those copyholders were so farre subject to the lords will that seasonably and unseasonably the lords could at will resume and revoke their holdings from them, as Bracton and Fleta both speak; the lords upon the least occasion, sometimes without any colour of reason, onely upon discontentment and malice; sometimes againe upon some sudden fantasticke humour, onely to make evident to the world the height of their power and authority, would expell out of house and home their poore copyholders, leaving them helplesse and remedilesse by any course of law, and driving them to sue by way of petition. But now copyholders stand upon a sure ground. . . .' (Doc. 11).

Coke's statement, far from being a rosy view, or a new and startling assertion, or the consequence of recent legal innovation, was a truism enlivened only by historical discursion. That copyholders stood upon a sure ground was old and commonplace. The ground had been sure for ages.

To understand more fully the security enjoyed by customary tenants, it may prove helpful to examine closely certain procedures in manorial and equity courts.

In the manorial court, a jury of suitors gave the verdict. Here were maintained, by the forms of customary law, both actions of trespass and actions of right—of novel disseisin, of mort d'ancestor, of formedon in the descender, reverter or remainder, or any other real action. Here recoveries were suffered, uses made, leases granted, entails made and docked.[31] Here, too, were processes akin to those of Chancery or the Duchy Court, with depositions, interrogatories, petitions, traverses, demurrers, and so on.[32] The jurymen try cases carrying the penalty of forfeiture of copyholds for life on charges of unlicensed felling, of defrauding lords of their heriots, of refusal of services or of voluntary negligence tantamount to wilful refusal, and the like; and when they find against a guilty party this is plainly to the mutual advantage of lords and tenants.[33]

Only occasionally is this flow of customary justice interrupted. The jurors of a court of survey are fined £20 apiece for contempt of court in refusing information on matters enquired of.[34] A steward presented a copyholder for felling a tree without licence and ordered the bailiff to seize the tenement; but forfeiture 'wolde not be founde by the jurye', and the bailiff's presentment of seizure was firmly struck

---

[31] *Ibid.* 271; Coke, *Copyholder*, sect. 48, 51, 56; Straton ii. 385; Plucknett, pp. xxxii, xxxvi, 126–7; Leconfield, *Sutton & Duncton Manors*. London 1956, p. 5.

[32] Farrer i. 480; BM, Add. MS. 23949, f. 67; Glouc. Lib. R. 66. 30; Herts. RO, G'bury X.C. 6c, X.B. 3a, Fitzherber, *Svying*, f. 15.

[33] Moore (KB) 350; Bannister, p. 228; T. W. Hall, *A Descriptive Catalogue of Sheffield Manorial Records*, Sheffield 1926–34, ii. 21; P. D. Mundy, *Abstracts of Star Chamber Proceedings relating to Co. of Sussex*, Suss. Rec. Soc. 1913, xvi. 97–8; Dors. RO, D. 12 Long Burton ct September 30, 31 Eliz.; PRO, Exch. KR, Deps. by Commn 21–2 Eliz. Mich. 8.

[34] PRO, DL, MB 119, f. 67; and Ess. RO, D/DL M. 81 Ct Bk no 1, p. 7.

from the record of the court, for it was against custom.[35] The steward
of Castle Donington was accused of peculation, of reviling and re-
buking the homage so unfittingly that the understeward walked out,
and, worst of all, of dispossessing a copyholder in the teeth of a presentment by the jury in his favour.[36] Elsewhere another steward
attempts to seize a tenant's land without authority, only to be foiled
by the jury's refusal to find a forfeiture.[37] The lord farmer of a
royal manor tries to grant copyholds to his own son, contrary to the
custom.[38] A lord farmer to the bishop of Salisbury enters William
Flower's copyhold tenement in Upavon and forcibly ejects him, on
the pretext that he has felled more than five hundred young oaks,
mostly one foot in breadth, which was sufficient ground for action of
trespass. Yet the homage testify that all titles in question should be
settled in the manor court on their presentment and that otherwise
any vexation is contrary to custom. As for the felling of trees, the 'tree
of waste' has to contain one foot of timber 'at the mote' and be 20 feet
long. The lord cannot enter a copyhold unless its forfeiture has been
presented in open court, which in this case has not been done, although 'the defendant by his steward hath sought divers ways and
means to have the forfeiture fownde ageinst the plaintiff, and hath
thretained divers of the seyd homage with diverse threttes to the tenent
to bringe a forfeiture ageinst the seyd compleynent'.[39] If he attempts
to thwart customary law, redress may be had against the lord by
subpoena or trespass. The lord can only have his way if it does
not conflict with the custom, with common law, or with equity
(Docs. 1, 2).

It was not unknown for a lord or steward to attempt to browbeat
a jury or threaten them with a fine for perjury.[40] The lord, too,
might well be a justice of peace and perhaps might then contrive to
use his power and influence to incarcerate refractory suitors or
witnesses.[41] It is not surprising, then, that customary tenants sometimes had to have recourse to subpoena. In petitions in Chancery or
Requests, it is pleaded that no redress can be had in the manor court;
that the lord is a man of 'great power, substance and alliance'; or
that the jury has been made agreeable to a false judgment. Pleas of this
kind are either accepted in Chancery, referred to the relevant honour
or duchy court, or dismissed because they have not as yet been tried

[35] Northants. RO, Mont. old box P, pt i, Ct R. Foxley c. Bawdswell October
12, 30 Eliz., April 9, 31 Eliz.
[36] PRO, DL, Ct R. 80/1100, m. 1.
[37] Willcox, p. 296.
[38] PRO, Exch. LR, MB 207, f. 13 (11).
[39] PRO, Req. 80/47; & Norden, p. 63.
[40] Willcox, pp. 296-7; PRO, Req. 41/74; 30/8, 70.
[41] Ibid. 21/33; Hall, Soc. p. 7.

in the manor court in the first instance.[42] In order to prefer a suit in equity one had to allege matter of equity, so the pleas cannot be taken at their face value, but they nevertheless show that some false judgments were made in manor courts. But it should not be imagined that the lords were the only persons seeking to corrupt manorial courts. Seven years after Robert Hancock had brought an action of debt against William Jennynges, the latter was alleged to have tried secretly to obtain the forfeiture of the former's copyhold in Melksham manor.[43] Mistaken or false judgments arose in various ways.

Much more frequent than the plea of false judgment was the one of detinue, that is, that no lawsuit was possible in the absence of the relevant deeds and proofs. One needed not only the copy itself, but also the court records or a sworn custumal. The homage normally had access to these manorial records and could make searches in the rolls and files to decide issues. Sometimes the chest of records might be kept in a dwelling or a school, but more usually in a church-house, the chest having, say, three locks and keys, one of which was in the keeping of the court bailiff and two in that of the customers.[44] Without these records, recourse could be had only to equity. When the Nettleton tenants complain of being deprived of their common in the marsh, they say the custom is too old for any record of it to be available. In their dispute with the St Johns, the Midgehall tenants 'have not any remedye by the due order and course of the common lawe of the realme for want of some speciall and directe proffe of there said ancient custome to be used tyme out of mynde'.[45] Sometimes it is alleged the lord or another has detained copies of court roll and seized the court rolls and books to prevent inspection.[46] Nor was it unknown for copyholders to use the same weapon. Sir John and Bridget Hungerford, lord and lady of Latton, allege in their Chancery petition that, with intent to falsify the custom by extending the executor's year, 'divers of the customary tenants of the said manor, as namely Anthony Tommes, Edward Ware, Christopher Hinton, Richard Neweman, William Beames and William Stone' have 'casually gotten into their hands and possession the court rolles and court

---

[42] Boyd, 'Chanc. Proc.', pp. 75–6, 106–7, 126–7, 179–80, 182–3; Leadam, 'Security', p. 686; PRO, ECP 1472/10; Chanc. Proc. ser. ii, 76/3; Req. 14/97; 21/61; 91/44.

[43] Ibid. 26/67.

[44] 'Eliz. Chanc. Proc. 1558–79', p. 65; Lancs. RO, DD. K. 1526/5 Ct Bk Rainford April 17, 6 Geo. II; Shrewsbury Lib. 5384; BM, Harl. MS. 6006, f. 3v.; Add. MS. 37270, f. 54.

[45] PRO, Chanc. Proc. ser. ii, 29/17, 213/65.

[46] Ibid. 57/23; Req. 26/116; 74/95; 24/14; DL, MB 119, f. 14; Sp. Coll. Shaftesbury Papers 32/7; Shak. Bpl. Man. Docs. & Ct R. Attleborough ct 1587; Leadam, 'Security', p. 691.

books of the said mannor, wherein many of the ... customes were recorded, being partly led and seduced by the said Anthony Tomes, whom they doe conceave to be a polliticke and understandinge man'.[47] But these difficulties were not peculiar to customary tenures. It was quite common for the disseisin of frank tenants to be accompanied by a seizure of all the deeds of the premises. The ousted party could then have no action at law, unless by detinue of charters, and usually had to have recourse to a petition in equity. The petitioner pleads that he cannot proceed at common law because he 'knoweth not the certaine dates and contents of the said deedes, evidences and writings, nor whether the same be in chest, bag or cupboard, sealed, locked or unlocked, and is therefore remediles to recover them by the strict course of the common law'.[48] Thus Sir Edward Coke, when chief justice of the Common Pleas, petitioned in Chancery for a subpoena on the grounds that the deeds relating to one of his fold-courses had been seized and he did not know their number or whereabouts. The Earl of Suffolk and Lord Berkeley both made similar petitions at one time or another.[49] We need not take all these petitions at their face value, but it is certain that frank tenants no less than customers often had no choice but to seek an order compelling the discovery of records.

Impediments to redress might also arise from lack of 'ability'. Even in Requests the fees were considerable. To proceed there, a man complains, he has had to sell off his plough cattle.[50] But the lack of financial ability to maintain suits was by no means peculiar to customary tenants. The game of ruining people by lawsuits they cannot afford is confined to no time, place, tenure or estate. Sir Giles Overreach knows how to break Master Frugal, whose manor he covets:[51]

> 'I'll therefore buy some cottage near his manor,
> Which done, I'll make my men break ope his fences,
> Ride o'er his standing corn, and in the night
> Set fire on his barns, or break his cattle's legs:
> These trespasses draw on suits, and suits expenses
> Which I can spare, but will soon beggar him.
> When I have harried him thus two or three year,
> Though he sue in forma pauperis, in spite
> Of all his thrift and care, he'll grow behindhand ...

[47] PRO, ECP 1472/10; Chanc. Proc. ser. i, Jas I, H. 2/48.
[48] *Ibid.* A. 10/55; B. 21/7; C. 26/6; S. 36/47; ser. ii, 211/3; 244/54; Req. 30/95; HMC, *Rep. on MSS. in Var. Colls. iii*, HMSO, Cd. 1964, 1904, Tresham Papers, p. 61; Mundy, p. 79; Boyd, 'Chanc. Proc.', pp. 43, 45, 91; T. I. J. Jones, pp. xi-xii.
[49] PRO, Chanc. Proc. ser. i, Jas I, B. 17/19; C. 6/24; S. 39/53.
[50] PRO, Req. 15/48.
[51] P. Massinger, *A New Way to Pay Old Debts*, act ii, sc. 1.

> Then, with the favour of my man of law,
> I will pretend some title: want will force him
> To put it to arbitrement; then, if he sell
> For half the value, he shall have ready money,
> And I possess his land.'

In fact, poor persons could not so easily be ruined if they sued *in forma pauperis* from the outset. Under the Act of 11 Henry VII c. 12, they had full and free legal aid, including the costs of all processes, in all courts of record. By no means all customary tenants were poor and some were affluent, but if all the disputes in which poor customary tenants were involved had been with rich lords of manors, the latter would have had a slight advantage, in this only, that they had a somewhat wider choice of counsel.[52] But, of course, many frank tenants were of the poorer sort and customers as such suffered no disadvantage, rather the contrary, for proceedings were cheaper in manorial than in royal courts.

It is no part of our argument to deny that there were many disputes between the lords of manors and claimants to customary tenements, but it would be sheer prejudice to assume that the former were usually in the wrong. When a customary tenant in a lifehold manor claims to hold by a copy in reversion for 70 years, the surveyor is bound to note that 'yt ys ageynst the custome of the lordshypp to have a copy for yerys. Wherfor youre pleasure'.[53] Another surveyor credibly remarks, 'Thys copy ys enterlynyd and suspicious and he denythe the rentt'.[54] We have no reason to disbelieve the surveyor who notes about three copies, 'This coppie is entered... in a newe hand and new inck, out of all order... *heredibus* interlined... *heredibus* interlined in the booke and copie razed and *heredibus* there written'.[55] In western England, and wherever copyhold was for lives, parents sometimes named all their children after themselves, Thomas and Ann Smith, for example, having three sons called Thomas and three daughters named Ann. By this they hoped to creep a child into the parent's estate and one child into that of another, so evading the expense of a new lease of life. Only the imposition of heriots and the strictest supervision could frustrate such fraudulent intentions.[56] Customers who did that kind of thing deserved to forfeit all their holdings for infidelity. Yet they could, if they chose, enter a plausible enough petition in the courts of Requests or Chancery.

[52] Hall, *Soc.* p. 7; *Cals. Proc. Chanc. R. Eliz.* iii. 90; *Wilts N. & Q.* 1902, iii. 157–9; W. J. Jones, *The Elizabethan Court of Chancery*, Oxford 1967, pp. 323 sqq.; PRO, Req. 26/67.
[53] PRO, R. & S. GS 4/2, f. 11.
[54] PRO, Ct R. GS 208/48, f. 17v. & pass.
[55] PRO, Exch. KR, MB 47, f. 23.
[56] Leigh, op. cit.

F

That some customary tenants were disturbed in their possession does not argue any insecurity of tenure, for even frank tenants, whose security is never to be doubted, were sometimes disturbed. In ousting an owner of an estate of inheritance at the common law, it was not unknown to muster an armed band, cut off cart-wheels, overturn laden wains and reap the other man's wheat.[57] One could compile a catalogue of such ousters and create the impression that frank tenants were in constant danger of eviction, but it would be an illusion. Forcible entry was illegal and most intrusions were made with the intention of drawing on a suit of trespass by which the title could be tried, rather than of defying the law. Trespass *quare clausum fregit* was a personal action much used for this purpose. The need for such intrusions redoubled when freeholders began to grant leases to their friends and attorneys merely to have a trial of title by writ of trespass *de ejectione firmae*, which became the usual way of trying titles in the sixteenth century. There was thus a vast growth in purely nominal intrusions. Then, in Commonwealth times, when the action of ejectment finally became perfectly fictitious and it was no longer necessary for the nominal plaintiff to goad the nominal defendant into ejecting him or for such a pretence to be made, the intrusions died away as fast as they had sprung up.[58] These were not really lawless times. People were highly litigious, perhaps, but this was because it no longer occurred to them to take the law into their own hands. Ouster was not so much a defiance of law as a recognized gambit in a lawsuit. A customer of Gillingham manor explains how he put his horse into another tenant's enclosure merely to bring about a trial of right in the manor court. The horse was impounded, as intended, and suit commenced according to plan.[59] A roll-call of customers supposedly ousted must therefore fall far short of showing the insecurity of their tenure. Similarly, many charges of violent entry, with weapons offensive and defensive, were merely intended, often in vain, to show Star Chamber matter. And this criminal equity of Star Chamber was abused and its jurisdiction extended by fictitious pleadings to cover essentially civil cases.[60] Anyway, the court files give an unbalanced picture of the copyholder's security. One might as well learn how to drive a car by studying running-down cases. Wide reading in manorial records would leave the student in no doubt that the overwhelming

[57] PRO, St. Ch. Hy VIII vol. 2, ff. 113 sqq.; Jas, 168/16.

[58] 5 Co. Rep. 105b; A. W. B. Simpson, *An Introduction to History of Land Law*, London 1961, pp. 42, 136 sqq.; A. Smith, *Wealth of Nations*, ed. E. Cannan, London 1930, i. 367; NLW, Kentchurch Ct. R. 888 for lease made for trial of title by ejectione firmae.

[59] PRO, SPD, Chas I, vol. 200 no. 42.

[60] Yale, *Manual*, p. 12; P. H. Williams, 'St. Ch. & Council of Marches of Wales', *Bull. Bd Celtic Studs*, 1956, xvi. 289.

majority of customary tenants lived out their whole lives without so much as a whisper of a hint of the least threat to their security of tenure.

It is almost impossible, indeed, to find an instance of copyholders being wrongfully ousted by persons whom they dared not gainsay. The nearest thing to such an instance is the allegation, which found some support, that copyholders of inheritance in Moore were forced to take leases for years in the early seventeenth century under the duress of threats from the Dean and Chapter of Worcester Cathedral.[61] Some copyholds for lives, it is true, were replaced by leases for lives by indenture, but it can rarely or never be shown that this was an illegal or oppressive act. When enclosures were made, the lord of the manor might insist on substituting for copyholds for lives, leases by indenture for three lives or for 21 years. This could hardly have been any skin off the tenants' noses, for the terms of lease were thereby altered only slightly, and even if the copyholds had been continued they would not have had the sanction of either customary or common law, since customary and demesne lands had been exchanged by the enclosures. The effectual change was really from tenancy at will to a frank tenancy for life or a common-law estate for years.[62] The change might bring some slight incidental advantage to the landlord. It permitted him to bind the tenant to a course of husbandry mutually agreed between the two of them instead of to a course agreed by the whole township. But the tenant would likely welcome this move. Enforcement of covenants against waste and sub-letting, too, might be more effective than the provisions of customary law.[63] But in so far as this enforcement impeded the sitting tenant it further safeguarded the rights and property of his successors. If an individual were disadvantaged, the whole class of tenants gained. The term of lease might be somewhat shortened in some instances by the cessation of customary free bench; but this was open to abuse in a loose and disreputable manner, as when an aged and ailing customer took a young wife merely in order that she or a third party might enjoy the holding during her expected widowhood.[64] All in all, the balance of advantage in a change from copy to indenture generally lay with the tenants. In lifehold leases, an indenture was at least as good as a copy and the change from one to the other was often made on the initiative of the copyholders themselves, 'for good consideration given

[61] Cave & Wilson, p. 96; 1 Brownl. & Golds. 31.

[62] PRO, Exch. KR, Deps by Commn 5–6 Chas I, Hil. 17; Tawney and Power, i. 19 sqq.

[63] B'ham Lib. Winnington 52; Northants. RO, F(M) Misc. 77, 202, 205, 211, 459, 1033; BM, Add. Ch. 18821; Add. MS. 21608. ff. 130–1.

[64] Ibid. 23151, f. 11v.; Laurence, Diss. pp. 23–5; Marshall, S. Dept. p. 570; Smyth, Hund. Berk. p. 20.

to the lord', in order to avoid the burden of customary dues and services.[65] This, after all, was enfranchisement, and it would be perverse to argue that the copyholder had less security than the indenture-holder and then to complain that copies were replaced by indentures.

It is instructive to compare the security enjoyed by the customer with that finally won by the common-law lessee for years. The estate for years was no freehold, but a mere chattel estate, and the termor, having no franktenement, was excluded from real actions in common law just as the customer was, and yet had no protection from customary law as the customer had. A writ of novel disseisin sued by his landlord could give the lessee for years adequate protection against ouster by a third party and it was no disadvantage that restitution could be obtained only in this way. A bill to enable the lessee to take action himself was rejected as superfluous by the House of Commons in 1621. Of the remedies open to the termor himself, the writ of *quare ejecit infra terminum* only enabled him to recover his farm from someone else claiming possession through the lessor, and an action of trespass *de ejectione firmae*, though it could be brought against any ejector, at first gave the termor no more than damages for his rent laid out, which could never amount to the real loss sustained. It was not until 1499 that it was finally and certainly judged possible to recover the farm itself by a writ of *ejectione firmae*, so at last endowing the termor with security of tenure.[66] Thus the customary copyholder won his security long before the termor and always had more lines of defence than the termor could hope for.

It could conceivably be argued that the dissolution of the monasteries, and perhaps some other changes of landownership, brought a threat to customary as well as common-law tenants. What if the new lord should pick holes in grants made by his predecessor? As an instance of the difficulties that might arise we may cite from a survey book of 1542: 'This is the offer made by the tenantes ther for that their copyes be not good for that they were made by Mr Bruyne deceased, being tenant for terme of liffe, to have new copyes for . . . lyves and to gyve for a fyne of every yardland xls.' True the fine was modest, but then the fines previously paid for the estates surrendered were presumably taken into account. And it is far from certain that the customers had such a bad bargain. This, after all, may explain why they did not take the matter further. But the fact remains that the law favoured them, for estates granted by a lord for life or by any lord *pro tempore*, *de jure* or *de facto* were valid in law, even if their terms exceeded that of the grantor, for the grant itself was paramount

[65] Willcox, p. 278.
[66] Fitzherbert, *NB*, f. 220; A. Smith i. 367; Notestein & al., iv. 190.

because the custom was paramount (Doc. 7). This was the existing
state of the law that was declared in the statute of 32 Henry VIII c. 28.[67]
Occasionally, in course of the alienation of estates, copyholds became
severed from the manor they had formerly been part of, and thereby
placed in jeopardy. Thus Richard Mody bought the manor of Lea
from the Crown as an entire manor of itself, set up his own court, as
legally he might, and refused to recognize copyholds in the former
manor of Lea and Cleverton. Legally, severance in no way defeated a
customary estate, but in practice it could create some knotty problems.[68] Nevertheless, the law offered security to customers even in
these unusual circumstances. If they then failed to avail themselves of
the law, this may have been for three possible sets of reasons. Circumstances make the case and these we cannot always learn, but in some
instances the pretending customers may not have had a leg to stand
on in law. In others they may not have had much to lose and thought
it not worth the candle to make an issue of the matter. In yet others
they may simply have been ignorant of the law and too foolhardy to
take advice. By 1540, however, such ignorance as there was must have
been virtually invincible. The act of 31 Henry VIII c. 13 declared the
existing law to be that all monastic leases by common or customary
law, by indenture or copy, for years or for lives, were good and
effectual in law. The act of 32 Henry VIII c. 28 similarly declared
leases in being and in reversion good against all heirs and successors.

The second of these declaratory statutes, in its preamble, makes
our flesh creep by speaking of a 'great numbre' being 'daily with greate
cruelty expulsed'. But it also provides an essential clue to the whole
problem when it goes to great pains to exclude from legal protection
all leases by indenture where the accustomed rent was not reserved,
all those without covenant for impeachment of waste, and all leases
in reversion for terms exceeding 21 years or three lives. An indenture
of lease without covenant of waste was no lease in nature, but a
camouflaged grant for ulterior motives. A reversion of more than
21 years or three lives was not an ordinary conveyance, but an attempt
to defeat a successor of his rightful income. Such leases were legally
invalid. Yet the act confirmed leases in being for such exorbitant
terms as 99 years. These were indefensible by common law, the
courts holding that they were *ipso facto* suspect of fraudulent intent.
The effect of the act was thus to extend statutory protection to these
exorbitant and otherwise invalid leases.[69] This, then, was the gist of

[67] Wilts. RO, acc. 192, Figheldean Svy Bk, f. 7; Moore (KB) 236–7; Brook's
New Cs, 175–6; Dalison 19; Jenk. 242, 276; Coke, *Copyholder*, sect. 34.
[68] *Ibid.*; Savine, 'Customary Tenure', pp. 59–60; PRO, Req. 14/97; Gray,
pp. 239 sqq.
[69] Coke, *Copyholder*, sect. 53; Moore (KB) 128; 2 Brownl. & Golds. 156;
Savile 66–7.

the statute. It is well known that the heads of religious houses made a general attempt to estate out all monastic lands for exorbitant terms, under peppercorn or nominal rents, on leases in being and in reversion, and these often false or antedated, to their own kinsmen and henchmen, in order to prolong their own interest in the land and cheat their successors of theirs.[70] These successors, for their part, held courts of recognition to weed out invalid copies and indentures.[71] The second act, in part declaratory, struck, in addition, some compromise, allowing certain leases of less flagrantly fraudulent intent to stand. And these circumstances explain why what was probably the most sensational case of attempted eviction at this time related to a lease by indenture of an entire manor and lordship for six lives successively to a family of the old religion where the wife was said to have been the concubine of the abbot who made the grant.[72]

It is noteworthy that in all this *furor* precious little is heard about customary tenants. Some copies are said to have been voided—mostly on good grounds for all that we can learn—but the second act makes no specific mention of copyholders or customary law, and Henry Brinklow's, and so the age's, fiercest complaint, was against the eviction not of lessees, far less of customary ones, but of mere tenants at will, who had no leases at all. His grudge is that, 'It is now a common use of the landlordys, for every tryfyll, even for his fryndys plesure, in case his tenant have not a lease, he shall put hym out of his ferme.'[73] Customary tenants evidently suffered far less than tenants at will at the common law and holders of dubious indentures. Least of all can it be maintained that customers were worse off than common-law tenants.

Hitherto, in all this treatment of security of tenure, we have always used the word 'copyhold' in the sense of customary tenure and 'copyholder' in the sense of customer, in contradistinction from franktenement and frank tenant. But we have already had occasion to notice that 'copyhold(er)' could be used to mean all holding or holders by copy whether by the customary law or not. All customary tenure was not necessarily copyhold and some copyhold was certainly not customary. Demesne land arrented by copy was held by copy of court roll at the will of the lord, but not according to the custom of the

[70] A. Savine, *English Monasteries on Eve of Dissolution*, Oxford 1909, p. 54.

[71] G. Baskerville, *English Monks & Suppression of Monasteries*, London 1937, pp. 196 sqq.; Stewart-Brown, *St. Ch.* i. 74.

[72] E. M. Richardson, *The Story of Purton*, Bristol 1919, pp. 25 sqq.; 'Purton, case in St. Ch.', *Wilts. Archaeol. Mag.* 1903–4, xxxiii. 204 sqq.; PRO, Ct R.GS 208/28, f. 18.

[73] H. Brinklow, *Complaynte of Roderyck Mors*, ed. J. M. Cowper, E.E.T.S. 1874, pp. 9, 25; *A Supplication of the Poore Commons*, same ed., E.E.T.S. extra ser. 1871, xiii. 80.

manor, even if this phrase were erroneously included in the habendum. Since these tenancies were not under the custom of the manor,
they were in no wise protected by it. Since they were not made by
indenture, they were not leases at the common law. Irrespective of
the terms of their grants they were in law nothing but tenancies at
will pure and simple. As such they were carefully distinguished in
most survey books by such appellations as *overland, bordland, new
copyhold, netehold, runningland, courtdeal, barton land,* and *roveless*
(as opposed to tenements of old astre). Generally these holdings
formed a minute fraction of the whole and it was rare for a man's
holding to be composed solely of such demesne land. But in the
Midland Plain, and even more in the North-eastern Lowlands, it was
earlier the common practice to parcel out demesnes in such non-
customary copyholds.

Many of these tenants at will, when the occasion arose, were treated
strictly on their legal merits and displaced from their holdings at
short notice. In law they could claim no more than the safe harvesting
of the crops they had put in the ground.

By dint of repetition, the locus classicus for the displacement of
demesne copyholders has become the case of the tenants of Abbots
Ripton v. Sir John St John. Ruined at the time of the Wars of the
Roses, the tenants had thrown up their customary copyholds because
they were unable to keep up repairs and pay the rents. The lands they
surrendered were let back to themselves or others at abated rents
as tenancies at will, but did not thereby cease to be demisable by
copy, and the last monastic lord, shortly before the Dissolution, let
them out again by copy of court roll, yet not according to the custom
of the manor. When St John acquired the manor he took actions of
trespass against those of the tenants who would not comply with his
notice to quit, and they in turn complained that he had evicted them
and was compelling them to take common-law leases for terms of
forty years. What they found objectionable in this does not appear,
but they petitioned the court of Requests, presumably in the pious
hope of having the customary copyhold reconstituted which they had
first wilfully abandoned and then extinguished by the acceptance of
tenancies at will. The court decided for St John, but enjoined him to
bear no grudge, to extend his offer of common-law leases for years at
suitable rents, and to restore goods distrained for non-payment of rent.
If anyone was hardly dealt with, it was St John himself, except, of
course, that the abbot may have been guilty of false pretences, causing
much unnecessary hardship to both the tenants and St John.[74] Other
similar cases normally took much the same course. In Chatterton v.

[74] Leadam, 'Security', pp. 686, 688; *Select Cases in Court of Requests 1497–
1569,* Selden Soc. 1898, xii. 64 sqq.; Coke, *Copyholder,* sect. 62.

Poole in 1573, Requests ordered the plaintiff to surrender his copy to Sir Giles Poole in return for a good lease in law for 21 years. A Coggleshall tenant in 1574 was given a lease for 40 years. Some Rochdale tenants compounded with Sir John Byron and were granted leases for 21 years.[75]

Numerous demesne copyholds were swept away in the north of England, particularly in the North-eastern Lowlands, and especially after the Rebellion of the Earls. Some tenants offered to take leases for 21 years at double or treble the old rent; but many hoped against hope, clung to worthless copies, and forced trials that could only go against them. Sometimes the lord leased the entire demesne at the old rent, without a fine, to a man willing to shoulder the burden of clearing the estate to the mutual advantage of lessor and lessee. Alternatively, the tenants would concert to withold their rents, leaving themselves open to prosecution for debt and to the forfeiture of any estates they may have had pretensions to. One way or another the matter was often tried out. If the tenants had paid entry fines, the judges, as usual, normally recommended landlords to follow the common practice of granting them good leases for 21 years at easy rents and fines.[76] Where tenants had confused their 'copyhold' and freehold lands, landlords sometimes substituted leases for both. The same might occur when an enclosure or exchange of lands had been agreed upon. Elsewhere again, tenants were confirmed in two thirds of their holdings in return for surrendering the rest. Some tenants tried to buy their farms, while others with leases by both copy and indenture were willing to surrender the copy in return for a common-law lease of the whole.[77] The exchange of bad copies for good leases was no disadvantage in itself; but there was no longer any scope for smallholders combining subsistence cultivation with a little cattle breeding and much fighting and stealing. The sad plight of these anachronistic survivors from a more barbaric age is well depicted in this letter from one of them to the Earl of Northumberland:[78]

'Whereas your saide peticioner and his predecessors being ayncient tenauntes to your honour holdinge one tenement on ferme in Upper Bustone by vertue of coppieholde tenure out of the memorie of mann, which coppies both of your said poore peticioners great grandfather, his fathers father and his owen father are yet extant and to bee seene; and now of this late time your saide poore peticioner, being

---

[75] PRO, SPD, Eliz. Add. vol. 23 no 38, ff. 91–2; DL, R. & S. 2/11, f. 41v. (p. 82); APC, xxiv. 31; Fishwick, Rochdale, p. viii.

[76] Bateson, ii. 384 sqq., 427–8, 455–6, 482–3; v. 259–60; viii. 238, 264; x. 276; xv. 159, 285–6; xvi. 230–1.

[77] Ibid. ii. 428; v. 259–60; viii. 264; ix. 322; xv. 285–7.

[78] Ibid. v. 210.

under age, helplesse and none to doe for him, and forced (God knowes) by some of your honours officers to take a lease and paye double and tribble rent, insomuch as that your saide poor peticioner, his wife and eight poore children is utterly now beggered and overthrowen, unlesse your worthie good honour will be pleased to take a pittifull commiseracione hereof. . . .'

Many demesne copyholds were voided likewise on the royal estates. In the manor of Pickering, one Tusser sold as copyhold of inheritance lands formerly let at low rents. His commission was to grant copyholds according to the custom; but this manor had never had customary copyhold before, nor any custom for estating land, so the copyholds of inheritance created were invalid, and were subsequently replaced by tenancies frankly at will. The demesne copyholders at Clitheroe fared no better. In 1505–56 the Duchy told the steward of the manor that his predecessors had granted demesne lands by unlicensed and legally invalid copies. His grants were to be limited to holdings of over £2 annual value and to terms of twelve years or more. Next year special commissioners came to Clitheroe empowered to grant unlimited demesne copyholds. Two years after it was forbidden to partition these new holdings lest the demesne become unduly fragmented, but otherwise they continued without let or hindrance until 1607. Then the Duchy suddenly demanded 20 years' rent for confirming the copyholds to their tenants. They accepted the principle of composition, offered 12 years' rent, and in the end agreed to 20, making a total composition of £3,950, in return for a Duchy decree of confirmation of title. But this was not thought sufficient security and the tenants offered as much again for a private Act of Parliament to confirm the decree.[79]

A lease for years in common law was a good exchange for what was no more than a tenancy at will; but there was this other alternative of assuring titles by private act. The Protector Somerset promoted an act lending demesne copyholds in some of his manors the force of customary estates. Tawney's starry eyes saw this as an application of a 'popular agrarian policy', but we do not know what was paid in consideration. Similar acts were made for Hounslow Heath and Walsingham.[80]

But it often happened that the lord of the manor was concerned not to put demesne copyholds on a sound legal footing but to absorb them into a large demesne farm. We have seen this in the North-eastern Lowlands on a wide scale, and more isolated examples of the practice

[79] Savine, 'Customary Tenure', pp. 58–9; Priv. Act 7 Jas I no 3; G. H. Tupling, 'Causes of Civ. War in Lancs.', *Trans. Lancs. & Ches. Antiq. Soc.* 1956, lxv. 17–20; Turton i. 52.
[80] Stats. 2 Ed. VI c. 12; 37 Hy VIII c. 2, 3; Tawney, pp. 294, 365.

may be found in many farming countries. In the Oxford Heights Country, Sir Thomas Freke withdrew portions of the demesne previously held by copy by all but one of the customers of Hannington. When the demesne was in common field, it was often the best course to let it out by copy to the customary tenants. Then, if it were later decided to enclose the demesne into a small number of enclosed farms, these tenancies at will could easily be terminated at short notice.[81]

Leadam saw it with commendable clarity, but it is understandable that Savine, who, as he regretted, had breathed little of the happy atmosphere of English common law, should have misread some of these demesne copyhold cases and confused one of them with the question of the security of tenure of customary tenants. He cites a case purporting to show the insecurity in law of the customer, when the Chancery petition itself states that 'by color that is conteyned in his copy "to have and to hold to him and his heirs at the will of the lord", in which case your seid suppliaunt can have no remedy agenst his saide lorde by course of the comen lawe of this lande'. He was unprotected in law just because his copy was not customary; he did not hold 'according to the custom of the manor'.[82]

Finally, to the serfs, villeins, natives or bondmen, the security of tenure enjoyed by other tenants was not applicable. Bondmen existed in declining but far from negligible numbers in the sixteenth century, especially on monastic estates. Some still survived even in the early seventeenth, the last instances as yet discovered being in 1635, though after Pigg v. Caley in 1618 no case appears to have come before the king's courts.[83] Bondmen by blood had no remedy by law or equity, and their lords might, and frequently did, seize their holdings at pleasure. Their position was that ascribed by Coke to all 'copy-

---

[81] Bland, Brown & Tawney, p. 245; PRO, Chanc. Proc. ser. i, Jas I, P. 17/14; DL, MB 115, ff. 31v. sqq.; Bristol Univ. Lib. acc. 31 Ct Bk Hannington vol. A.

[82] Savine, 'Customary Tenure', pp. 33, 63.

[83] A. Savine, 'Bondmen under the Tudors', *Trans. R. Hist. S.* 1903, xvii; H. E. Malden, 'Bondmen in Sy under Tudors', *ibid.* 1905, xix; Fitzherbert, *Svying*, f. 27v.; Moore (KB) 90–1); Noy, 37, 171; E. Sfk RO, S1/10.9.4; Earl Soham Custom R. 1635; Bland, Brown & Tawney, p. 231; Straton i. 9; *VCH Beds.* ii 90–1; *Berks.* ii. 203–4; *Glos.* ii. 165; J. A. Tregelles, *A History of Hoddesdon*, Hertford 1908, p. 325; R. J. Hammond, 'Soc. & Econ. Circes Ket's Rebellion', ts. thesis M.A. Ldn Univ. 1933, p. 96; F. Hull, 'Ag. & Rural Soc. in Ess. 1560–1640', ts. thesis Ph.D. Ldn Univ. 1950, pp. 339–40; Herts. RO, 47295, 47297, 47299; Dors. RO, D. 54 Terrier w. rental Ryme 1563; Leadam, 'Inq. 1517', vi. 190; Shak. Bpl. Throckmorton: Sambourn rental 24 Hy VIII; Wilts. RO, acc. 84 Ct Bk Durrington & Knighton 1609–17, f. 2 v.; Savernake, Svy Burbages 1574–5, f. 3; Oxon. RO, DIL. II/a/2; BM, Egerton MS. 2994 ff. 45v.–6; 3034, f. 127v.; 3134, ff. 84, 123–4, 126, 156 sqq., 183 sqq.; C. M. Hoare, *The History of an East Anglian Soke*. Bedford 1918, pp. 252, 296–9.

holders' in Saxon and Norman times (Doc. 11). Manumissions were made from time to time, and occasionally out of grace or for services rendered, but lords knew well how to extract the uttermost penny even from enfranchisement, which often amounted to spoliation. In 28 Henry VIII the House of Lords rejected a bill for general manumission, presumably because it would have cut off this source of income. The consideration for manumission, which in practice was often compulsory, might be either cash in hand or the surrender of part of the bondman's holding. In order to ascertain the bondman's worth, it was usual, before proceeding further, to make an inventory and valuation of his goods. Sir Henry Lee, acting on behalf of Queen Elizabeth, sought out bondmen whose servitude might otherwise have lapsed and compelled some of them to be manumitted at great expense. An alternative course was to seize the bondman's holding and then grant it back for a high fine. One had then only to wait for the unfortunate to accumulate enough to pay another fine and repeat the process. Even when the bondmen lived outside the manor precincts, all was not lost, for chevage was exacted and their goods could be seized at pleasure. When Enford was surveyed in 1552 a memorandum was made of the 'Bondemen otherwyse called due men belongynge to the seid manor', who 'ar to be sesed and putt to fines or as the lorde pleses, after the custom of the sayd mannor'.[84] Manumission was made under the high-sounding principle that all men were created free by nature and by God, but really depended on the depth of the bondman's purse. Paupers were not worth manumitting. When John Norden finds bondmen of blood at Falmer in 1607, he is immediately concerned to discover their 'ability'. It was disappointing that the jury did not know what goods the bondmen had, only that they were 'all poore men'. 'But mee thinkes this kinde of advantage is nowe out of season,' says the surveyor, adding with a touch of regret, 'Yet were the men of abilitie they might be upon some consideration infraunchized.'[85] Bondmen could expect no security of tenure, rather to be summarily evicted or clapped in irons at the whim of an abbot.

[84] *Ibid.* pp. 252, 299–301; Richardson, p. 193; F. G. Davenport, *The Economic Development of a Norfolk Manor 1086–1565*, Cambridge 1906, pp. 96–7; Rec. Commn, *Ducatus Lancastriæ*, London 1823–34, iii. 147; Savine, 'Bondmen', pp. 253, 270; Jones-Pierce, 'Rural Caerns.', pp. 35–6; *Arch. Camb.* 1847, ii. 215–7; A. F. Pollard, *The Reign of Henry VII from Contemporary Sources*, London 1913–4, ii. 234–5; W. Hooper, 'Bondmen at Reigate under Tudors', *Sy Archaeol. Colls.* 1930, xxxviii, pt ii, pp. 150 sqq.; F. J. Baigent and J. E. Millard, *A History of Ancient Town & Manor of Basingstoke*, Basingstoke 1889, p. 328; Shak. Bpl. as prev. n.; B'ham Lib. Elford Hall 76; PRO, Exch. KR, Deps. by Commn 39–40 Eliz. Mich. 31; Wilts. RO, acc. 7 Enford Ct Bk 1537–1723, ff. 19–20; BM, Add. Ch. 24440; Add. MS. 41305, f. 78v.

[85] PRO, Exch. TR, MB 157, f. 99v. (p. 180); and DL, MB 108, f. 8v.; BM, Add. MS. 6027, f. 133 (123) v.

When copyhold remaindermen petition Chancery against depriva-
tion of their succession to a tenement, the steward simply answers
that the first taker was a villein regardant to the manor, so that the
seizure of all his belongings was justified, while the remaindermen
were amply compensated with £5. The complainants allege their
copies were seized on pretext of scrutiny and that 'when he had their
coppyes he asked of them what they could doo', to which they,
poor souls, replied they could trust their landlord. When petitioners
complain that a dispossessed nief is a blind widow with six young
children, 'at this present tyme yet goen agooding, which is pitious and
hevy to see', the steward promptly replies that blindness was reason
enough for turning her out, for how could she hope to manage the
holding.[86] This was how bondmen were treated. This was the face
of rural society before the advent of agrarian capitalism.

In fine, it has been seen that the confusion of judgments on writs
of trespass with those on writs of false judgment and other similar
errors, with a dash of misquotation, gave Tawney the false idea that
customary tenants only came to enjoy security of tenure in the course
of the sixteenth century. If this were correct, one would expect to
find numerous instances of customary copyholders being ousted and
left without remedy. But this one cannot do. With the worst will in
the world, Tawney was only able to scrape together ten instances
purporting to prove insecurity of tenure and the widespread clearance
of estates by the ousting of customers. The reader can see for himself
how Tawney makes this stage army of ten serve all his occasions and
fight all his battles. And the reader can see also how unfitted for his
part is each and every member of this stage army. At Ormsby in 1516
the lord of the manor is found holding 219 acres lately in farm to
six tenants, suggesting the possible consolidation of demesne farms,
which were perhaps demesne copyholds. There was some similar
consolidation at Damerham in 1568. In neither instance is there anything to suggest illegal or harsh evictions and in neither is any mention made of any displacement, far less of copyholders or of customers.
The case of Abbots Ripton, as we have seen, concerned demesne
copyholders, mere tenants at will, who resisted in equity St John's
efforts legally to substitute good leases for bad copies. There was
never any question of eviction or oppression. In North Wheatley, the
issue was not even between landlord and tenant, but between clients
and a lawyer accused of fraud. The remaining six incidents are all
from the North-eastern Lowlands and relate to the displacement not
of customary copyholders, but of tenants at will. No single instance
has ever been brought forward of a customary tenant wrongfully

[86] I. S. Leadam, *Select Cases before King's Council in Star Chamber*, Selden
Soc. xvi, xxv, 1903–11, xvi. pp. cxxiii sqq., 118 sqq.; PRO, ECP 1197/34–5.

evicted who did not have redress in law or equity. Tawney's belief that 'copyholders were not safe even on the sacred customary land itself' is refuted even by his own meagre evidence.[87]

Bondmen apart, everyone had security of tenure as befitted their estates, and nearly all were quite untroubled in their possessions, never needing even to defend them in law or equity. Had it been otherwise, had farmers not been secure in their farms, they would hardly have undertaken any improvement, let alone the agricultural revolution they actually achieved. Men will not travail long and risk all their capital in the nagging fear of sudden confiscation. Tenures arose in feudal society; the doctrine of estates evolved to meet the needs of the capitalist farmer and his landlord, both of whom imperatively required security of tenure. To assert that capitalism throve on unjust expropriations is a monstrous and malicious slander. Security of property and tenure answered capitalism's first and most heartfelt need. Where insecurity reigned, it was because of the absence, not of the advent or presence of capitalism.

[87] Tawney, pp. 257–8, 260, 283, 302–4, 362; Bland, Brown & Tawney, pp. 258–60; and see above, pp. 87–9.

4

Enclosures

SINCE security of tenure was firmly established in law and equity, enclosure could only be accomplished in three main ways, either by custom, or by unity of possession, or by agreement, which, in turn, might be by composition or by commission.

The customs of manors, especially in hill-farming and other countries where the commons were abundant, often gave their lords the right to enclose portions of the waste. These customs varied greatly, but most applied to common of estover and of turbary as well as of pasture, and none allowed limitless enclosure; either the lord might make grants from the waste with the consent of the homage, or, more usually, he was bound to leave enough waste to meet the requirements of all the commoners. This latter custom was so general that it was conveniently consolidated in the statutes of Merton and Westminster II in 1235 and 1285. The former of these Statutes of Approvement, as they are generally called, applied only to common appendant, i.e. rights of common attached to a corporeal hereditament by operation of law, but the second extended the same principle to common appurtenant, i.e. to rights so attached only by grant or prescription. The statutes were continued in 1549 by another that trebled the damages for hedge-breaking and exempted houses built with grounds not exceeding three acres, but did nothing to sweep away the safeguards of the Statute of Merton, as Tawney alleged it did.[1] These statutes were especially intended to cover the intakes, many of them for industrial dwellings, so frequently made in northern England in particular.

To ensure that when intakes were made from the waste, freeholders were not deprived of necessary commons, was the purpose of the Statutes of Approvement, and freeholders' rights were also protected in law by the action of novel disseisin. Although Coke argued against it on the grounds that one person should not be deprived

[1] Stats. 20 Hy III c. 4; 13 Ed. I, Stat. 1 c. 46; 3 Ed. VI c. 3; Tawney, pp. 371–2.

of remedy simply because others had it, it was ruled that a commoner, as such, could not maintain an action of trespass for intrusions into the common, but only the owner of the soil. If the intruder were a a tenant of the manor, the remedy was in the court baron, and if an outsider, the lord of the manor had the right and duty to bring an action of trespass or proceed by writ of novel disseisin.[2] But approvement (improvement) was often carried out by the lords of manors from the waste of the manors themselves and if harmed by this the customary tenants had no redress but in equity, to which they frequently resorted.[3] Because customary tenants had this means of redress, still more because they themselves generally took the initiative in dividing the commons, it became usual for approvement to be conducted under a formal agreement. In the long run it was the easiest way of going about the business.

Not a few allegations (and denials) of arbitrary enclosure are nevertheless to be found. Most of these relate to approvements or intakes made from the waste and common of pasture, and in them the commoners are concerned to prove their rights, if necessary by a suit compelling the discovery of documents, and then to show that the common left to them was insufficient, making the enclosure contrary to both customs and statutes.[4] One of the bones of contention in the long struggle between the lord of Thingden and his tenants was the enclosure of the common pastures.[5] Very similar was the protracted strife between Lord Berkeley and the tenants of Frampton for the possession of Slimbridge warth. They had suits in the courts of King's Bench, Common Pleas, Chancery, Wards and Star Chamber, and other trials of law lasting a half-century.[6] Several instances might be brought forward to show that commons were sometimes wrongfully enclosed.[7] John Turbeville esquire enclosed the sheepdown and much of the common fields of Bere Regis without compensating the

[2] 2 Brownl. & Golds. 146–9: PRO, Chanc. Proc. ser. i, Jas I, C.16/66, ans.; Boyd, 'Chanc. Proc.', 112–3.

[3] PRO, Chanc. Proc. ser. i, Jas I, C. 16/59, compl. & 66, compl.; T. 1/5, compl. & ans.

[4] E. C. K. Gonner, Common Land & Inclosure, London 1912, pp. 48–51; Fishwick, DL, i. 3–5; W. Brown, Yorkshire Star Chamber Proceedings, Yks. Archaeol. Soc. Rec. Ser. 1909, xli. 53–4; L. A. Parker, 'Enclo. in Leics.', ts, thesis Ph.D. Ldn Univ. 1948, pp. 104–5; F. E. Hyde & S. F. Markham, A History of Stony Stratford, Wolverton & London 1948, p. 38; Tawney. pp. 412–3; HMC, 3rd Report, App. London, HMSO C. 673, 1872, pp. 31–2; PRO, Req. 26/116, 65/52, 74/95, 87/7, 121/30; St. Ch. Hy VIII, 19/11, 25/34; Ed. VI, 6/107; P. & M. 10/49; Jas, 55/13; Exch. KR, Deps. by Commn 30 Eliz. Hil. 3; Chanc. Proc. ser. i, Jas I, B. 35/66, S. 6/37, S. 8/45, S. 22/71, T. 13/70; Northants. RO, F-H 1382, 1386.

[5] Savine, 'Customary Tenure', pp. 72–3.

[6] Smyth, Hund. Berk. pp. 330–1; Glouc. Lib. RF. 274. 12.

[7] E.g. PRO, DL, MB 115, f. 10v.

tenants of the lord of the other half of the manor.[8] Francis Smyth
of Wootton Wawen enclosed part of the common only to have the
court baron order the levelling of his hedges and ditches.[9] But events
at Warslow, in the Peak-Forest Country, perhaps provided a more
typical specimen of these disputes. In a Chancery petition grounded
on a plea of detinue, the lord of the manor rehearses the history of
the period 1547–67. 'At the earnest entreaty of divers of his poor
tenants and cottages there, and for the better maintenance of tillage
and corn, which they then greatly wanted,' he recounts, he 'granted
to certain of them licence to enclose and sow certain acres of waste
ground adjoining unto several cottages.' But now a certain William
Fynney has brought an action of novel disseisin at Stafford assizes,
'making his outward show thereby that he would be a Commonwealth man and put down enclosures, whereas in truth he seeketh to
destroy tillage and the increase of corn'.[10]

Enclosure by unity of possession occurred in various farming
countries but especially in the North-eastern Lowlands and the Midland Plain. If the so-called 'farmers' had no estates and the demesnes
or other freeholds were let to halves and thirds, or the tenancies were
merely annual, the landlords had only to wait until the end of the
year to have all their land at their immediate disposal, when it could
be enclosed without asking leave of anyone, simply by unity of possession.[11] It was under such circumstances that the Elizabethan Earl
of Essex was able to license his farmer at Keyston to enclose all the
common fields of the manor, which he did.[12] Unity of possession was
occasionally brought about also by the engrossment of estates through
purchase or similar acquisition. The land could then be enclosed at
pleasure.[13] This is what Sir Edward Duncombe did at Battlesden.[14]

The clearance of landed estates in the North-eastern Lowlands,
where not only farmland but also coal deposits were to be won or lost,
was facilitated by the circumstance that the tenants were mostly without genuine estates in the land; they were mere tenants at will.[15]
Sometimes one of the tenants,[16] but more usually the landowner or
the farmer of his demesnes strove to enclose the whole township

[8] BM, Add. MS. 6027, ff. 94(93)v.–95(94)v.; PRO, Exch. TR, MB 157,
f. 67 (pp. 127–8).
[9] W. Cooper, App. pp. 13, 17.
[10] Boyd, 'Chanc. Proc.', pp. 111–3.
[11] See above, pp. 44–6, 87–90.
[12] PRO, Exch. LR, MB 216, f. 73.
[13] Gonner, pp. 44 sqq.
[14] PRO, Chanc. Pro. ser. i, Jas I M. 18/30, compl.
[15] J. U. Nef, The Rise of the British Coal Industry, London 1931, i. 316–7;
and see above, pp. 44–6, 58–60, 88–9.
[16] Bateson, i. 350–1, 353–4.

for himself. Early in the seventeenth century William Carr leased from his uncle the manor of Hetton and proceeded to enclose all the land to his own use.[17] In 1586 the farmer of Bambergh was trying to monopolize all the commons and not long after Sir Thomas Gray of Chillingham took a hand in furthering this end.[18] Whitehead, the demesne farmer of Alnmouth, whose burgesses he had dispossessed of their commons by 1613,[19] joined with Delavale, another of the Earl of Northumberland's officers, in securing for one Slegg the lease of Bilton demesne, this being the first step in the enclosure of the lordship.[20] The outstanding hero of the enclosures in this country was this Robert Delavale of Seaton Delaval and Hartley, both of whose demesnes he cultivated under his own management. Towards the end of the sixteenth century he displaced all the tenants of Hartley and threw all the land into one enclosed farm.[21] What he did at Seaton Delaval is best told in the words of Joshua Delavale:[22]

'Seaton Delavale being a lordship and the inheritance of Robert Delavale esquire, whereof on his demayne ther he had two plowes going of ancient time; and since or about the tenth yeare of the queene, ther was in Seaton Delavale towne twelve tenements, whereon dwelt twelve able men, sufficientlie furnished with horse and furniture to serve her maiestie, who paid 46s. 8d. rent yearlie apiece or three-aboutes. All the said tenantts and their successors saving five the said Robert Delavale either thrust them out of their fermolds or weried them by taking excessive fines, increasing of their rents unto £3 apiece, and withdrawing part of their best land and medow from their tenements, and by not permittinge theim to malt their own malt corne they grew of their fermes for hindring the vent or saile of their said landelord's, by taking their good land from them and compelling theim to winne morishe and heath ground, and after hedging heth ground to their great chardge, and payed a great fine, and bestowed great reparations on building on ther tenementes, he quite thrust them of in one yeare, refusing either to repay the fine or to repay the chardge bestowed in diking or building, as the tenants do bitterlie exclame. The said seven fermolds displaced had every one of them 60 acres of arable land, viz., 20 in every feild at the least, as the tenannts affirme, which amounteth to 480 acres of land yearlie or thereaboutts, converted for the most part from tillage to pasture, and united to the demayne of the lordship of Seaton Delavale. So that wher was twelve tenantts with sufficient horse and furniture able to serve, they are now brought to five ... who have not one serviceable horse emongst them, all for the causes aforesaid.'

[17] *Ibid.* xiv. 230.
[18] *Ibid.* i. 274–5.
[19] *Ibid.* ii. 482–3.
[20] *Ibid.* 455–6.
[21] *Ibid.* ix. 124–5.
[22] *Ibid.* 201.

G

By 1610 the clearance of this estate was complete, all the 2,500 acres being enclosed.[23]

Where enclosure by unity of possession bore most hardly on the poorer sort was perhaps in urban centres where the owners were closed corporations and the erstwhile commoners numerous and utterly dependent upon one single common. The oligarchic governments of commercial capitalists in most free boroughs and cities[24] proved even more dangerous enclosers than the lords of manors and manorial boroughs. The usual policy adopted, for instance in Marlborough, was one of leasing the borough lands as enclosed farms, so depriving the poorer sort of pasture for their cows.[25] Coventry was the scene of a long struggle between the rich burgesses and the mass of commoners who objected to the enclosure of the town fields.[26] Similar disputes flared up in Lincoln at various times between 1511 and 1722.[27] In 1517 Southampton corporation made an ordinance for the enclosure of part of the saltmarsh to defray the charges of the sea-wall. This met with strong opposition and the enclosures were set up, levelled, raised again and once more thrown open in 1549, when the rebellious atmosphere enabled the popular party to have its way.[28] After 1624 the corporation of Leicester leased the South fields out to farmers, endangering common rights, and in the eighteenth century attempts at enclosure led to the outbreak of riots.[29] In 1630, 'to prevent popular tumult', the old common council of Huntingdon was dissolved and an oligarchic government was instituted by a new and restrictive charter. This was followed by complaints that the mayor and aldermen had been using their power to deprive the burgesses of their common rights. Oliver Cromwell, who was a magistrate, made 'disgraceful and unseemly speeches' of protest to the mayor and recorder and was taken into custody. The dispute was finally settled by the arbitration of the Earl of Manchester, who insisted on the amendment of the charter to ensure to the burgesses sufficient common for their needs.[30] About 1613 a Malmesbury glover complained that the richer burgesses had divided and enclosed the heath for their own private advantage. Farmers who had leased heath enclosures from

[23] *Ibid.* 201–2.
[24] G. Unwin, *Industrial Organisation in the 16th and 17th centuries*, Oxford 1904, p. 74.
[25] See below, p. 98.
[26] Tawney and Power, iii. 12–3; *VCH War.* ii. 157.
[27] J. W. F. Hill, *Medieval Lincoln*, Cambridge 1948, pp. 335–6, 353.
[28] A. L. Merson, *The 3rd Book of Remembrance of Southampton 1514–1602*, vol. i, *1514–40*, Southampton Rec. Ser. 1952, ii. 20–2, 24–5, 51.
[29] C. J. Billson, 'Open Fields of Leicester', *Trans. Leics. Archaeol. Soc.* 1925–6, xiv, 25–7; *VCH Leics.* iv. 99, 100, 102, 165–6.
[30] C. Firth, *Oliver Cromwell*, London 1953, pp. 30–2.

the new and exclusive borough government were forced to defend possession against a crowd of 'the meanest and basest sort of people'. Led by a baker, a blacksmith and a strongwaterman, the rioters levelled hedges, fences, gates and stiles. Although the town rulers complained loudly that the place was 'very full of poore people' and were not backward in attributing unrest to the activities of a paid agitator, the enclosures clearly aroused the hostility of most of the crafts and tradesmen.[31]

Generally speaking, however, the usual form of enclosure was by express consent or agreement.[32] Some enclosure agreements were merely permissive of piecemeal division, a custom being established that lands might be taken in at will provided they were thrown open at Lammas, or that it was permissible to keep such enclosures in severalty throughout the year, if only the encloser surrendered all his own rights of common and obtained his neighbours' consent.[33] Another type of enclosure by agreement, sometimes styled enclosure by composition, entailed the consent of common-field farmers to the enclosure of the demesne lands or of a part of the waste proportionate to the rights of common enjoyed by the demesne, the extinction of the demesne rights of common and the preservation of those of all the other farms. Enclosures of this kind frequently necessitated formally agreed exchanges of land between the lord and the tenants (Doc. 21).[34]

Enclosure by composition was frequently employed in emparkment. In the late fifteenth century and the first half of the sixteenth there was a widespread movement of emparkation, both for the creation of new parks and the enlargement of old ones. This was not peculiar to particular farming countries, but ran its course wherever landowners found suitable situations for their seats, that is, everywhere

---

[31] [J. Waylen], *A History Military and Municipal of the Town . . . of Marlborough* . . . , London 1854, pp. 110, 117, 120, 122–3; *Wilts. Archaeol. Mag.* 1936, xlvii. 322–3; *APC* 1613–4, pp. 92–3; PRO, St. Ch. Jas, 93/2, 138/8, 290/22; Exch. KR, Deps. by Commn 9 Chas I Mich. 75.

[32] Gonner, pp. 51–4. Supporting references too voluminous to publish.

[33] Baigent & Millard, pp. 330, 334, 340; Campbell, p. 90; E. M. Leonard. 'Inclo. of Com. Fds in the 17th century', *Trans. R. Hist. S.* 1905, xix. 110; H. C. Brentnall, 'A Document from Gt Cheverell', *Wilts. Archaeol. Mag.* 1949–50, liii. 436; *Sy Archaeol. Colls.* 1871, v. 136–7; PRO, Exch. AO, Parl. Svys Herts. 7, f. 18; Mx 16, f. 8; Leics. RO, DE. 10, ct files Quorndon October 26, 1756; Glos. RO, D. 184 M7, nos 2, 8.

[34] Leonard, pp. 107, 110; Finch, pp. 17, 146; Cornwall, p. 196; Bradney, ii. pt ii. 135–6; Leconfield, *Sutton & Duncton*, pp. 47, 49; PRO, Exch. AO, Parl. Svys Herts. 9, f. 5(4); KR, Deps. by Commn 21–2 Eliz. Mich. 28; DL, MB 115, f. 17; NLW, Pitchford Hall 2038, 2434; Shak. Bpl. Leigh: Ct R. Longborough March 16, 34 Eliz.; W. de B. 1250; Northants. RO, I(L) 697–707, 760, 802–3; Deene ho. Brudenell A. iv. 10(1), (2), (3).

except in the fens and marshes.[35] Perhaps the best known example of emparkation is that carried out by Wolsey at Hampton Court.[36] Sir William Herbert enclosed several tenements in Wilton Suburbs into his park, together with some of the land of Washern Grange.[37] Henry VIII himself was one of the foremost emparkers. He enclosed into Vasterne Park some of the common lands of Tockenham and Wootton Bassett[38] and into Worthy (or Castle) Park at Ham the manor farm of Alkington and other grounds.[39]

That some emparkments were carried out tyrannically is alleged by the persons who considered themselves aggrieved. When Sir John Rodney enclosed into Stoke Moor Park two hundred acres of common on the Mendips and part of the Brent marshes, he was said to have pulled down several tenements and taken land from his tenants.[40] Guy Willistrop was accused of destroying the whole town of Wilstrop for his park.[41] When John Palmer was emparking at West Angmering, he allegedly threatened the tenants, saying, 'Doo ye not knowe that the kinges grace hath putt downe all the houses of monks, fryers and nunnes? Thierfor nowe is the tyme come that we gentilmen will pull downe the houses of suche poore knaves as ye be.' If such tales evoke memories of the opening scenes of *The Grapes of Wrath*, it has, nevertheless, to be remembered that there are two sides to all these stories. Tawney's malicious gossip that 'The gentle Sidney's *Arcadia* is one of the glories of the age, and it was composed, if we may trust tradition, in the park at the Herberts' country-seat at Washerne, which they had made by enclosing a whole village and evicting the tenants', will not bear repeating. Washern was never more than a hamlet and it was only the site of the grange and part of the demesnes that were enclosed in the park, quite apart from the fact that *Arcadia* was written at Ivychurch.[42] Palmer claimed that the West Angmering enclosure was by agreement, with land allotted in exchange, and the

[35] E.g. C. Gill, *Studies in Midland History*, Oxford 1930, p. 113; Aubrey, *Wilts. Topog. Colls.* pp. 130–3; Brinklow, pp. 16–7; Lennard, p. 75; Leconfield, *Petworth*, p. 55; *Cals. Proc. Chanc. R. Eliz.* ii. 237; Hist. MSS. Commn, *Report on MSS. of Duke of Portland at Welbeck Abbey vol. vi*, London, HMSO, Cd. 676, 1902, p. 88; P. A. J. Pettit, 'Economy of Northants. Royal Forests 1558–1714', ts. thesis D.Phil. Oxford Univ. 1959, p. 325.

[36] See below, p. 102, n. 51.

[37] See below, p. 102, n. 54.

[38] *Cals. Proc. Chanc. R. Eliz.* iii. 131.

[39] Smyth, *Hund. Berk.* 209.

[40] Bradford, pp. 72 sqq.

[41] H. B. McCall, *Yorkshire Star Chamber Proceedings vol. ii*, Yks. Archaeol. Soc. Rec. Ser. 1911, xlv. 166–8.

[42] Straton, i. pp. xlvi, 11 sqq.; Wilton ho. Svys of Manors in Co. Wilts. in the 16th cent. ff. 12 sqq.; Compotus R. of Receiver General 1633, f. 8; Tawney, p. 194; *Wilts. N. & Q.* 1893, i. 24.

most his tenants complained of was that the compensation was in-
adequate.[43] Even in apparently arbitrary emparkation, adequate compensation was usually given, by an exchange of land normally, and
even when there is no record of it, such compensation is not easily
disproved, especially if one bears in mind that without such compensation parks were not exempt from statutory penalty. Such exchanges of land took place when Sir John Thynne emparked at Longleat, the Earl of Arundel at Fersfield, the Earl of Suffolk at Somer-
sham, the Duke of Somerset at Savernake, and Edward IV at Castle
Donington.[44] The conditions under which these exchanges took place
are exemplified by a report to the Duke of Somerset from his agent
during the enlargement of Savernake Park:[45]

'The tenants of Wilton should have no maner of common for their
rudder beasts in that side, which would have been to their utter undoing ... I brake with the tenants afar off therein, but I perceive that
should be much grief to them. And as it is an old saying, "Inough is as
good as a feste", I pray God we may finde owte land, medowe and
something to satisfy them for that which they shall now forego.'

Similar emparkations continued by composition throughout the
sixteenth century and, to a lesser extent, in the seventeenth.[46]
Charles I made Richmond New Park and expanded Grafton Park by
taking in common-field lands.[47] Graphic illustration of such emparkment is provided by survey maps of Holdenby. In 1580 a small
park may be seen near the manor house, but by 1587 the pale has
been widened to include Wood Field and a large part of Brampton
fields.[48] A survey of Petworth in 1557 shows that part of the park
had been hedged in while the manor was in the hands of the Crown
by attainder, and next year the seventh Earl of Northumberland obtained the consent of the court baron to this. The ninth earl emparked

[43] Mundy, pp. 12 sqq.
[44] PRO, Exch. LR, MB 220, f. 238v.; AO, Parl. Svys Hunts. 7, ff. 19, 35;
DL, Sp. Commn 370; Req. 20/64, 24/6; Wilts. RO, Savernake: Svy Gt Bedwyn
Prebend 1552; Longleat ho. Thynne Papers, Ct Bks Manors Sir Jn Thynne sen.
1567–77, box liv, bk 4, ff. 6, 8.
[45] J. E. Jackson, 'Wulfhall & the Seymours', Wilts. Archaeol. Mag. 1875,
xv. 179–80.
[46] E.g. Smyth, Hund. Berk. pp. 36, 303; VCH Herts. iv. 216; R. Holinshed
& W. Harrison, Chronicles, London, 1586, p. 205; P. M. Handover, The 2nd
Cecil, London 1959, p. 275; Beds. RO, L. 26/281; PRO, Exch. LR, MB 216,
ff. 21 sqq.; 220, f. 238; AO, Parl. Svys Herts. 27, f. 10; Hunts. 7, ff. 19, 35;
SPD, Jas I, vol. 153, no 5; St. Ch. Jas, 219/23, m. 21; BM, Add. MS. 24787,
ff. 18, 25.
[47] Clarendon, The History of the Rebellion & Civil Wars in England, ed.
W. D. Mackay, Oxford 1888, bk. i. 208–11; PRO, Exch. KR, Deps by Commn
17 Chas I, East. 16.
[48] Northants. RO, F-H 272, ff. 59v.–60 (58v.–9), 62.

a common wood after overcoming in Chancery the objections raised by his tenants. Thenceforward the park spread rapidly northwards and in 1610 over 800 acres were enclosed into New Park.[49]

Still, even with compensation, emparkation purely for purposes of pleasure, as some of it was, was generally disfavoured by countryfolk. There was a rooted objection to the withdrawal from production of good farmland merely to provide landowners and aristocrats with 'houses built alone like ravens' nests, no birds building near them.'[50] In response to such complaints, and because the chase was no longer needed by a king too fat to go further afield, the Duke of Somerset disparked Hampton Court and let the land to its old tenants at the former rents.[51] Three or four years after Sir George Huntley had emparked farmland at Nimsfield, he fell from his horse and died. Years later, it is related, 'The inhabitants, out of a rurall reluctacion against such enclosures, ascribe to the injustice of that act not only his suddaine death forthwith at that place, but the sale of that and all the rest of his land made by his sonne.'[52] From about 1550 onwards, emparkation was more than counterbalanced by disparkment, but existing parks were a constant affront to countryfolk. A hundred years after Edward IV had emparked at Castle Donington, giving land in exchange, some of the tenants of the manor were intent on bringing a lawsuit they hoped would return the land to the farms whence it had been taken.[53]

Disparkment might only exacerbate hostile feelings. Hardly had Sir Francis Englefield been granted the Great and Little Parks at Vasterne than he disparked them and let them out, partly in two large leasehold farms and partly to two large partnerships formed by the Wootton Bassett burgesses, who returned this land to its original use as cow pasture for their domestic dairies. In addition, the inhabitants continued to hold at will and allot amongst themselves the hundred-acre Wootton Lawn which Henry VIII had allowed them. According to John Rosyer *alias* Hooper, later mayor, the burgesses had only agreed to hire the parkland from Englefield, in place of rights of common they had never renounced, because he was powerful and their landlord. Francis Englefield, the grand nephew, refused to renew the tenancy at will of Wootton Lawn, and Rosyer and his fellow burgesses laid claim, in Chancery, to the occupation of either the Lawn or of their former commons in the Great Park. This failed and two years later Englefield leased the Lawn to a freeholder at a pepper-

[49] Leconfield, *Petworth*, 56–7, 59, 62–3.
[50] Brinklow, pp. 16–7.
[51] *VCH Mx*, ii. 88; *APC*, ii 1547–50, pp. 190–2.
[52] Smyth, *Hund. Berk.* p. 303.
[53] PRO, DL, Sp. Commn 370.

corn rent. At the same time the burgesses were drawn to sign individual surrenders of their pretensions to rights of common. These submissions, made by the mayor and burgesses, included an undertaking to pay Englefield what he wished for the pasture of the Lawn. This situation persisted until the overthrow of royal government created circumstances favourable to the petty tradespeople of the town. The burgesses then petitioned Parliament for redress, expatiating colourfully on their grievances, one of which was that Englefield had seized their charter. Englefield was said to be ruining them with lawsuits and trying to dominate the borough government. More would have signed the petition but for the fact that Englefield was their landlord and they feared he would put them out. The final touch is put to the picture by the claim that divine help had been extended to the saints in their struggle, for whenever Englefield tried to put his cattle in the Lawn claps of thunder drove them away.[54]

Enclosure by composition or consent was, however, of less import than the multilateral agreement for the mutual extinction of common rights and the general enclosure of whole tracts of common fields or wastes by those who had freehold estates in the premises. This type of enclosure by agreement was sometimes styled enclosure by commission, because the two or more contracting parties commissioned disinterested persons to supervise the division and award of the allotments.[55] It was for this enclosure by commission that the experts reserved their heartiest recommendation.[56]

Enclosures by commission were conducted in much the same way throughout the whole of the period from the sixteenth century to the nineteenth. Whoever took the initiative, be it the chief landowner,[57] a group of landowners,[58] the capital farmers,[59] the family and part-

[54] Aubrey, *Wilts. Topog. Colls.* pp. 204–5; *Topographer & Genealogist*, 1858, iii. 225; PRO, Exch. KR, Sp. Commn 2395; Chanc. Proc. ser. i, Jas I, W. 30/53; Wilts. RO, acc. 212a, unsorted deeds & docs. rel. to Wootton Bassett and Vasterne; Archdeaconry Wilts. inv. Roger Harding als North yeo. Wootton Bassett December 31, 1635, proved October 12, 1636.

[55] Marshall, *Yks.* i. 52, 98.

[56] Fitzherbert, *Svying*, ff. 52–4; W. Blith, *The English Improver Improved*, London 1652, p. 79; PRO, Exch. LR, MB 194, f. 307.

[57] E.g. Willcox, pp. 280–3; Bateson, x. 130–1; xii. 109–10; Leonard, p. 115; T. G. Barnes, *Somerset 1625-40*, London 1961, pp. 155–6; Deene ho. Brudenell O.viii. 8; PRO, Chanc. Proc. ser. i, Jas I, B. 8/69; B. 27/59.

[58] E.g. Bateson, v. 212; xii, 239; H. R. Thomas, 'Encl. of Open Fds & Coms. in Staffs.', *Colls. Hist. Staffs.* 1933 (1931), p. 67; T. Lawson-Tancred, *Records of a Yorkshire Manor*, London 1937, p. 95.

[59] E.g. W. H. Hosford, 'An Eye-witness's Account of a 17th century Enclo.', *Econ. Hist. Rev.* 1951, iv. 215–6; T. M. Blagg, 'N. Collingham Customary Agrt to Enclose 1567', in *A Miscellany* pt. ii, Thoroton Soc. Rec. Ser. 1944–5, xi. 114–6; Wilts. RO, Ct Bk Andr. Baynton 1547–57, ff. 29v.–30; PRO, DL, Sp. Commn 700; R. & S. 9/31; BM, Harl. MS. 71, ff. 34 sqq., 45 (56)v.

time farmers[60] or both farmers and landowners together,[61] the advocates of enclosure 'drew into communication' and made 'speeches towards agreement'.[62] Sometimes petitions or draft proposals were circulated[63] and if necessary lawyers conducted negotiations on behalf of the various parties (Docs. 12, 15).[64] It might happen that one or two 'trooblesome fellowes' vetoed the proposals, so that the scheme fell through;[65] but often the opposition, if any, was brought to a formal agreement. This was more easily accomplished if the lord of the manor favoured enclosure and was prepared to use his influence. Indeed, tenants sometimes complained that they were 'very hardly drawn to give their consents'.[66] The leaseholder could only oppose his landlord at the risk of the non-renewal at the drop of the next life or the end of the next septennium, and it was not uncommon practice to grant customary and common-law leases only to those who entered covenants not to oppose equitable enclosure.[67] If the lord of the manor or some other freeholder opposed enclosure, steps might be taken to bring him to heel, vexatious lawsuits being the most efficacious form of persuasion (Doc. 20).[68] Edward Hussey, lord of Caythorpe, set his face against the enclosure promoted by the capital farmers, mainly because, as he himself exercised no common rights, he would have been little benefited, but partly because of conscientious scruples. The promoters thereupon engaged him in a lawsuit and the lawyers were nothing loth to multiply and protract the proceedings, 'ther being a purse on the one part and stomack on the other'. Under this pressure and because, though the 'improvment would not be very great as is usyuall in other lordships, yet it would be an improvement', Hussey abandoned his main objections and had only to be dissuaded from a superstition that he would not live long enough

[60] E.g. PRO, Chanc. Proc. ser. i, Jas I, H. 8/53.
[61] E.g. Thomas, pp. 73–4; Leonard, p. 110; G. H. Tupling, *The Economic History of Rossendale*, Chetham Soc. 1927, lxxxvi. 51–2, 54, 69; Beds. RO, WG. 1/19; Glos. RO, D. 444/M. 1; PRO, Chanc. Proc. ser. i, Jas I, D. 8/77; Req. 56/18; Exch. KR, Sp. Commn 2424; Deps. by Commn 1 Jas I, East. 4; 19 Jas I, East. 11.
[62] Northants. RO, Mont. old box 10 no 32, Ct R. Newton April 11, 28 Eliz.; PRO, Chanc. Proc. ser. i, Jas I, F. 11/62, compl.
[63] B'ham Lib. 344741; Deene ho. Brudenell O. xii. 10; I. iii. 13; Oxon. RO, DIL. III/n/2.
[64] B'ham Lib. 508625.
[65] Bateson, viii. 264.
[66] Leonard, p. 115; PRO, Chanc. Proc. ser. i, Jas I, B. 8/69.
[67] N. Riches, *The Agricultural Revolution in Norfolk*, Chapel Hill 1937, p. 72; J. L. & B. Hammond, *The Village Labourer*, Guild Bks, i. 44–5; Wilts. RO, Savernake: Ct R. Bk 1741–58, p. 127.
[68] Gonner, pp. 53–4.

to reap much advantage.[69] Generally, when all the freeholders, by both common and customary law, had been brought into agreement or made conformable, formal articles of agreement were drawn up, usually in the form of a multipartite indenture with up to three score seals and signatures (Docs. 16, 20).[70] These articles were often preceded by a preamble that argued the benefits of enclosure, as that the wastes were apt for corn, the common fields too cold for sheep-and-corn husbandry, or the grasslands insufficient for the plough-beasts.[71] The articles that followed then laid down the procedures to be adopted.

Surveyors, whose fees were borne jointly by the enclosers, were appointed to measure out the land to be divided and the new allotments, (Docs. 12, 14-15, 21),[72] employing for these purposes rods, chains, plain tables and theodolites.[73] The freeholders also commissioned impartial men to award the allotments. Often there were as many as four commissioners, one of whom might also be the surveyor, to safeguard the interests of the various parties—the lord of the manor, the parson, the other freeholders and the lesser farmers (Docs.

[69] Hosford, pp. 215-6.

[70] E.g. H. L. Gray, *English Field Systems*, Cambridge, Mass. 1915, p. 117; W. Cunningham, 'Com. Rights at Cottenham & Stretham in Cams.', in *Camden Miscellany xii*, R. Hist. S. Camd. 3rd ser. 1910, xviii. 193-4, 196-9, 201-3; Bateson, ix. 325; BM, Add. MS. 5701, ff. 133-8; Bucks. RO, Woolston enclo. agrt January 4, 27 Chas II; Northants. RO. I(L)3947; XYZ 991 Greatworth enclo. agrt September 28, 13 Chas I; Claycoton S(g)79, enclo. indre August 1, 15 Chas I; Abington arts. agrt November 22, 1659; Shak. Bpl. W. de B. 1386; Beds. RO, WG. 1/19; EN/E. 1/2; Berks. RO, D/EBy E71; B'ham Lib. 508624; Leics. RO, DE. 53/278; PRO, Chanc. Proc. ser. i, Jas I H. 22/19, B.8/69; Req. 71/4.

[71] Leonard, p. 117; W. Morris, *Swindon Fifty Years Ago*, Swindon n.d. p. 507; C. B. Fry, *Hannington*, Gloucester 1935, p. 27; PRO, Chanc. Proc. ser. i, Jas I, A. 10/47, K. 8/48; BM, Harl. MS. 71, f. 45 (56)v.; Glos. RO, D. 444/M.1.

[72] Gonner, pp. 77-8; Bland, Brown & Tawney, p. 525; Tawney & Power i. 83; Hosford, p. 216; G. N. Clark, 'Enclo. by Agrt at Marston', *EHR*, 1927, xlii. 89; C. T. Clay, *Yorkshire Deeds iv*, Yks. Archaeol. Soc. Rec. Ser. 1924, lxv. 74; M. W. Beresford, 'Habitation versus Improvement', in *Essays in Economic & Social History of Tudor & Stuart England in Honour of R. H. Tawney*, ed. F. J. Fisher, Cambridge 1961, p. 60; BM, Add. Ch. 15156; Add. MSS. 5701, f. 133v.; 37682, f. 60; Deene ho. Brudenell ASR. 562; O. viii. 8; Bateson, ii. 424; v. 202; ix. 4-5, 326; Wilts. RO, Keevil & Bulkington Ct Bk 44 Eliz.-2 Chas I, Bulkington ords. April 16, 11 Jas I; PRO, Exch. KR, Sp. Commns 2409, 2418; Deps. by Commn, 4 Chas I Mich. 6; 9 Chas I Trin. 4; DL, Sp. Commn 700; R. & S. 9/31; Chanc. Proc. ser. i, Jas I, A. 10/47, F. 12/8.

[73] Rathborne, op. cit.; Norden, op. cit.; E. G. R. Taylor, 'The Surveyor', *Econ. Hist. Rev.* 1947, xvii; Smyth, *Hund. Berk.* p. 36; Tupling, *Rossendale*, p. 53; J. Harland, *The House & Farm Accounts of the Shuttleworths*, Chetham Soc. xxxv, xli, xliii, xlvi, 1856-8, ii. 235; Beds. RO, AD. 1651; BM, Add. MS. 37682, f. 61; PRO, Req. 56/18, 393/128; Exch. KR, Deps. by Commn 40 Eliz. Hil. 17; Chanc. Proc. ser. i, Jas I, C. 10/44, H. 22/19.

14, 20–21).[74] If, however, a court were appealed to for the sanctioning of the enclosure, this authority might formally issue the commission and, especially if the court was one of the lord paramount and his interests were also concerned, even choose one of the commissioners. Such commissions were made by the Duchy Court of Lancaster, the Exchequer, Chancery and Parliament (Doc. 21).[75]

Allotments, for which lots were actually cast, were awarded in proportion to former holdings and interests, taking into account variations in soil, hill and vale land being allotted separately if need be.[76] This entailed numerous exchanges of land, some of which might be ancient enclosure. Other exchanges, with the object of rendering farms compact, might be effected at the same time (Docs. 13, 17–9, 23).[77] Even after they had been awarded, closes were sometimes exchanged between neighbours.[78] Usually accompanied by maps showing the disposition of the new allotments, and sometimes also of the former parcels,[79] the awards were then engrossed for record purposes.[80] Such, for instance, was the Bedfont 'Boke of the Heithe'

[74] Gonner, p. 74; Gray, p. 118; Tupling, *Rossendale*, p. 51; Bateson, v. 202; xii, 239; Beresford, p. 59; *VCH, Durh.* ii. 238; *Lincs.* ii. 335; Leonard, pp. 114–5; Hosford, p. 216; Bland, Brown & Tawney, pp. 525–6; W. M. Palmer, *A History of the Parish of Borough Green*, Camb. Ant. S. 8vo pubns, 1939, liv. 154; W. Harrison, 'Commons Inclos. in Lancs. & Ches. in 18th century', *Trans. Lancs. & Ches. Antiq. Soc.* 1888, vi. 118; Cartwright Hall, Swinton: Ct R. Leeming in Tanfield October 4, 7 Chas; Clark, *Marston*, p. 12; Wilts. RO, Keevil & Bulkington Ct Bk, Bulkington ords. April 16, 11 Jas; Beds. RO, AD. 1651; NLW, Pitchford Hall 905; BM, Add. MS. 37682, f. 62; PRO, Chanc. Proc. ser. i, Jas I, A. 10/47, B. 27/59, S. 39/64 compl.; Req. 393/128; Exch. KR, Sp. Commn 2424; Deps. by Commn 40 Eliz. Hil. 17; I Jas I, East. 4; Tawney & Power, i. 81–4.

[75] *Ibid.*; Gonner, pp. 63–4, 74–6; Leonard, p. 110; Tupling, *Rossendale*, p. 52; R. Somerville, *History of Duchy of Lancaster*, London 1953, i. 308; Farrer, ii. 393–8; R. C. Shaw, *Kirkham in Amounderness*, Preston 1949, p. 270; Bland, Brown & Tawney, pp. 525–6; Harland, ii. 241; Beds. RO, AD. 1651; PRO, DL, Sp. Commn 700; Exch. KR, Sp. Commns 2409, 2418; LR, MB 221, f. 325; Chanc. Proc. ser. i, Jas I, F. 11/62 compl.; N. 1/68, m. 2.

[76] Leonard, p. 111; Tupling, *Rossendale*, p. 54; Bateson, ix. 325; PRO, Chanc. Proc. ser. i, Jas I, S. 39/64 compl.

[77] My *Ag. Rev.* pp. 21–2; Brown, *Yks. Deeds*, iii (lxiii). 41–3; Shak. Bpl. W. de B. 1250; Beds. RO, WG. 1/19; Glouc. Lib. 28899(7); Northants. RO, Mont. old box 10, no 32 Ct R. Newton April 11, 28 Eliz.; I(L) 697–707, 760, 802–3; Leics. RO, DE. 53/275; Berks. RO, D/EBy E71; D/ELl T6; PRO, Exch. KR, Deps. by Commn 19 Jas I, East. 11; Chanc. Proc. ser. i, Jas I, D. 8/77 m. 1; BM, Add. MS. 34683, ff. 4v.–6; Add. R. 28281.

[78] Wilts. RO, Keevil and Bulkington Ct Bk, March 14, 1 Jas, September 4, 9 Jas, April 1, 10 Jas.

[79] Leics. RO, DE. 53/417; Northants. RO, I(L) 3947; XYZ 990–1; Stanwick enclo. map 1663 (ex box 14); Deene ho. Brudenell ASR. 562, pp. 17, 27, 41, 45, 53; Berks. RO, D/EBy E71; Oxon. RO, Dashwood VIII/35.

[80] Deene ho. Brudenell ASR. 562, pp. 5–8, 39, 44, 51 sqq.; Leics. RO, DE 53/417; BM, Add. Ch. 15156; PRO, Exch. KR, Sp. Commn 2409.

and the Glapthorne and Cotterstock 'Booke of Instructions' of 1630 (Doc. 14).[81]

Frequently the various freeholders and owners of chattel leases continued to hold their land after enclosure just as before; but this needed the assent of the lord of the manor, who sometimes demanded a slight increase in reserved rent (Doc. 13).[82] At Kirkbibidon cum Witlingham and Wadker manor in Wymondham, land taken from the Great Marsh continued to be held by copy only on payment of one penny fine and a halfpenny rent an acre of marsh.[83] A special order of Bromham court overruled the lord, Sir Edward Baynton, in declaring that, according to the true intent of the enclosure agreement, both customary and common-law leaseholders and socage tenants were to hold their allotments by their old tenures and estates, even though the lands themselves had been exchanged.[84] Any change in tenures or estates was likely to be advantageous to the tenant. As advised by Fitzherbert, Norden and Blith,[85] landlords usually offered long leases to farmers who were parties to enclosure, for otherwise their co-operation could hardly be expected. In various enclosures, copyholders were granted three new lives gratis or at reduced rates or allowed to exchange their customary leases for common-law ones, with terms of three lives or twenty-one years, even though the former terms were partly spent;[86] tenants at will were given common-law leases at easy rents or, if they preferred to leave town, were allowed a pension;[87] and leaseholders were sometimes offered the fee-farm of their land.[88] As it was not otherwise good in equity or law for customary and frank tenants to interchange lands, special assurances were needed for

[81] Deene ho. Brudenell E. vii. 1.

[82] B'ham Lib. 508624; Beds. RO, WG. 1/19; W. Marshall, *A Review . . . of Reports to Board of Agriculture from Midland Department of England*, London 1815, p. 350; Stat. 37 Hy VIII c. 2; BM, Add. MSS. 5701, f. 135; 36906, f. 155; Wilts. RO, Keevil & Bulkington Ct Bk, March 3, 45 Eliz.; Enclo. Awards, Bishopstone 1792, p. 142; PRO, KB, Plea Side, 20 Geo. III, 1780, Hil. roll 124, rot. 12; 56 Geo. III, 1816, Trin. roll 800; Chanc. Close R. 8 Geo. III, 1767–8, pt 16, no 1, rots. 38, 42–3; 1841, pt 69, no 1, rots. 41 sqq ; Com. Pleas, Recovery R., 19 Geo. III, 1778, Mich. rot. 150.

[83] BM, Add. Ch. 14054.

[84] PRO, Chanc. Proc. ser. i, Jas I, E. 1/51; Wilts. RO, acc. 122, Svys Bromham, Bremhill, Rowden & Stanley, Bromham Ct September 25, 16 Jas

[85] See above, p. 103, n. 56.

[86] Bateson, viii. 264; BM, Egerton MS. 3007, ff. 29–30, 41, 43; PRO, Chanc. Proc. ser. i, Jas I, K. 8/48, ans. & replic.; Decree R. 2nd Div. 1st pt, pt 360, no 5; Exch. KR, Deps. by Commn 5–6 Chas I Hil. 17.

[87] B'ham Lib. 344741, 508624; Beds. RO, WG. 1/19; Deene ho. Brudenell O. viii. 8; Leonard, p. 115.

[88] Deene ho. Brudenell ASR. 562, p. 55; I. i. 11.

these new estates, and these were best concluded at the outset, lest disputes be occasioned later.[89]

Over and above the other allotments, there had to be one in lieu of the rights of common of ancient cottages. This was usually a residual close, already hedged and ditched, that the cottagers could use as a common cow-pasture.[90] Such allotments were often generous: in Clifton-upon-Dunsmore $1\frac{1}{2}$ or more acres a cottage, at Marston a close of 65 acres between twelve and at Ayston 19 acres between nine. In Deene the cottagers' close contained $12\frac{1}{2}$ acres.[91] The eight cottagers of Barford St Martin were allotted the Ham, a close of four or five acres, that the commissioners said was 'very profitable for them considering litell or no lande at all did belong unto the said cottages'.[92]

Occupiers of poor law and other newly erected cottages, and generally all squatters on the waste, were not entitled to rights of common, so no allotment was due to them;[93] but they often received ex gratia grants, for it was to the general advantage that day-labourers and others should have a cow for the pail.[94] Thus at Charlton the Earl of Berkshire assigned fifty acres of his own allotment as a common for the poor cottagers.[95] Blith was not alone in considering that the poor cottager or day-labourer, who had been more abused by enclosures than anyone else, should have his allotment laid out first. Where this had been neglected, it had often to be remedied with much difficulty later.[96]

Both tithes and customary works were often commuted when a general enclosure took place. In return for surrendering his claims to the latter, the lord of the manor usually received an extra allotment.[97] Tithes were normally commuted to a rate tithe or modus, a fixed annual payment secured by an article of the agreement, thus leaving the farms 'tithe-free' and burdened only with a rent-charge.[98]

[89] PRO, Chanc. Proc. ser. i, Jas I, B.27/59 ans.; D.8/77; E.1/51; Exch. KR, Deps. by Commn, 5–6 Chas 1, Hil. 17; VCH Durh. ii. 238.

[90] Lawson-Tancred, p. 98; PRO, Exch. KR, Deps. by Commn 1657, East. 9.

[91] Deene ho. Brudenell ASR. 562, pp. 8, 39, 55; A. Gooder, Plague and Enclosure, Coventry & N. War. Hist. Pmphlts 2, 1965, p. 18.

[92] PRO, Exch. KR, Sp. Commn 2418.

[93] E.g. Wimbledon, p. 147; Shak. Bpl. Leigh: Stoneleigh custumal c. 1560; Northants. RO, Wmld 5. v. 1 Ct R. Farcet September 19, 10 Jas.

[94] Gonner, pp. 78–9; Gooder, pp. 16–8; PRO, Chanc. Close R. 8 Geo. III, 1767–8, pt 16, no 1, rot. 38; Wilts. RO, Enclo. Awards, Fovant Award 1785, p. 6.

[95] Wilts. RO, acc. 88, Charlton Este Papers, Moores box 1, enclo. agrt 1631.

[96] Blith, pp. 76–7.

[97] E.g. N. S. B. & E. C. Gras, The Economic & Social History of an English Village, Cambridge Mass. 1930. p. 611.

[98] Notestein & al. vii. 91; J. Lee, A Vindication of a Regulated Inclosure, London 1656, p. 3; W. Pitt, A General View of the Agriculture of County of

Tithes were, nevertheless, the greatest single obstacle to the enclosure of common fields. Even if a rate tithe were agreed with one incumbent, his successors did not necessarily see themselves bound to it. It therefore became the practice to have the modus ratified. This could be done in Chancery, only taking care that the agreement, which this court held to be against common right, was clear and certain in itself and not dependent on doubtful or further documentary proofs, else no help was to be had. Even if one complied in all these respects and proved the modus beyond doubt, Chancery would still refuse a decree and give no more than a verdict *pendente lite* (with lawsuit pending), that is, the modus would be declared proved as a matter of fact, but its enforcement left to common-law courts and processes. This was because a court of conscience, especially one so often in the charge of clerics, could not decree something against conscience. On account of these difficulties, ratification was frequently sought in the Court of Exchequer Chamber, citing as Exchequer matter the parson's debt to the Crown of first fruits, for this court was always willing to decree a proven modus.[99] But any generally satisfactory agreement for a rate tithe was difficult to achieve. The great fear of tithe-owners was that enclosure would lessen their receipts, for even if the small or vicarial tithes were raised by increased stocking and breeding, there was a chance that the great or rectorial tithes of corn and grain might diminish. At enclosure the area of tillage might be halved, while yields per acre usually only doubled, so that the gross product was much as before, while if corn prices, and consequently tillage areas fell, it might be reduced. High rates of commutation could therefore hardly be afforded.[100]

Northampton, London 1806, pp. 36, 38, 40–1; M. James, 'Political Importance of Tithes Controversy in Eng. Rev.', *History* 1941–2, xxvi. 1–2; D. M. Barratt, *Ecclesiastical Terriers of Warwickshire Parishes* vol. i, Dugdale Soc. 1955, xxii. 68, 73, 75, 108–10, 128; Northants. RO, Wmld Misc. Vol. 42; Abington arts. agrt November 22, 1659; Leic. Mus. 35/29/272, 340; PRO, Maps & Plans MP. L. 55 i; Req. 106/60 compl. & ans.; Chanc. Proc. ser. i, Jas I, B. 21/7 compl., B. 30/59 compl., F. 11/62 compl., S. 20/65 compl. & ans., S. 39/64 compl.; Exch. KR, Deps. by Commn 26 Eliz. Trin. 4; 31 Eliz. Trin 2; 42–3 Eliz. Mich. 2, art. 13; 10 Chas I Trin. 4; 10–1 Chas I Hil. 31; 12 Chas I East. 24, ex parte quer. m. 2; East 34, ex parte def.; 13 Chas I Mich. 59, arts. 4, 7; 14 Chas I, Trin. 9, m. 1; 1654–5 Hil. 5; 1655–6, Hil. 23; 1656, Mich. 17; 1657, East. 9.

[99] Yale, *Manual*, p. 322; *Chanc. Cs*, i. 63; ii. 451; *Cals. Proc. Chanc. R. Eliz.* i. 195, 202, 355, 365; ii. 167, 220, 271; iii. 63.

[100] H. R. Trevor-Roper, *Archbishop Laud*, London 1940, p. 169; P. S. Clarkson & C. T. Warren, *The Law of Property in Shakespeare & Elizabethan Drama*, Baltimore 1942, pp. 92–3; C. M. Ingleby, *Shakespeare & Enclosure of Common Fields at Welcombe*, B'ham 1885, p. 1; *VCH, Durh.* ii. 238–9; *Ruts.* i. 223: Deene ho. Brudenell C. iv. 2; PRO, Exch. KR, Deps. by Commn 16 Jas I, Hil. 18; St. Ch. Jas, 221/1, compl.

Yet whatever the rate agreed, the real income from it fluctuated with corn and other prices.[101] Furthermore, it usually happened that rate tithes were settled when tillage was being laid down to grass, and when this was in turn ploughed up for corn, the tithe-owner was prone to break his agreement and demand tithes in kind. For these reasons, the enclosure of common fields and the substitution of up-and-down husbandry produced a flood of tithe disputes.[102] The owners of rectorial tithes, especially, were frequent objectors to enclosure agreements. They feared for their tithes and prophesied the decay of tillage.[103] In order to secure the consent of the owners of rectorial tithes, therefore, it was often necessary to inflate the rate of commutation (Doc. 21),[104] and it later became a practice to allot land in lieu of tithes, usually on a generous and often on an extravagant scale (Docs. 12, 15).[105] At this point the reader may ask how it was that an act of Parliament was needed to commute tithes in 1836, by which time previous enclosures must already have entailed commutation almost everywhere. The answer is that the act was passed precisely because commutation was already general. The Tithe Rent-Charge Commutation Act, to give it its proper name, was not to commute tithes, nor even to legalize existing commutations, but to stabilize them in relation to the existing price level.[106]

Enclosure awards generally gratified the allottees, but individuals sometimes expressed their dissatisfaction by revoking their agreement to the enclosure itself (Doc. 21).[107] Glebe lands were a particularly fruitful source of friction, for they might well be enclosed without the knowledge of an absentee parson and their farmer might have neglected to preserve the boundary between the glebe allotment and his own.[108] There were occasionally even allegations of conspiracy with the surveyor and commissioners, in the hope of obtaining larger or better allotments.[109] Commissioners sometimes entered bonds to

[101] PRO, Exch. KR, Deps. by Commn 15 Chas I, East. 19, mm. 1d, 2, arts. 19, 20, ex parte quer.; Northants. RO, Wmld 7. xv Apethorpe tithe agrt 1700; F-H 1145; Leic. Mus. 35/29/376.

[102] My *Ag. Rev.* p. 189.

[103] Gonner, pp. 316–7; Ingleby, p. 1; Willcox, p. 281; Blith, p. 77; Tothill 110–1; PRO, Exch. KR, Sp. Commn 2418; Chanc. Proc. ser. i, Jas I, M. 18/30 compl.

[104] Tothill 110.

[105] Gonner, pp. 79, 315–8; Barratt, pp. 6, 73.

[106] J. A. Venn, *Foundations of Agricultural Economics*, Cambridge 1933, p. 168; Stat. 6 Wm IV c. 71.

[107] Tothill 110; PRO, Exch. KR, Sp. Commns 2418, 5711; Bland, Brown & Tawney, pp. 525–6.

[108] Beds. RO, AD. 1651; PRO, Req. 71/4, compl. & ans.; 79/48; Exch. KR, Sp. Commn 2424; Deps by Comm. 1 Jas I, East. 4.

[109] PRO, Req. 393/128, compl.; Exch. KR, Deps. by Commn 4 Chas I, Mich. 6, ex parte def.

be forfeited if anyone had good reason to be discontented with his allotment;[110] but forfeiture must have been extremely rare, for the consensus of opinion was that the awards were almost invariably equitable[111] and the impression derived from them is one of meticulous accuracy and studied impartiality.[112]

The allotments had to be mounded with walls, hedges and ditches, or at least balks, and provision had to be made for ponds and watering pools.[113] Drainage works might also be necessary.[114] The costs of mounding fell usually upon the allottee, while those of surveying, division and all other matters of common concern, from pond-making to litigation, were defrayed from the common purse collected in the usual way by a levy rated according to the values of the estates and interests of the various parties (Doc. 15).[115] But let it not be forgotten that lords of manors sometimes offered to supply quicksets free of charge[116] or to meet half the charges of hedging and ditching,[117] and that certain persons, in return for their consent to the enclosure, might have all the cost of their mounding, or even all their enclosure expenses, paid out of a public rate to which they contributed nothing, or out of the lord's own pocket.[118]

[110] PRO, Chanc. Proc. ser. i, Jas I, A. 10/47, compl.
[111] PRO, Exch. KR, Deps. by Commn 40 Eliz. Hil. 17; 19 Jas, East. 11; 10 Chas I, Mich. 48, art. 21; Chanc. Proc. ser. i, Jas I, H. 22/19, compl.
[112] Gonner, pp. 75–7, 80–1, 95; & see e.g. Bateson, ix. 4–5; BM, Add. Ch. 15156; Deene ho. Brudenell ASR. 562.
[113] PRO, Chanc. Proc. ser. i, Jas I, F. 11/62, compl.; K. 8/48, ans;. Leics. RO, DE. 53/278.
[114] E.g. PRO, Chanc. Proc. ser. i, Jas I, B. 1/37, mm. 1, 4, 7; W. 11/61 compl. & ans.
[115] *Ibid.* N. 1/68 compl., m. 2; P. 9/24, compl. mm. 1, 2, ans. m. 9; Exch. KR, Deps. by Commn 9 Chas I Trin. 4, ex parte def.; Gonner, pp. 72–3; Hosford, pp. 216–7; Bateson, ii. 425; ix. 326.
[116] Deene ho. Brudenell O. viii. 8.
[117] Bateson, x. 276.
[118] Leonard, p. 115; Gooder, p. 19; Wilts. RO, Enclo. Acts & Awards, Fifield; PRO, Chanc. Proc. ser. i, Jas I, N. 1/68, compl. & ans. mm. 1, 2; K. 8/48, ans. & replic.

5

The Ratification of Enclosures

THE parties to an enclosure might sometimes content themselves with an indenture of agreement and conveyances by the usual instruments, but the interchange of lands held by various tenures and estates was often considered to demand more express and general legal sanction or ratification, and enclosure agreements themselves frequently stipulate that they shall have 'such ratification as learned counsel shall devise and advise'.[1]

In this the manor court had an especial part to play. Customary land passed in it and the lord of the manor had to consent to exchanges and enclosures of demesne and customary land and to grant licences in respect of the latter. Many exchanges and enclosures, therefore, were necessarily registered or ratified in manor courts,[2] and enclosure agreements already arrived at were frequently promulgated there and recorded in the court rolls.[3] Thus in the court of Whaddon in 1548:[4]

'Yt is agreed betweyn the fermor Henry Long and the tenantes there that the said fermor shall have and inclose the xiiij acres of land now in the holding of the said tenentes in the Myl furlong upon Almed, in recompence wherof the said tenantes shall have and inclose other xiiij acres of the said fermors which he now occupieth lying in Long-

[1] Shak. Bpl. Throckmorton: Sambourn: Petition of tenants to Sir Robt 1707; PRO, Chanc. Decree R. 2nd Div. 1st pt, pt 361, no 1.
[2] E.g. Bateson, v. 212; Tregelles, p. 324; Thomas, pp. 66–7; Boyd, 'Chanc. Proc.' p. 111; BM, Add. R. 28281; Northants. RO, Mont. old box 10 no 32 Ct R. Newton April 11, 28 Eliz.; Glos. RO, D. 444/M.1; D. 326/E.1, f. 89v; B'ham Lib. Fletcher 91; Shak. Bpl. Leigh: Ct R. Longborough October 3, 1638; Wilts. RO, Keevil and Bulkington Ct Bk March 14, 1 Jas; PRO, R. & S. roll 763.
[3] Bateson, ii. 424; v. 202; Tupling, *Rossendale*, p. 50–1; Blagg, p. 117; C. T. Clay, *Yks. Deeds*, lxv. 100–1; A. F. J. Brown, *English History From Essex Sources 1750–1900*, Chelmsford 1952, p. 29; Shak. Bpl. Leigh: Ct R. Longborough March 16, 34 Eliz.; Wilts. RO, Keevil and Bulkington Ct Bk March 3, 45 Eliz.; acc. 122, Svys Bromham, Bremhill &c. Bromham ct September 25, 16 Jas; acc. 88, Charlton Este Papers, Moores box 1, Charlton enclo. agrt 1631; PRO, Chanc. Proc. ser. i, Jas I, B. 8/69, D. 8/77 compl.
[4] Wilts. RO, acc. 84, Ct Bk Andr. Baynton 1545–57, ff. 29v.–30.

lond and at the Yate. The lord dothe graunt and agre that at any tyme hereafter that it shalbe lefful to the said fermor and tenantes to per- mute and exchange any other their landes to inclose and make severall for the welthe of theyme or any of theyme as nede shall requere and thexchange so made to be recorded at the next court following. And it is further agreed by assent and conscent of the lord and his tenants that the land that the said fermor hath inclosed called Almershe conteyninge viij acres shalbe and remayne severall still without lett or interupsion of any of the said tenantes.'

Similarly at the court of Bremhill manor in 1578 (Doc. 13): [5]

'Yt ys condescendyd and agred ... betweene Sir Edward Baynton knight lord of the mannor ... and his tenantes ... that they shall in- close and make severall their landes in the comon fields of Foxeham and Aven, and also to exchaunge one with another for the same. And the said tenantes that so dothe exchaunge and inclose doth agree to pay yeerely to the sayd Sir Edward and Dame Anne now his wyfe one bushell of beanes for every yeardland they have.'

Each encloser agrees that he will not

'challenge, have or demaund any maner of comon within the said mannor, but utterly seclude hymselfe and his heyres of all his comon for all maner of cattell in the said mannor for ever, and for affyrmance hereof he hath to this order and agremente putte his hand, as appereth in the old court book'.

Legal sanction was given to some enclosures by a special com- mission of the Duchy of Lancaster on the petition of its tenants.[6] For others, similar facilities were provided by the Exchequer Chamber.[7] The sanction most sought after, however, was a decree in Chancery. The same kind of fictitious and collusive actions used to confer legal sanction upon other agreements served also for enclosure ones.[8] All that was needed, provided adequate provision had been made for tithes, was a complaint alleging violation of the recited enclosure agreement, an answer denying this and a decree that the agreement should stand. Such actions were carefully prearranged, plaintiffs and defendants being chosen amicably and covenants en- tered for the filing of complaint and answer as planned, the object

[5] BM, Add. MS. 37270, ff. 105v.–6, 112, 114, 121, 130v., 208v.
[6] Tupling, *Rossendale*, p. 52; Farrer, ii. 393–8; Somerville, i. 307–8; *Ducatus Lancastriae*, iii. 133, 157, 185.
[7] PRO, Exch. KR, Sp. Commns 2409, 2418, 2424, 5711; Deps by Commn 1 Jas I, East. 4.
[8] Tothill 109–11. From a legion of examples, I take 3: Blagg, p. 112; *Cals. Proc. Chanc. R. Eliz.* i, 109, 190.

H

being expressly stated in the agreements themselves to be the assurance of estates by a confirmatory decree.[9] Similar ratifications were made also in the chancery of the bishop of Durham.[10]

Some actions in the royal Chancery, however, bear no indication of collusion and some were certainly not fictitious, but started with the object of obtaining a decree for compulsory enclosure. Enclosure agreements required the consent only of the owners of freehold estates and sometimes pressure was needed to secure even this. Opposition might come not only from parsons, tithe-owners and some of the freeholders, but also from those without freehold estates. Only the parson of Barford St Martin objected to the first commission, but later six others joined with him, and of these three almost certainly had naught but chattel leases.[11] Opposition might be voiced by freeholders who denied they had ever given any but forced consent,[12] or expressed merely by a refusal to pay the enclosure rate[13] or to accept the allotment awarded (Doc. 21).[14] In some instances arguments against enclosure were put forward. Some copyholders in Stour Provost say that their estates for one life only do not warrant the charges involved. In Aynho it is declared that enclosure will lead to sheep-rot and the decay of tillage and population. From Stalbridge comes the answer that enclosure will spoil the roads and lead to amercements on their account at the quarter sessions, and that the neatherds will lose their jobs. Enclosure, it is averred, will make the fens of Hockwold and Wilton too dry.[15]

Some of these answers were evidently intended to stop the enclosure altogether and others merely to impose certain conditions or set up a good bargaining position. At all events, the chancellor usually attempted to reconcile the two parties if the answers appeared well grounded and only overrode them if they did not. In the case of the Aynho enclosure, Francis Bacon ordered a commission of reconciliation, probably to devise guarantees against the decay of tillage, and,

[9] Yale, *Chanc. Cs*, i. 108; Gonner, p. 55; Ritchie, p. 63; Hosford, p. 217; W. Holloway, *The History of Romney Marsh*, London 1849, p. 165; Clark, 'Enclo. by Agrt', p. 87; Morris, App.; Gooder, p. 23; BM, Add. MS. 37682, ff. 60 sqq.; Shak. Bpl. Throckmorton: Sambourn, 'A True Copy of the Patent', April 18, 34 Eliz.; PRO, Chanc. Proc. ser. i, Jas I, A. 10/47, C. 7/14, D. 8/77, F. 12/8, H. 22/19, S. 39/64; Decree R. 2nd. Div. 1st pt, pt 361 no 1; pt 374 no 8.

[10] Leonard, pp. 111–3; *VCH Durh.* ii, 238; Bland, Brown & Tawney, pp 525–6.

[11] PRO. Chanc. Proc. ser. i, Jas I, E. 1/51.

[12] *Ibid.* B. 8/69 ans.; B. 27/59 ans.

[13] *Ibid.* N. 1/68 ans.

[14] Tothill 110.

[15] PRO, Chanc. Proc. ser. i, Jas I, K. 8/48 ans.; C. 10/44 ans. mm. 2–4, 10; C. 26/36 ans.; B. 1/37, ans. mm. 4, 7.

in response to further objections from the parson, decreed an increased rate for the commutation of tithes. These measures removed objections and it was decreed that the enclosure and award should stand (Doc. 21).[16] Disagreement over the Stour Provost award led to the appointment of commissioners to supervise an impartial allotment, which was followed by a decree that it should stand.[17] The objections of the parson of Holcote to the diminution of his glebe were met by a commission of admeasurement and a decree followed.[18] In 1673 Nottingham noted of the Water Stratford enclosure that it had begun by the consent of the major part (notwithstanding the coverture and infancy of some parties, which always happened), but the rector had retracted his consent. He was inclined to decree an enclosure because of the evident melioration and the ordinary's and the patroness's consent, but eventually proposed mediation. A mortgagee tried to defeat the enclosure at Ashley, despite an offer of compensation at double value. In the end, the township itself agreed to pay off the mortgage, and a decree to establish enclosure in perpetuity immediately ensued.[19] Despite objections, Chancery decreed the Buscot agreement, conceiving that 'inclosure (being well ordered) might tend to the greate good of the commonwealth'.[20] Many other decrees were in a similar sense (Doc. 21).[21] Those who raised the danger of the decay of tillage were reconciled to enclosure by making the decree provisional upon its maintenance. Sometimes it was stipulated that the arable should not be decreased (nor the tillage more than halved) and sometimes that a third or a half of the old common-field tillage remain under the plough (Doc. 21).[22] The need for some such provision was widely understood, and Blith considered that the owners and occupiers of all enclosing townships should enter solemn legal engagements to keep one third or so of the land in tillage.[23] Occasionally the covenants were even more specific, guaranteeing the maintenance of all existing houses of husbandry.[24] Decrees with similar provisos were made also by the chancellor of Durham.[25] With such a decree, a plaintiff in Chancery could obtain a further

---

[16] Tothill 110.
[17] PRO, Chanc. Proc. ser. i, Jas I, N. 1/68 compl. & ans.
[18] Beds. RO, AD. 1651.
[19] Yale, Chanc. Cs, i. 6; ii. 603.
[20] PRO, Chanc. Proc. ser. i, Jas I, F. 11/62 compl.
[21] Tothill 110–1.
[22] Tothill 110–1; PRO, Chanc. Proc. ser. i, Jas I, C. 10/44 ans. mm. 2–4, 10; Exch. KR, Deps. by Commn 10 Chas I Trin. 12, ex parte quer.; 1657 East. 9, dep. by Jn Place/Isham.
[23] Blith, pp. 79, 81.
[24] Lee, p. 6; Leonard, p. 119.
[25] VCH Durh. ii. 239.

decree overthrowing the whole enclosure, if he could show that provisions had not been complied with and that he was unable to recover from the defendants adequate compensation for any prejudice suffered on account of depopulation or the decay of tillage.[26] To objections that exchanges of land would break customary tenures, Chancery responded by a commission of reconciliation with the task of arranging the necessary assurances; but if this failed, a decree confirming the enclosure would be refused. This was the practice also in the Durham chancery.[27] Without good grounds for complaint and in the event of the break-down of efforts at reconciliation, Chancery would not heed belated objections to enclosure from those who had been willing parties to the original agreement, but decreed that this should stand.[28] Although it often decreed against one refractory person, Chancery would never compel a significant minority that had not freely consented in the first instance, unless the enclosure was to the general benefit of the inhabitants, as it often was (Doc. 21).[29]

Only a proportion of the enclosures made were ratified by Chancery decree and even then not always immediately after the event, for delays in procedure were often excessive.[30] Chancery actions provided, at moderate expense,[31] varied and flexible procedures for ensuring and confirming well-regulated enclosures and preventing those that were inequitable or injurious to agriculture. Once obtained, confirmatory decrees could be invoked at any time, for their infraction was a contempt of court. For instance, in 1613, despite the refusal of Robert Broxholme to honour it, Chancery decreed that the Owersby enclosure agreement should stand. Shortly afterwards, Broxholme set two servants to plough newly allotted land formerly his, and these unfortunates were straightway committed to the Fleet for contempt.[32]

Ratification was generally more convenient in Chancery than in Parliament, but resort was also had to the latter court as an alternative or additional procedure. It was written into the Cottenham agreement in 1587 that it was to be ratified either in Chancery or by act of Parliament or both or otherwise, as learned counsel might agree.[33] In 1693 a private act ratified a Hambleton enclosure agreement that

[26] Tothill 110–1.

[27] VCH Durh. ii. 238.

[28] Tothill 109–11.

[29] Tothill 110–1; Leonard, pp. 114–5; Yale, *Chanc. Cs*, i. 108.

[30] Boyd, 'Chanc. Proc.', pp. 111–3; *Cals. Proc. Chanc. R. Eliz.* i. 180; PRO, Chanc. Proc. ser. i. Jas I, C. 16/59 compl.; H. 36/74, mm. 1 sqq., 9; T. 1/5 compl. & ans.; W. 1/7, mm. 1–2; Decree R. 2nd Div. 1st pt, pt 376 no 11.

[31] Harland, ii. 241.

[32] Ritchie, pp. 63–4.

[33] Cunningham, p. 224.

had already been ratified in Chancery forty years before.[34] A thin stream of such parliamentary enclosure acts flowed throughout the sixteenth and seventeenth centuries.[35]

Two circumstances encouraged such private legislation: the necessity, as in royal fen drainage projects,[36] for wide compulsory powers, and the occasionally severe overburdening of Chancery. To take an extreme example of this latter situation, when Chancery was in temporary abeyance, from 1654 to 1656, private-bill procedure was widely resorted to. It was originally intended that the Caythorpe enclosure should be established by act of Parliament.[37] In 1656 a private bill was introduced in the Commons to confirm the agreement between the Earl of Carlisle and his tenants for dividing Nasing common; but it was rightly objected that the Statute of Merton and a Chancery decree would serve the purpose, now that the court had been reconstituted.[38] It was not until the mid-eighteenth century, when the volume of suits in Chancery was increasing rapidly, and delays and congestions became intolerable,[39] that private acts came to be generally preferred to Chancery decrees for ratifying enclosure agreements.[40] Private-bill procedure was extremely expensive[41] and only to be adopted if imperative. Thus the proprietors of Marsh Baldon agreed to divide their common fields in 1724, 'but the interests too complicated to be settled but by an Act of Parliament', which apparently was not then economic.[42] The increase in the numbers of parliamentary enclosures is, therefore, more indicative of the parlous state of Chancery than of any increase in the numbers of enclosures.

Changing the instruments of ratification made little or no difference to enclosure by commission. The lawyers were simply instructed to secure a private act instead of a Chancery decree.[43] For instance, in

[34] Priv. Act 4 W. & M. no 31.
[35] Stats. 37 Hy VIII c. 2; 4 Jas I c. 11; Priv. Acts 5 Eliz. no 36; 8 Eliz. no 22 (25); 14 Eliz. no 15 (14); 14 Chas II no 18; 16 Chas II no 5; 19 & 20 Chas II no 12.
[36] W. Dugdale, *The History of Imbanking & Drayning*, London 1662, p. 63; C. H. Firth & R. S. Rait, *Acts & Ordinances of Interregnum*, London, HMSO, 1911, ii. 130 sqq.; Gonner, pp. 56–7; *Jnl H.C.* 1547–1628, p. 308; Stat. 37 Hy VIII c. 11.
[37] Hosford, p. 217.
[38] J. T. Rutt, *The Diary of Thomas Burton Esq.*, London 1828, i. 20.
[39] Yale, *Manual*, pp. 66–7; Holdsworth, i. 635–6; E. Halévy, *A History of the English People*, Penguin edn, i. 57–8.
[40] Gonner, pp. 58–9.
[41] Marshall, *Yks.* i. 98; *S. Dept*, p. 64; *A Review of Reports to Board of Agriculture from Northern Dept of England*, London 1808, p. 141; T. Davis, *A General View of the Agriculture of County of Wilts.*, London 1813, p. 252.
[42] Oxon. RO, Wi. X/34, 1st pag. 14, 2nd 98.
[43] Gonner, pp. 60–1, 183; Man. Lib. Lancs. Deeds L. 96.

1775 in an agreement for the enclosure of Englefield common fields and for the exchange of old enclosures, after detailed provisions for division and allotment, the eleven parties undertake 'to apply for and endeavour to obtain an Act of Parliament for ratifying, confirming and establishing these present articles'.[44] In Parliament, no less than in Chancery, enclosures might be completed by agreement and then merely confirmed; or it might happen, after general agreement, that the implementing of the enclosure was impeded by a minority, in which case surveyors and arbitrators might be commissioned. Many enclosure acts were little more than recitals of agreements already made and of enclosures already partly carried out.[45] But some private bills met with no less opposition than similar suits in Chancery and not a few were rejected.[46] In 1733, for instance, the bill for enclosing Bisley commons and wastes was thrown out by the Commons on the petition of some of the inhabitants, copyholders, labourers and small freeholders that the common was used by carders, spinners, weavers and other woollen workers and that there were already 800 industrial dwellings on 1,000 acres of waste.[47] Thus an attempt to circumvent the Statutes of Approvement was defeated. Finally, by the General Enclosure Consolidating Act of 1801, private enclosure acts were simplified and perhaps rendered slightly less expensive. By its terms a majority of landowners still could not concert to compel an enclosure on a large minority, and by the General Enclosure Act of 1845, the agreement of two-thirds of the proprietors was required.[48]

[44] Berks. RO, D/EBy E71.
[45] W. Cooper, *History of Lillington*, Shipston-on-Stour 1940, p. 127; Gonner, pp. 60–1.
[46] W. E. Tate, 'MPs & Proc. upon Enclo. Bills', *Econ. Hist. Rev.* 1942, xii. 68 sqq.
[47] *VCH Glos.* ii. 167.
[48] Gonner, pp. 67–70; Stats. 41 Geo. III c. 109; 8 Vic. c. 118.

Depopulation and Impopulation

APPROVEMENTS of wastes, forests and flooded lands resulted in the extension of cultivation and the peopling of the countryside, as likewise did the breaking up of old grasslands. In contradistinction, agricultural progress by the intensification of cultivation tended to reduce the numbers of people engaged in farming. Between the progress of enclosure in general and agricultural depopulation there thus could be no clear or constant relation. As Marshall says,[1]

'All general remarks on the effects of 'inclosures', in regard to population, must necessarily be inconclusive. Appropriating common pastures, and completing the appropriation of common arable fields—distinctly considered—will ever, in their opposite tendencies, have a contrary effect. Common pastures, mostly, and frequently common mowing grounds, are broken up for a succession of corn crops, and of course give employment to numbers, where little or none was required before. Whereas newly inclosed arable fields, especially those of a deep fertile soil, which they mostly are (the best of the lands of a parish or township having almost invariably been set apart for that purpose) are frequently laid down to grass:—permanent, perhaps, if a cool, deep, rich quality; or for a length of time proportioned to their specific natures. Hence in this case, after the draining, fencing and roadmaking are finished, fewer hands are required to manage them ... Calculations founded on arable fields alone, without including the pasture and meadow grounds that inseparably belong to them, can only proceed from gross ignorance of the subject, or some less excusable source.'

Although increases of agricultural population were apparent in many places, notably in the Norfolk Heathlands, the Fen and Cheese countries and the Lancashire Plain,[2] it is depopulation that has attracted most attention, and this especially in the Midland Plain. Here there had been much conversion to permanent grass in the later

[1] Marshall, *M. Dept*, p. 243.
[2] Marshall, *E. Dept*, p. 302.

middle ages. The attractions that this held for the grazier and land-owner, often combined in the same person, were clearly understood by contemporaries. As Thomas More says, 'One shepherde or heard-man is ynough to eate that grounde with cattel, to the occupying wherof about husbandrye many handes were requysyte.'[3] 'Bicause grasing requireth a smaller household and less attendance and charge,' conversion to permanent grass was a prime cause of depopulation.[4] This, however, was a small price to pay for an improvement of rent. As Thoroton remarks,[5]

'Enclosing and converting arable to pasture . . . certainly diminishes the yearly fruits, as it doth the people, for we may observe that a lord-ship in tillage every year affords more than double the profits which it can in pasture, and yet the latter way the landlord may perhaps have double the rent he had before; the reason whereof is that in pasture he hath the whole profit, there being required neither men nor charge worth speaking of; whereas in tillage the people and their families necessarily employed upon it . . . must be maintained, and their public duties discharged, before the landlord's rent can be raised or ascertained. But this improvement of rent certainly causes the decay of tillage.'

Where the soil was suitable, some new enclosures continued to be laid to permanent grass, therefore, even at the end of the eighteenth century, when there was an acute shortage of grain.[6]

Conversion to permanent grass was generally regarded as a canker to the commonwealth that 'un-houses thousands of people, till desperate need thrusts them on the gallows'.[7] It is 'apish', 'woolvish' and 'an apparant badge of atheisme'.[8] In Norden's words,[9]

'It hath bene a matter formerlie opposed and much disliked of the vulgar that comon feyldes shoulde be inclosed; grounding their mislike especially upon some abuses and injuries done therby unto the inhabitantes and tenantes of such manors whose comon feyldes have bene inclosed without the consent of the inhabitantes; and have depopulated the places and converted the soyle to such endes and uses

[3] *Utopia* ed. J. C. Collins, Oxford 1904, p. 17.
[4] Holinshed & Harrison, pp. 202, 205.
[5] Cited in J. D. Chambers, *Notts. in 18th century*, London 1932, p. 152; Pitt, *Northants.* pp. 58–9, 61–3; *A General View of the Agriculture of County of Leicester*, London 1809, p. 78; *A Comparative Statement of Food produced from Arable & Grass Land*, London 1812, p. 23.
[6] Pitt, *Leics.* pp. 78, 87.
[7] T. Fuller, *The Holy State & Profane State*, ed. J. Nichols, London 1841, p. 91.
[8] Norden, p. 224 (1st occ.).
[9] PRO, Exch. LR, MB 194, f. 307.

as have beene neyther pleasinge to God, beneficiall to man nor fitt for a comonweale. Theis kindes of inclosures are not onlie not toller-able but greyvously punishable; and although the sworde of the majestrate passe by suche offenders, because they are comonlie great, yet doth the hande of God find them owt, and suffereth seldome the issue of suche depopulators to enjoye such extorted revenewes manie generations.'

Blith inveighs against those who make[10]

'for the great depopulation in the nation that hath devoured poor and tenant, overthrow corneing and good husbandry, and in some parts minister and all, and yet persist by keeping their lands from tillage, when it wants it, when country, the landlords profit, the markets, the labourer, poore and lande itselfe and all calls for it, is no lesse than grand oppression'.

That 'Cain and Abel were borne and planted together, and ordained to live together' and that permanent-grass grazing should be put down by law were opinions to which most Englishmen subscribed.[11]

In the early modern period most of the enclosed land in the plain countries were converted to an up-and-down system. Employment was increased where old commons or permanent grass were broken up, and diminished where permanent tillage was enclosed. Generally speaking, the enclosure of common-field townships for up-and-down husbandry led to a degree of agricultural depopulation. The propor-tion of tillage was necessarily reduced from about one half to a third or even a quarter. The labour force was therefore reduced. But up-and-down husbandry was conducted on capital farms and enclosure was usually accompanied by the consolidation of small holdings into large.[12] In these farms costs were cut by the reduction in horses and men needed to the acre: labour was abridged while production was increased. On the average, in the common fields, family farmers had about 7 acres of corn to each horse and working farmers about 10, while capital farmers working an up-and-down system had about 11.[13] Hedging and ditching may have absorbed the labour of displaced common herdsmen,[14] but halving the tillage area meant in practice more than halving the labour force.

Literary evidence of depopulation is not far to seek, but deserves

[10] Blith, p. 78; also pp. 71–4.
[11] *Ibid.* 81, 92; also 71–2; Marshall, *M. Dept*, pp. 284–5.
[12] *Ibid.* 33, 285, 585; J. Wedge, *A General View of the Agriculture of County of Warwick*, London 1794, p. 21; J. Moore, *The Crying Sin of England*, London 1653, p. 11; J. Morton, *The Natural History of Northants*. London 1712, p. 15.
[13] My *Ag. Rev.* p. 209.
[14] Fitzherbert, *Svying*, f. 53.

close scrutiny rather than acceptance at its face value. John Rous, who wrote in 1486, relates something of depopulation in the south-west of the Midland Plain and nearby parts of the Vale of Evesham, and lists no less than sixty-one towns and hamlets either destroyed or mutilated.[15] Thomas More probably exaggerates little when he says that noblemen, gentlemen and abbots, 'not contenting themselfes with the yearely revenues and profyttes that were wont to grow to theyr forefathers and predecessours of their landes ... enclose all in pasture; they throw down houses; they plucke downe townes; and leave nothing stondynge but only the church, to make of it a shepehowse'.[16] Later, Ascham, as befitted his times, blamed the abbots' lay successors, and especially the imparkers among them.[17] As for Goldsmith, his 'Deserted Village' probably depicts Lissoy in West Meath as much as anywhere else, but it gives a good description of a deserted village site, though nothing is said of a depopulated township, and, as we shall see, sites could be deserted without towns being dispeopled.

Turning now to record evidence, a survey[18] of Apethorpe tells us that

'the lord hath a freehaye which was somtyme a hamlet called the Hale and was inhabyted, as there remayneth a mencion of old walls at this daye, the habytacions wherof were decayed, by the reporte of dyverse ancyent persons, long before the remembrance of anie manne lyvyng and as they suppose in the latter end of the reygne of Kyng Henry the Fyft and the begynnyng of the reygne of King Henry the Syxt'.

The villages of Whatborough[19] and Childerley[20] and the hamlet of Hamilton[21] all appear to have been deserted in medieval times. Other deserted sites in the Midland Plain were known in the sixteenth and seventeenth centuries, and although contemporaries wisely hesitated to venture an estimation of the dates of their destruction, these were probably medieval. Such were Redreth hamlet and Dovedales in Litlington.[22] Of Gamblethorpe in 1616 Norden says, 'There is now neyther tofts, tenements or cotage standinge, onlie the ruynes of the

---

[15] BM, Cottonian MSS. Vespasianus A. xii, ff. 72(73)–73(74) (pp. 143–6).

[16] p. 16; & Tawney & Power, iii. 46.

[17] R. Ascham, *Familiarum Epistolarum*, Hanover 1610, p. 381.

[18] Northants. RO, Wmld 4. xvi. 5; also 4. xx. 3; 2. iv. 2/F.9; 2. x. 1/B.8; F-H 143, f. 87v.; *VCH Northants.* i. 318b.

[19] Tawney, pp. 222–3; Savine, *Eng. Mons.*, p. 193; M. Beresford, *History on the Ground*, London 1957, p. 121.

[20] Palmer, *Layer*, p. 101; cf. M. Beresford, *The Lost Villages of England*, London 1954, p. 343.

[21] W. G. Hoskins, *Essays in Leics. History*, Liverpool 1950, p. 74.

[22] Palmer, *Layer*, pp. 103, 106.

towne appeareth at the south end of the lordship.'[23] At Somerby, 'There are now noe particular tenementes within this township, onlie an auntient capitall house there yet standeth, moated about, much decayed.'[24] Another place[25]

'is called and retayneth the name of East Lilling township, thowgh at this daye ther doe remayne but onlie one howse . . . But by tradition and by apparent stepps and track of aunctient buyldinges and ways for horse and carte, visibly discerned, leading unto the place where the town stood, within Sheriffe Hutton parke, it hath bene a hamlet of some capacitie, thowgh now utterlie demolished.'

Even in the Cheese Country, says Aubrey, upon the felling of some oak trees at Knapwell juxta Draycot, were discovered many foundations of former houses and the ruins of a smith's forge,[26] and a village formerly adjoined Blunsdon St Andrews, 'as appears by the ruines, which houses were swallowed up by the mannour house'.[27] As late as the middle of the sixteenth century, allegations were still being made that persons had destroyed whole townships by enclosure;[28] but they seem unlikely.

It would be wrong to exaggerate the extent to which towns were destroyed. The most that Rous asserts is that two former centres of population were deserted, two reduced to the manor house alone and forty-three 'either destroyed or mutilated'.[29] Some of these latter remained, or were reduced to, very small settlements; many shrank; some grew; and few indeed were destroyed.[30] To prove that villages and hamlets no longer existed is a task beyond the capacity of final concords, tax assessments and inquisitions of depopulation. Many places that may appear at first sight to have been deserted were not so in fact,[31] and some that were eventually deserted suffered this fate at times not yet ascertained.[32] To take the single example of the village of Godington, Domesday Book is said to have recorded a

[23] Jn Rylands Lib. Eng. 216, f. 19.
[24] *Ibid.* f. 39.
[25] BM, Harl. MS. 6288, f. 26; and PRO, Exch. LR, MB 193, m. 123(55).
[26] J. Aubrey, *Collections for Wilts.*, ed. T. Phillips, London 1821, p. 67.
[27] Aubrey, *Wilts. Topog. Colls.* p. 150.
[28] PRO, St. Ch. P. & M. 3/8 compl.
[29] BM, Cottonian MSS. Vesp. A. xii, ff. 72(73)–73(74) (pp. 143–6); cf. Beresford, *Lost Vils.* pp. 388–9, 435; 'Deserted Vils. of War.', *Trans. B'ham Archaeol. Soc.* 1950 (1945–6), p. 85.
[30] S. C. Ratcliffe & H. C. Johnson, *Warwick County Records ii & iii: Quarter Sessions Order Book*, Warwick, 1936–7, iii. 151; W. Smith, *History of Co. of Warwick*, Birmingham 1830, pp. 91, 93.
[31] Beresford, *Lost Vils.* pp. 343, 367–8, 379; Palmer, *Layer*, p. 101; Hoskins, pp. 86 sqq., 93–4, 97–8; and below, p. 124. Let the reader check by the gazeteers.
[32] Hoskins, *Essays*, pp. 72 sqq.

population of 19, the 1279 hundred rolls 36 tenants, the 1327 *Nomina Villarum* 23 taxpayers, the 1377 poll tax return 43 heads over fourteen years of age, the 1524 assessment 10 subsidy men, the 1665 hearth tax list 7 households, an unnamed return of 1676, 65 adults, the 1801 census 99 inhabitants, and that of 1841, 117. These figures, even if correct, do not justify the conclusion that has been drawn from them, that the village was definitely deserted at some time between 1450 and 1700. Rather do they pose questions to be addressed to the fiscal records and warn demographic historians to follow Darwin in trusting to true counting and the rule of three.[33] Appearances are often deceptive and the complaints of contemporaries misleading. Ruined churches or manor houses do not prove deserted towns. Some villages were removed a short distance away to more convenient sites.[34] Not a few were deserted for reasons other than enclosure. War destroyed some.[35] Others were abandoned, perhaps because inconveniently situated, the farmers and others removing to neighbouring villages.[36] Occasionally the inhabitants emigrated as a complete community.[37]

After the earlier years of the sixteenth century, since most enclosure was for up-and-down husbandry and not for permanent grass, the usual result was not the desertion but the shrinkage of villages and the concentration of their inhabitants into one or two capital farms and some outlying cottages (Docs. 24–27).[38] A good example of this situation is provided by Kirby, since 1576 the seat of the Hatton family. About 1530 the manor only had five tenants, but the survey and map of 1584 show the hall, its outhouses and stables, a church, a farm-

[33] *History*, 1966, li. 210–1.

[34] Bateson, vii. 305; HMC, *Portland MSS.* vi, London, HMSO Cd. 676, 1901, p. 96; *Montagu of Beaulieu MSS.* London, HMSO Cd. 283, 1900, pp. 84–5; M. Spufford, 'Rural Cams. 1520–1680', ts. thesis M.A. Leic. Univ. 1962, p. 31.

[35] W. Marshall, *The Rural Economy of the Midland Counties*, London 1790, ii. 225; Leics. RO, DE. 40/22/4, ff. 2(1)v., 7(6)v.

[36] Leic. Mus. 35/29/340; B. Blackstone, *The Ferrar Papers*, Cambridge 1938, p. 63.

[37] A. N. Cooper, 'How Rowley in Yks. lost its Population in 17th cent. & how Rowley in Mass. was founded', *Trans. E.R. Archaeol. Soc.* 1909, xv. 85 sqq.; M. Campbell, in *Conflict in Stuart England*, ed. A. Aiken & B. D. Henning, London 1960, p. 183.

[38] Lee, p. 22; Leonard, p. 117; L. A. Parker, in *Studies in Leics. Agrarian History* ed. W. G. Hoskins, Leicester 1949, pp. 42–3, 68–9; 'Depopulation Returns for Leics. in 1607', *Trans. Leics. Archaeol. Soc.* 1947, xxiii. 286; K. J. Allison, 'Wool Supply & Worsted Cloth Ind. in Nfk in 16th & 17th cents.', ts. thesis Ph.D. Leeds Univ. 1955, p. 182; Jn Rylands Lib. Eng. 216, f. 21; PRO, Exch. KR, Deps. by Commn 26 Eliz. Trin. 4; LR, MB 231, m. 40; St. Ch. Jas, 295/22, mm. 8–9; 304/6; Northants. RO, F-H 2601; Leics. RO, Archdeaconry invs. 1626: 169; 1638: 91; 1669: 35; 1671: 15; 1693 V.G.: 16; 1710: 100.

stead and eleven cottages. Even after some enclosures and exchanges of land, these buildings still appear in the map and survey of 1587. By 1638 the Hattons possessed here only the hall and a shepherd's cottage and a map of 1708 shows no housing outside the park walls. Yet the fields were being energetically cultivated, largely by the employment of labour accommodated in the outbuildings of the hall itself.[39] The most usual effect of enclosure now became not desertion, but the dispersal of crowded townships into scattered homesteads, giving an illusion of desertion and leaving a derelict site. As is well known, nucleated townships, where the farmhouses were all crowded into a main street, usually went hand in hand with common fields, and dispersed settlement with enclosures. Now there were changes from the one to the other.

Enclosure for cultivation was not unknown in the early sixteenth century, nor for permanent grass in the eighteenth; the latter was overtaken by the former and the usual became the unusual. Change in time was thus superimposed upon local diversity and was reflected in views that were first clear, then discordant and at last clear again. The earlier writers, as is well known, were almost unanimously hostile to enclosure, which was regarded as anti-social. The unanimity was broken up by controversies between the opponents and the advocates of enclosure. The enclosure of Marston, for example, was argued between the lord of the manor, Brudenell, and the rector, Nelson; the latter stigmatizing the original petition as a plan to 'lett thistles grow instead of wheat or cockle instead of barley', and the former pointing out that in enclosures the land would be 'noe whit farther from tillage then in common fields'.[40] Part and parcel of the social and intellectual ferment that marked the Interregnum was the ventilation in print of conflicts of opinion that had long engaged the various rural interests.

This discussion was opened by John Moore, the minister of Knaptoft, who published the sermons he preached at the Lutterworth lectures in 1653. He was bound to concede that corn was grown in the 'pastures', but deplored the decrease of the tillage area and the consequent redundancy of self-employed farmers and day-labouring cottagers. It was true that enclosures were by agreement, but this was all too often forced.[41] In his reply, Pseudomisus was concerned to shift the balance of emphasis. There were, he granted, some depopulating enclosures; but Cain and Abel could live together amicably and up-and-down husbandry was far superior to permanent tillage or

[39] Northants. RO, F-H 272, ff. 2v.–3, 4v.–5, 5v.–6; 2859; PRO, Wds, Feodaries' Svys no 566; J. Wake, *The Brudenells of Deene*, London 1954, p. 31; *A Copy of Papers relating to Musters &c. in Co. Northampton 1586–1623*, Northants. Rec. Soc. 1926, iii. 113.

[40] Deene ho. Brudenell I. iii. 7, 12, 13; O. ix. 2. Nelson cites Job, xxxi. 40.

[41] Moore, *Crying Sin*, pp. 9, 11–4, 23.

permanent grass, for more corn and more grass were produced at lower cost.[42] All enclosure, Moore rejoined in 1656, led sooner or later to depopulation. Well-regulated enclosure was a myth, for tillage was always diminished. In short, opposition only excited Moore still further to exaggerate the productivity of common fields and belittle ley farming.[43] He thus left himself open to a stunning retort from Pseudomisus, who showed that Moore was still opposing enclosure in principle. That the decay of tillage and depopulation were evil was generally agreed, but these were not the inevitable consequences of enclosure; the fault lay in men's hearts, not in the nature of the ground. The fact was that up-and-down husbandry could be practised only in enclosures. Just because some closes had been kept in permanent grass, this was no reason to prevent tillage in others.[44] These exchanges cleared the way for a final analysis by Joseph Lee, who had been in-stituted to the rectory of Cotesbach by Parliament in 1645.[45] By a wealth of illustration from the Midland Plain itself, Lee showed that most of the enclosures were cultivated in an up-and-down system, corn and grass yields greatly increased, and costs reduced. What sense was there in lamenting that some closes were still kept in permanent grass and at the same time quarrelling with enclosure for up-and-down husbandry, which, because of the greater volume of meat put upon the market, was destroying the price-structure of permanent-grass meat production, and, because of the boosting of yields, had made tillage more profitable than mere grazing. To com-plain of depopulation was absurd, for the labour force was only deci-mated. It might be conceded that three or four shepherd's boys might be dismissed from their desultory work; but they should have been at school or church instead of playing nine-hole under a bush. The consolidation of farms, it was true, did abridge labour, but this was also possible in common fields. In any event, the abridgement of labour was not to be deplored.[46]

'Let it be granted that our land and businesse lying nearer together, fewer servants will be kept; are any bound to keep more servants then are needful for their businesse; or may they not cast how to do the same businesse with least labour? . . . In vain that is done by more, which may be done by lesse.'

[42] Pseudomisus, *Considerations concerning Common Fields & Inclosures* London 1654, pp. 10–2, 39–40. Cf. Fuller, *Holy State*, p. 91.
[43] J. Moore, *A Scripture-word against Inclosure*, London 1656, pref., pp. 5–7, 9–11, 13.
[44] Pseudomisus, *A Vindication of the Considerations concerning Common Fields & Inclosures*, London 1656, pp. 19, 22, 43 sqq.
[45] *Jnl H.L.* viii. 165 (2nd occ.).
[46] Lee, pp. 2 sqq., 12, 14–5, 22, 25, 30.

The arguments expounded by Lee found general acceptance, for they corresponded to the new reality. Enclosure no longer reduced production or dispeopled the countryside. With up-and-down husbandry, production was vastly increased, labour abridged and unit-costs reduced. Thus ineffective and outmoded diatribes against greed gave way to a utilitarian philosophy of free capitalist enterprise, actuated by profit motives, spurred by competition, guided and controlled by market forces, and producing the greatest happiness of the greatest number.

Lee clearly distinguished between rural depopulation and the abridgement of agricultural labour and realized that the more labour agriculture was able to dispense with, the more could be employed to advantage in industry. Many of the rural poor, especially in enclosed districts, worked in the clothing industry.[47] Labour spared from agriculture might be employed in processing wool, flax, hemp, woad and other materials essential to the economy, so that 'they need not labour in vain'.[48] One of the mainsprings of industrialization is thus revealed. It was generally agreed that family farmers and others made redundant by enclosures in the Midland Plain, removed to common-field or market towns and took to industrial employments.[49] Most of the expanding industries, such as hosiery, lace, boot and shoe, and nail making, and metal-working, were sited in the countryside and organized by merchant employers who exploited the labour of self-employed persons, thus providing openings for displaced family farmers who had conserved enough capital to set themselves up with a loom, knitting-frame or some such. Others took employment in the extractive or heavy industries. Many industrial workers were able to establish themselves in dwarf farms and to devote part of their time to accommodation closes, domestic dairies or even a few acres in a common field. In this way industry spread throughout the countryside, industrial villages appeared on the scene and industrial towns and cities developed.[50] The expansion of the stocking manufacture at Catthorp was simultaneous with the enclosure of the township and many other villages underwent a similar transformation.[51] The relative ease with

[47] Lee, p. 4.
[48] Lee, p. 8.
[49] Tawney, pp. 150, 276-7; Morton, p. 15; Wedge, pp. 20-1; Pitt, *Northants.* pp. 248-51; *Leics.* pp. 80, 337; H. Stocks, *Records of Borough of Leicester 1603-88*, Cambridge 1923, pp. 396, 429; Moore, *Scripture-word*, pp. 9, 11; PRO, Exch. KR, Deps. by Commn 1651, Mich. 15; Marshall, *M. Dept.* pp. 285-6.
[50] *Ibid.* 202-3, 285; Wedge, p. 21; Hoskins, *M. Peasant*, pp. 211-2, 228; *Anns. of Ag.* 1786, v. 488.
[51] C. Holme, *A History of the Midland Counties*, Rugby 1891, pp. 22-4; M. Bloxsom, *History of Parish of Gilmorton*, Lincoln 1918, p. 57.

which small masters switched from agriculture to industry strengthened the hands of the merchant employers and in some degree retarded the mechanization and concentration of the hosiery, shoemaking and metal-working industries. In the event, agricultural depopulation largely became transformed into rural depopulation only during the great agricultural depression after 1873.

In the North-eastern Lowlands, however, this transformation was accomplished more drastically. The way in which the family farmers here were rudely swept into great industrial centres is best described by citing cases. In 1567 the 11 husbandmen, 8 cottagers, 4 cottiers and 1 smith of Tuggal had recently been reduced to 8 farmers.[52] By 1597 the Dean of Durham could observe that private men had dispeopled whole villages.[53] About this date Sir Thomas Gray of Chillingham is reported to have expelled 340 men, women and children from Newham in one day.[54] Robert Delavale displaced all the tenants of Hartley, defaced their houses and threw all the land into one great farm that he cultivated with three teams instead of the fifteen previously kept.[55] At Seaton Delaval he effected similar cost reductions.[56] William Carr knocked all but one of the farms at Hetton into his own.[57] Edward Adams engrossed nearly half the farms in Little Houghton.[58] Depopulation thus took the form it assumed in Scotland in the eighteenth century, 'the turfen huts of the petty tenants being profitably spread over the land, as manure'.[59]

In the Chalk, Cotswold, Southdown, Northwold and Oxford Heights countries depopulation took a third course, one of slow attrition, to which enclosure itself was inessential. The engrossment of farms was accompanied by agricultural depopulation because capital farms needed less labour to an acre than did family ones.[60] Bishops Wilton in the Northwold Country serves to illustrate the process. In 1611 there were 42 farmsteads and 24 cottages, but 'the povertie and wante of the tenantes' of the cottages had led to them being severed from their land, which was sold to farmers. The cottagers were bereft of rights of common and could hardly meet their rents, so nothing was now to be expected but the decay of their dwellings.[61]

In the Chalk Country, by the middle of the seventeenth century, family farms had undergone such a decline that they embraced only a

[52] Bateson, i. 350.
[53] Tough, p. 178.
[54] Bateson, i. 275.
[55] Ibid. ix. 124–5, 202.
[56] Ibid. 201–2.
[57] Ibid. xiv. 230.
[58] Ibid. ii. 385.
[59] Marshall, M. Dept, p. 350.
[60] My Ag. Rev. p. 209; 'Ag. c. 1500–c. 1793', in VCH Wilts. iv. 50; Marshall, S. Dept, p. 247; T. Stone, A General View of the Agriculture of County of Lincoln, London 1794, pp. 40–1; A. Harris, 'Lost Vil. & Landscape of Yks. Wolds', Ag. Hist. Rev. 1958, vi. 98.
[61] PRO, Exch. LR, MB 229, f. 222.

minor fraction of the farmland. By the beginning of the eighteenth century only one occupier in three was a family farmer. In the next half century attrition continued only slowly and the final crisis of the class of family farmers was postponed until the second half of the eighteenth century, when many lifeholds were mortgaged and leases often allowed to run out instead of being re-lifed. By the last quarter of the century, even in townships with common fields, family and part-time farmers had either disappeared altogether or had been reduced to a small minority, in respect both of numbers and of the area occupied. The final liquidation of these classes was not long delayed.[62]

At this juncture enclosure accelerated. Long lists of enclosure acts and awards, it is true, give a false impression of the incidence and progress of enclosure itself, for the townships to which they referred had long had a considerable, and often the greater part of their land in severalty.[63] Moreover, even in parliamentary enclosures, not only were some of the lands left in open severalty;[64] others were allotted in tenantry and laid out in common fields, downs, marshes and meadows, where common husbandry was regulated by the awards themselves.[65] Nevertheless, the total acreage in common was much reduced in the last quarter of the eighteenth century and the first half of the nineteenth. It cannot be said that enclosures either did or did not cause depopulation. Generally speaking, the decline of the family farmer may be ascribed to the advantages of the lower working costs of the capital farm; and these exerted their influence whether the land was put into severalty or not. At this time the rate of decline of the family farms was accelerated, even where no fresh enclosures were undertaken; but where they were, it was sometimes still further speeded up, sometimes slowed down. Family farms could only be managed in common and it was, therefore, not the years of enclosure alone that were crucial, but the score or so that spanned the prospect and realization of enclosure, for some family farmers threw in their hand as soon as enclosure seemed likely and others struggled on until ruin itself convinced them they had no place in the new order of things. In the whole period of accelerated enclosure the rate of decline of the family farmers was vastly increased, save only where new common fields were laid out, and there the rate increased less sharply after division than before. Some substance is thus lent to the contemporary opinion that enclosure hastened the end of family farms, but not enough to prove it true; and it must not be forgotten that the presence of any considerable number of family farms itself imposed

[62] *VCH Wilts.* iv. 57–8.
[63] *Ibid.* 46; my *Ag. Rev.* pp. 17–9.
[64] *Ibid.* 20–2; *VCH Wilts.* iv. 47–8.
[65] *Ibid.* 48, 50–2.

I

on the enclosure commissioners the task of laying out new common fields. Since farms needed less labour an acre the larger they were, the decline of family farms led to a diminution of the agricultural population. Up to five or six farms might be laid into one and the consequent reduction of costs was considerable. In Monkton Deverill 4 farmers with 19 horses between them replaced 7 farmers with 29 horses; and in Brixton Deverill 3 farmers with 26 horses replaced 6 with 43. As horses and men were employed in about even proportions, it is clear that labour was much abridged and the agricultural population reduced by about a third. It is true that the numbers of freeholders were augmented during enclosure, but this is compatible with a diminution of the area occupied by them and most of the new freeholders were landless cottagers. In some instances, too, the number of self-employed persons increased; but this was consistent with a decline in the area occupied by them.[66]

The upshot was that population declined in the agricultural, and increased in the industrial districts. The decline of the family farm undermined common-field management and practices; deprived of the common herd, flock and fold, and of the domestic dairy, family and part-time farmers necessarily succumbed, became labourers on the capital farms, emigrated, or went to industrial and commercial centres. On the other hand, the incipient mechanization of industry was itself helping to undermine the family and part-time farms, whose female labour was largely employed in carding and spinning for the clothiers. The spinning jenny first appeared at Shepton Mallet in 1776 and by 1793 it had come into general use throughout the district. This instrument was then mostly installed in cottages and worked, with the assistance of two or three children, by specialized, self-employed spinners. Its innovation, therefore, knocked the bottom out of part-time farmhouse spinning. In the early stages, mechanization did not transcend rural self-employment, but it did immensely sharpen the division of labour between agriculture and industry and deprive family farmers, and even more part-time farmers, of one source of income. In 1790 the carding engine first appeared at Bradford-on-Avon and by 1805 horse-driven carders were in general use. Scribbling mills were introduced at much the same time and although the mechanization of some other processes was delayed, these early innovations sufficed to throw the family and part-time farmers into industrial crisis, so that they were faced by a two-handed engine of destruction.[67] Enclosure merely carried out the sentence of death

[66] *Ibid.* 49–50, 57–8, 62–3.
[67] *Ibid.* 63–4, 167; R. P. Beckinsale, *The Trowbridge Woollen Industry as Illustrated by Stock Books of Jn & Th. Clark 1804-24*, Wilts. Archaeol. & Nat. Hist. Soc. Rec. Brch, 1951, vi. pp. xvii–xix.

already imposed by the harsh realities of farming costs and industrial mechanization. The decline of agricultural self-employment may have encouraged mechanization; but the simultaneous action of high costs and falling incomes was irresistible.

Enclosure was nowhere the fundamental cause of rural depopulation, and the proof of this is that in farming countries favouring labour-intensive enterprises, for example, the Cheese Country, enclosure was accompanied by the proliferation of family farms. The admittedly considerable expenses of enclosure,[68] be it noted, which might be thought to have burdened self-employed farmers in countries suited to capital farms, were taken in their stride by family farmers elsewhere.

The depopulation of farms and countryside came about in different ways and was confined to certain farming countries, certain villages and certain farms, while it was counter-balanced by impopulation in others. If depopulation should not be exaggerated, neither should it be unduly belittled. It has been argued that the increased number of freeholders, that is, of persons with freehold estates, shows an increase in the number of owner-occupiers and of agricultural population; but this is a case of mistaken identity.[69] Only some freeholders were owner-occupiers and an increase in the number of freeholders is consistent with rural depopulation. No single county, it is true, suffered a decline of population;[70] but neither was any of them purely agricultural or rural. It may be true that rural marriage rates rose,[71] but this could have been for a variety of reasons, (of which increasing population is not one, and some, possibly, rising death rate and changing economic and social structure), and could have had a wide range of possible results, amongst which a significant rise in population in the long run is not necessarily the most likely. It would be wrong, too, to ascribe the movement of labour from agriculture to industry or the growth of the industrial division of the population merely to the

[68] F. H. Goldney, *Records of Chippenham* s. l. 1889, pp. 201–2; E. C. Lodge, *The Account Book of a Kentish Estate 1616–1704*, British Academy, 1927, p. 11; Harland, i. 21, 27, 49, 63; ii. 235, 246; J. Humphries, 'Eliz. Este Bk of Grafton Manor', *Trans. B'ham Archaeol. Soc.* 1920 (1918), pp. 86, 89; BM, Add. MS. 34162, f. 40; Devizes Mus. shelf 63, 'Wm Gaby His Booke, 1656', p. 12; PRO, St. Ch. Jas 63/10; Exch. KR, Sp. Commn 4707; SPD, Chas I, vol. 288 no 80.
[69] E.g. E. Davies, 'Small Landowner 1780–1832 in Light of Land Tax Assessments', in *Essays in Economic History* ed. E. M. Carus-Wilson, London 1954, pp. 272, 277–80, 284, 286–9.
[70] T. S. Ashton, *The Industrial Revolution 1760–1830*, London 1948, p. 61; A. Redford, *Labour Migration in England, 1800–50*, Manchester 1926, p. 69.
[71] Cf. J. D. Chambers, 'Enclosure & the Labour Supply', *Econ. Hist. Rev.* 1953, v.

natural growth of population. Until the question is asked, 'What economic forces caused this 'natural' growth?', we shall only be scratching the surface of the problem. All we know is that industrial manpower was recruited from people who, for one reason or another, found themselves wholly or partially excluded from farming; and that some enclosures slightly assisted this exclusion.

Depopulation, as has been seen, could mean either the abridgement of agriculture manpower or rural depopulation; but it could have also a third meaning, namely, the liquidation of the class of family farmers. This usually entailed depopulation in the other senses; but it was considered by contemporaries to be depopulation in itself, since it reduced the 'active' population as distinct from the 'passive', the heads of enterprises as distinct from mere hands.[72] When depopulation was denounced, it was meant that ploughs were put down, perhaps because large-scale farming permitted a less laborious management of the land, not necessarily because the arable area was reduced (Docs. 25–27).[73] The plaint is, as at Hill Deverill, that 'whereas the ancyent tenantes kept ploughes ... the nowe cotagers do lyve ... but barely, only by theire day labor'.[74] By no means the least burden of complaint was that family farmers were deprived of their livings and replaced by wage-workers.[75] Depopulation in this sense was the fate of all farming countries where part-time and family farms were replaced by capital ones. When a township in the Midland Plain is enclosed, the family farmers all refuse new tenancies,[76] because they cannot afford them, and, in the nearby town,[77]

'the market is full of inquirie and complaint of such tennants to all they meet, "Can you help me to a farm or a little land to imploy my team? I am discharged and if I sell my horses and cattel, I shall never get a team again or so many milk-cowes to maintain my familie. Alas, all my money will be spent that I shall sell them for, ere I shall hear of any land to be set." '

[72] J. Hawarde, *Les Reportes del Cases in Camera Stellata*, ed. W. P. Baildon, s. I. 1894, p. 76; S. R. Gardiner, *Reports of Cases in Courts of Star Chamber & High Commission*, Camd. Soc. 1886, xxxix. 44; T. I. J. Jones, *Exchequer Proceedings (Equity) concerning Wales, Hy VIII–Eliz.*, Cardiff 1939, pp. 297–8; J. Aubrey, *Wilts. Topog. Colls.* pp. 9–10, 131; *Natural History of Wilts.*, ed. J. Britton, London 1847, p. 104; 'Intro. to Svy & Nat. Hist. of N. Div of Co. of Wilts.', in *Miscellanies on Several Curious Subjects*, E. Curll, London 1714, pp. 31–2; Ratcliffe and Johnson, ii. 153; PRO, St. Ch. Jas 17/24, m. 3; Exch. KR, Sp. Commn 5554; Deps. by Commn 26 Eliz. Trin. 4.
[73] See my *Ag. Rev.* p. 209; and above, p. 130.
[74] Hawarde, pp. 104–5; PRO, St. Ch. Eliz. A. 11/8, A. 34/10, A. 58/12.
[75] Hawarde, p. 76; S. R. Gardiner, *Reps.* p. 44.
[76] Finch, pp. 87–9; HMC, *Var. Colls. iii.* 112.
[77] Moore, *Crying Sin*, p. 9.

Depopulation in the sense of the destruction of the class of self-employed persons was found even in the Fen Country, where the numbers of people obviously increased. Not only the 'slodgers', but also the family farmers of the uplands townships were adversely affected by enclosure and drainage.[78]

The chief sufferers from enclosure and the loudest in their denunciations of depopulation were the family and part-time farmers of the countries that favoured large enterprises. Farm labourers, perhaps, were occasionally deprived of their cow-pastures or even of their kitchen gardens;[79] yet it was not they who were reduced to despair, but the family and part-time farmers: [80]

'Behold a crier of tripe for sale growling angrily about the pasture-land stolen from him and the food for want of which his ass is dying. His poor little wife weeps bitterly over her hungry geese and half-mad begs for her accustomed marshlands.'

The tripe-seller and the farmer selling his team in the market had been, in some sense, driven off the land; but 'In vain what is done by more, which may be done by lesse.'

In fine, although both no doubt entailed many hardships and many joys to those compelled to move, depopulation was as great a blessing in some farming countries as impopulation was in others.

[78] Gardiner, *Reps.* p. 61; Norden, p. 196; L. E. Harris, *Vermuyden & the Fens*, London 1953, pp. 26–7; Marshall, *E. Dept*, pp. 229, 238–40; J. Thirsk, *English Peasant Farming*, London 1957, pp. 147, 153; PRO, Chanc. Proc. ser. i Jas, B. 1/37, m. 1; Exch. AO, MB 419, f. 59; BM Cott. Augustus I/i/78; E. Sfk RO, V. 11/2/1.1.

[79] See above, p. 108.

[80] J. Tyley, 'Inclo. of Open Fds', *Northants. Past & Pres.* 1951, i/4, p. 39.

PART II: SELECTED DOCUMENTS

1. FROM Bracton, *De Legibus et Consuetudinibus Angliæ*, circa
1250, 'De dominico domini regis et de condicione personarum
tenentium de dominico: non dico de manerio.' (E. G. Woodbine,
ed., 4 vols., New Haven 1915–42).

In the domains of the lord king there are many kinds of men. For
there are there, before, at, and after the conquest, serfs or natives.
And they hold in villenage and by villein and uncertain services, they
who down to the present day do perform villein and uncertain customs
and whatever is required of them, so it be lawful and honest. There
were also at the time of the conquest free men who held their tenements freely by free services or free customs, and when they had been
ejected by those more powerful, they afterwards returned and received
back their same tenements to hold in villenage by doing servile but
certain and specified works. These are said to be bound to the soil,
and are nevertheless free, because although they do servile works, they
none the less do them by reason not of their persons but of their
tenements. And therefore they shall not have an assize of novel disseisin, because the tenement is in villenage, albeit privileged, nor an
assize of mort d'ancestor, but only the little writ of right according
to the custom of the manor. And therefore they are said to be 'bound
to the soil', because they enjoy this privilege, that they cannot be
removed from the soil as long as they do pay their accustomed dues and
services to whomsoever the domain of the lord king may have come.
Nor can they be compelled to hold such a tenement unless they choose.
  'De assisa novæ disseininæ.
  Likewise, suppose an exception of villenage be raised against a free
man holding by villein services, the exception will not harm him as
regards his status, it will harm him however as far as his recovery of
the tenement be concerned, but not as regards his status, because he
can give up his villenage and leave it a free man, as in Michaelmas
term in the third and fourth year of the reign of King Henry III
in the county of Sussex in the case of John de Montagu and Martin de
Bestenovere, where it was said by the aforesaid Martin that if he
wished to hold that land he must make and keep the customs as his
father did, but, if not, his lord should take the villein tenement in
hand, and hence it seems by this that although a free man hold a
villein tenement by villein customs, he is not to be ejected against his
will so long as he will perform the customs appertaining to the tenement and arising by reason of the villein tenement and not by reason
of his person.'
  'Breve ballivis maneriorum secundum consuetudinem maneriorum.'
  The King to his bailiff of such-and-such a township, greeting. We

enjoin you without delay and according to the custom of our manor in such-and-such a township to maintain full rights to so-and-so of so much land with its appurtenances in such-and-such a township which so-and-so deprives him of. Lest any longer we hear a clamour thence about defeat of right. Witness, etc.

2. FROM Britton, circa 1290, book III, chapter ii, section 9 (ed. F. M. Nichols, 2 vols., Oxford 1865).

Ancient demesnes are lands that were part of the ancient manors annexed to our Crown, in which demesnes dwell some who have been freely enfeoffed by charter,—and these are our free tenants,—and others who are free of blood and hold land of us in villenage, and these are properly our sokemen and are privileged in this way, that they are not to be ousted from such tenements so long as they perform the services that appertain to their tenements, nor can their services be increased or altered so that they shall do any other or greater services or in any other way than they have been used to do. And because such sokemen are the tillers of our lands, we will that they be not summoned anywhere to serve in juries or inquests, save in the manors they belong to. And because we will that they enjoy such immunity, the writ of right close is provided, which is pleadable before the steward of the manor for a wrong done by one sokeman to another, that the steward may do the plaintiff right according to the custom of the manor by means of simple inquests. Nevertheless we will that in pleas of trespass and other personal actions, sokemen be summonable and answerable as well as others.

3. FROM Sir Thomas Littleton, *Tenores Novelli,* sine loco, 1481.

TENANT BY COPY OF COURT ROLL is, as if a man be seised of a manor, within which manor there is a custom which have been used time out of mind of man, that certain tenants within the same manor have used to have lands and tenements to hold to them and their heirs in fee simple, or fee tail, or for term of life, &c. at the will of the lord according to the custom of the same manor. And such a tenant may not alien his land by deed, for then the lord may enter as into a thing forfeited unto him, but if he will alien his land to another, it behoveth him after the custom to surrender the tenements in court &c. into the hands of the lord to the use of him that shall have the estate in this form or to this effect. A. of B. cometh unto this court and surrendreth in the same court a mese &c. into the hands of the lord to the use of C. of D. and his heirs, or the heirs issuing of his body, or for term of his life. And upon that cometh the aforesaid

C. of D. and taketh of the lord in the same court the aforesaid mese &c. To have and to hold to him and to his heirs, or to him and to his heirs issuing of his body or to him for term of his life &c. at the will of the lord according to the custom of the manor, doing and yielding therefore the rents, services and customs thereof before due and accustomed &c. And giveth the lord for a fine &c. and maketh unto the lord his fealty &c. And these tenants are called tenants by copy of court roll because they have no other evidence concerning their tenements but only the copies of court rolls. And such tenants shall neither implead nor be impleaded for their tenements by the King's writ. But if they would implead others for their tenements, they shall have a plaint entered in the lord's court in this form or to this effect: A. of B. complains against C. of D. of a plea of land, viz. of one messuage, forty acres of land, four acres of meadow &c. with the appurtenances, and makes protestation to follow this complaint in the nature of the King's writ of assize of mort d'ancestor at the common law, or of an assize of novel disseisin, or formedon in the descender at the common law, or in the nature of any other writ &c. Pledges to prosecute, F.G. &c. And although some such tenants have an inheritance according to the custom of the manor, yet they have but an estate but at the will of the lord according to the course of the common law. For it is said, that if the lord do oust them, they have no other remedy but to sue to their lords by petition, for if they should have any other remedy they should not be said to be tenants at the will of the lord according to the custom of the manor. But the lord cannot break the custom which is reasonable in these cases.* Also there are other tenants who are called tenants by the verge. And these tenants are in the same nature as tenants by copy of court roll. But the reason why they be called tenants by the verge is that when they will surrender their tenements into the hands of their lord to the use of another, they shall by the custom have a little rod in their hand, the which they shall deliver to the steward or to the bailiff according to the custom of the manor, and he which shall have the land shall take up the same land in court and his taking shall be entered upon the roll and the steward or bailiff, according to the custom, shall deliver to him that taketh the land the same rod or another rod in the name of seisin, and for this cause they are called tenants by the verge, but they have no other evidence but by copy

---

* In the 1530 edition is added the following passage:—But *Brian* Chief Justice said, that his opinion hath always been and ever shall be, that if such tenant by custom paying his services be ejected by the lord, he shall have an action of trespass against him. *H.21 Ed. 4.* And so was the opinion of *Danby* Chief Justice in *7 Ed. 4.* For he saith that tenant by the custom is as well inheritor to have his land according to the custom as he which hath a freehold at the common law.

of court roll. And also in divers lordships and manors there is this custom, viz. if such a tenant which holdeth by custom will alien his lands or tenements, he may surrender his tenements to the bailiff or to the reeve or to two honest men of the same lordship to the use of him which shall have the land to have in fee simple, fee tail, or for term of life &c., and they shall present all this at the next court, and then he which shall have the land by copy of court roll shall have the same according to the intent of the surrender. And so it is to be understood that in divers lordships and in divers manors there be many and divers customs, in such cases as to take tenements and as to plead and as to other things and customs to be done, and whatsoever is not against reason may well be admitted and allowed. And these tenants which hold according to the custom of a lordship or manor, albeit they have an estate of inheritance according to the custom of the lordship or manor, yet because they have no freehold by the course of the common law, they are called tenants by base tenure. And there are divers diversities between tenant at will which is in by lease of his lessor by the course of the common law, and tenant according to the custom of the manor in form aforesaid. For tenant at will according to the custom may have an estate of inheritance (as is afore said) at the will of the lord according to the custom and usage of the manor. But if a man hath lands or tenements which be not within such a manor or lordship where such a custom hath been used in form aforesaid, and will let such lands or tenements to another, to have and to hold to him and to his heirs at the will of the lessor, these words (to the heirs of the lessee) are void. For in this case, if the lessee dieth and his heir enter, the lessor shall have a good action of trespass against him, but not so against the heir of tenant by the custom in any case, &c., for that the custom of the manor in some case can aid him to bar his lord in an action of trespass, &c. Also the one, tenant by the custom, in some places ought to repair and uphold his houses, and the other, tenant at will, ought not. Also the one, tenant by the custom, shall do fealty, and the other not, and many other diversities there be between them.

4. FROM Sir Edward Coke, *The first part of the Institutes of the Lawes of England, or a Commentarie upon Littleton,* London, 1628, book I.

CHAP. 9 Section 73
Tenant by Copy.

Tenant by copy, &c. Tenant by copy of court roll. Copy we call in Latin *copiam,* though *copia* in his proper signification signifieth plenty, but we have made a Latin word of the French word *copie* and this is ancient, for in the *Register fo.51* there is a writ *de copia libelli deliberanda,* which is grounded upon the statute of 2 H.4 cap.—. There is no tenant in the law that holdeth by copy, but only this kind of customary tenant, for no man holdeth by copy of a charter or by copy of a fine or suchlike, but this tenant holdeth by copy of court roll.

(*a*) *Bracton* calleth copyholders *villein sokemen,* not because they were bond, but because they held by base tenure by doing of villein services.

And *Britton* saith that some that be free of blood do hold land in villenage, and *Littleton* himself in the next chapter calleth them tenants by base tenure: and in *Fitzherbert, Natura Brevium, fo.12.C. And this term which is nowadays called copytenants or copy holders, or tenants by copy, is but a new-found name, for in ancient times they were called tenants in villenage, or of base tenure, &c.* (*b*) And yet in *1 H.5.11* they be called copyholders, in *14 H.4.34 tenant by the verge,* in *42 E.3.25 Tenant by roll according to the will of the lord,* and in the Statute of *4 E.1* called *Extent of the manor* they are called *Customary tenants,* and so doth *Fleta* call them, and before him *Ockam* (who wrote in the reign of *H.2*) spake of them and how and upon what occasion they had their beginning.

(*c*) *Land by writing, in Saxon Bockland: in ancient estates they had and held either by writing or without writing, which were called respectively Bockland, i.e. Bookland, or Folkland, of which possession by writing was fitter to free possession, and immune from, as estates without writing were obliged to, certain dues and servitudes; the former a great part of the nobles had and held, and the latter for the most part the native rustics and peasants.*

Court, curia. Court is a place where justice is judicially ministered and is derived *from 'cura' because they ruled cares in public courts.*

(*a*) Bracton bk 2, ch. 8, fo. 26 & bk 4, fo. 209. Britton 165. Fleta bk 1, ch. 8 & bk 2, ch. 6. Also of the custom relating to them, Ockam, Ch. Quid murdrum. F.N.B. fo. 12c.

(*b*) 1 H.5.11, 14 H.4.34, 42 E.3.25. See bk 4, fo. 2, Browne's case.

(*c*) Lambard, word terra ex scripto.

(*d*) The court baron must be holden on some part of that which is within the manor, for if it be holden out of the manor it is void, unless a lord being seised of two or three manors hath usually time out of mind kept at one of his manors courts for all the said manors, then by custom such courts are sufficient in law, albeit they be not holden within the several manors. And it is to be understood that this court is of two natures, the first is by the common law, and is called a court baron, as some have said for that it is the freeholder's or freeman's court, (for barons in one sense signify freemen), and of that court the freeholders being suitors be judges, and this may be kept from three weeks to three weeks. The second is a customary court and that doth concern copyholders, and therein the lord or his steward is the judge. Now, as there can be no court baron without freeholders, so there cannot be this kind of customary court without copyholders or customary holders. And as there may be a court baron of freeholders only, without copyholders, and then is the steward the register, so there may be a customary court of copyholders only, without freeholders, and then is the lord or his steward the judge. And when the court baron is of this double nature, the court roll containeth as well matters appertaining to the customary court as to the court baron.

And forasmuch as the title or estate of the copyholder is entered into the roll whereof the steward delivereth him a copy, thereof he is called copyholder. (*e*) It is called a court baron because amongst the laws of King *Edward* the Confessor it is said: *The barons are truly those who hold their court of their men, &c.*, taking his name of the baron who was lord of the manor, or for that properly in the eye of law it hath relation to the freeholders, (*f*) who are judges of the court. And in ancient charters and records the barons of London and barons of the Cinque ports do signify the free men of London and of the Cinque ports.

  Seised of a manor. Manor is said to be from the word for enduring, very agreeable to a great, fixed and stable seat. A lawman is one having soc and sac over his men, &c. (*g*) *And it is to be understood that a manor may by itself be combined of several edifices adjacent, whether towns or hamlets. For a manor may exist both by itself and with several towns and with several hamlets adjacent, no one of which can be described as a capital manor by itself, and it*

(*d*) See 4, fo. 24, between Murrell and Smith, *ibid.* fo. 27, between Clifton & Molineux.

  (*e*) Lamb. fo. 128 & 136. Camden, *Brit.* fo. 121b. Britton fo. 274.

  (*f*) *Mirror* ch. 1, sect. 3.

  (*g*) Domesday. Bracton bk 4, fol. 212. Fleta bk 4, ch. 15 & bk 6, ch. 49. Britton, fol. 124.

may contain under it several non-capital manors and several towns and hamlets as though under one head or dominion. And afterwards, *But a manor may be made up of several towns or of one, for several towns may be in the body of a manor thus as one may be.* And in these (h) ancient authors you shall see the difference between mansion, town and manor. Concerning the institution of this court by the laws and ordinances of ancient kings and especially of King *Alfred,* it appeareth that the first kings of this realm had all the lands of England in demesne, and the great manors and royalties they reserved to themselves, and the remnant they, for the defence of the realm, enfeoffed the barons of the realm with such jurisdiction as the court baron now hath, and instituted the freeholders to be judges of the court baron. And herewith agreed the aforesaid law of Saint *Edward.* And it is to be observed, that in those ancient laws under the name of barons were comprised all the nobility.

There may be a customary manor granted by copy of court roll, so although the word be *seised* which properly betokeneth a freehold, yet tenant for years, tenant by statute merchant, staple, elegit, and tenant at will, guardian in chivalry, &c. who are not properly seised but possessed are lords for the time being, not only to make admittance, but to grant voluntary copies of ancient copyhold lands which come into their hands. And therefore there is a diversity between disseisors, abators, intruders, and others that have defeasible titles, for their voluntary grants of ancient copyhold lands shall not bind the disseisors or others that right have. And voluntary grants by copy, made by such particular tenants as is afore said, shall bind him that hath the freehold and inheritance, because all these be lawful lords for the time being, but so is not a tenant at sufferance, because he is in by wrong, as hath been said, and so (i) was it adjudged *Easter 29 Eliz. between Rowse & Arteis,* bk 4, fol. 24. But admittances made by disseisors, abators, intruders, tenants at sufferance or others that have defeasible titles, stand good against them that right have, because it was a lawful act and they were compellable to do them.

(k) And yet in some special case an estate may be granted by copy by one that is not lord for the time being, nor that hath anything in the manor. As if the lord of a manor by his will in writing deviseth that his executor shall grant the customary tenements of the manor according to the custom of the manor for the payment of his debts, and dieth, the executor having nothing in the manor may make grants according to the custom of the manor.

(h) Bract. bk 5, fo. 434. Fleta where above. *Mirror,* ch. 1, sect. 3.
(i) Bk 4, fol. 24, E. 29 Eliz. between Rous & Arteis.
(k) Dier, Mich. 7 & 8 Eliz. manuscript.

Within which manor there is a custom, which have been used time out of mind of man, &c. Of this custom here spoken of there be three supporters. The first is time, and that must be out of memory of man, which is included within this word 'custom', so as copyhold cannot begin at this day. (*l*) The second supporter is that the tenements be parcel of the manor or within the manor, which appear by these words of *Littleton*, 'that certain tenants within the same manor, &c.' The third supporter is that it hath been demised and demisable by copy of court roll, for it need not to be demised time out of mind by copy of court, but if it be demisable it is sufficient. For example, if a copyhold tenement escheat to the lord, and the lord keepth it in his hands by many years, during this time it is not demised but demisable, for the lord hath power to demise it again.

At the will of the lord according to the custom. So as he is not a bare tenant at will, but a tenant at will according to the custom of the manor, as shall be spoken more hereafter in this chapter.

Certain tenements. What things may be granted by copy, is necessary to be known. First, a manor may be granted by copy. Secondly, underwoods without the soil may be granted by copy to one and to his heirs, and so may the herbage or vesture of land.* Thirdly, generally all lands and tenements within the manor and whatsoever concerneth lands or tenements may be granted by copy, as a fair appendant to a manor may be granted by copy, &c.**

Customs. The word *Consuetudo* being derived from *Consueto*, properly signifieth a custom, as here *Littleton* taketh it. But in legal understanding it signifieth also tolls, murage, pontage, pavage, and suchlike newly granted by the king, and therefore when the king grants such things, the words be, *We grant &c. in aid of the aforesaid town for paving &c. the undermentioned customs, viz. of whatever summage, &c.*

And it was an article of the justices in eyre to enquire, *Of new customs levied in the kingdom, either on land or on water, and who levies them and where,* where *custom* is taken for tolls and suchlike taxes or charges upon the subject.***

Section 74

And such a tenant may not alien his land, &c. And this is true in case of alienation, but when a man hath but a right to a copyhold, he may

(*l*) See bk 4, fol. 24, between Murrel & Smith.
* Bk 11.17, Sir H. Nevil's case.
** Bk 4, fols. 30–31, between Hoe & Taylor.
*** Regist. F.N.B. 270 d. Old Master, Certain ch. Itin. fol. 151. Bracton, bk 3, 117. Fleta, bk 1, ch. 20.

re-lease it by deed or by copy to one that is admitted de facto tenant.*

Alien by deed. Here it appeareth by *Littleton* that there must be an alienation, for the making of the deed alone, unless somewhat pass thereby, is no forfeiture, as if he make a charter of enfeoffment, or a deed of demise for life, and make no livery, this is no forfeiture, because nothing passeth, and therefore no alienation, but otherwise it is of a lease for years.

Forfeited unto him. This adjective in Latin is *forisfactus*, the verb is *forisfacere*, and the noun *forisfactura*; they are all derived of *foris*, that is, *extra*, and *facere*, as if to say to do a thing against or without law or custom, and that legally is called a forfeiture. *Littleton* useth this word but once in all his book, what shall be said (*k*) forfeitures of copyholds you may read at large in my Reports.

In court. (*l*) This is the general custom of the realm that every copyholder may surrender in court and need not to allege any custom therefore. So if out of court he surrender to the lord himself, he need not allege in pleading any custom, but if he surrender out of court into the hands of the lord by the hands of two or three, &c. copyholders, or by the hands of the bailiff or reeve, &c., or out of court by the hand of any other, these customs are particular and therefore he must plead them.

(*m*) *Bracton bk 4, fol. 209,* speaking of these kind of customary tenants, saith, *But they cannot give away their tenements nor convey them to others by way of donation, no more than absolute villeins, and hence if they are to be transferred, they give them back into the hands of the lord or his bailiff and they deliver them to others to be held in villenage,* but although it be incident to the estate of a copyhold to pass, as our author saith, by surrenders, (*b*) yet so forcible is custom that by it a freehold and inheritance may also pass by surrender (without the leave of the lord) in his court and delivered over by the bailie to the feoffee according to the form of the deed, to be enrolled in the court or the like.

A. of B. cometh unto this court, and surrendreth, &c. Here *Littleton* putteth an example of a surrender in court, and in this example three (*c*) things are to be observed.

First, that the surrender to the lord be general, without expressing of any estate, for that he is but an instrument to admit the party

---

* Bk below 131. Bk 4, fol. 25b, between Kite & Queinton.

(*k*) Bk 4, among the copyhold cases 21, 23, 25, 27, 28. Bk 8, 92, 99, 100. Bk 9. 75, 107. Bk 10. 131.

(*l*) Bract. bk 2, ch. 8 & bk 4. 49, 15 H. 4. 34, 1 H. 5. 11.

(*m*) Bract. bk 4, fol. 209 & bk 2, ch. 8 & 14. N.4.34.

(*b*) Coram rege Mich. 31 E.3, Ralph Huntingfeld's case. 3 E.3. Corona 310. 11 H.4.83. per Thewing.

(*c*) See bk 4 among the copyhold cases.

K

to whom the use is, for no more passeth to the lord but to serve the limitation of the use and he to whom the use is, when he is admitted, shall be in by him that made the surrender, and not by the lord.

Secondly, if the limitations of the use be general, then he to whom the use is taketh but an estate for life, and therefore here *Littleton* expresseth upon the declaration of the use the limitation of the estate, viz. in fee simple, fee tail, &c.

Thirdly, the lord cannot grant a larger estate than is expressed in the limitation of the use. *Littleton* here putteth his case of one. (*d*) If two joint tenants be of copyhold lands in fee, and the one out of court according to the custom surrender his part to the lord's hands, to the use of his last will, and by his will deviseth his part to a stranger in fee, and dieth, and at the next court the surrender is presented, by the surrender and presentment the jointure was severed, and the devisee ought to be admitted to the moiety of the lands, for now by relation the state of the land was bound by the surrender.

Into the hands of the lord. The lord of a manor is described (*e*) by *Fleta* as he ought to be in these words, *In and above aught else and to his uttermost every lord is behoven to be true in word and trusty in deed, loving God and justice and hating deceit and iniquity, contemning the wilful, the malevolent and the mischievous, and showing kindness to his neighbours with an open and sympathetic countenance, for it is to his interest to use discretion rather than force, and his own judgment rather than that of some impulsive youth, minstrel or flatterer, but to prefer the counsel of loyal and candid men learned in the laws and experience in affairs. Whosoever wants to make good provision for himself and his family will find he has to learn the true value of his lands that he may thereby become conversed with the extent of his means and the limits of his annual expenditure.* And the residue is fit for every lord of a manor to know and follow which were too long here to be recited, only his conclusion, having spoken of the lord's revenue and expenses, I will add, *And let all these matters be written separately on membranes, so that the lord may consequently order his life with greater wisdom and more easily convict falsehood in accountants.*

(*f*) If the lord of the manor for the time being be lessee for life or for years, guardian, or any that hath any particular interest, or

---

(*d*) Mich. 2 & 3 Ph. & M. in Common Pleas, by the whole court, in Constable's case of Pickenham in Norfolk.

(*e*) Fleta, bk 2, ch. 65 & 71.

(*f*) See more of this bk 4, the cases of copyholds. Trin. 1 Jas rot. 854, between Shapland & Ridler in repl. in Common Pleas, the case of the Guardians in Socage adjudged.

tenant at will of a manor (all of which are accounted in law lords for the time being) do take a surrender into his hands, and before admittance the lessee for life dieth, or the years, interest or custody do end or determine, or the will is determined, though the lord cometh in above the lease for life or for years, the custody or other particular interest or tenancy at will, yet shall he be compelled to make admittance according to the surrender, and so it was holden in 17 *Eliz.* in the Earl of *Arundel's* case, which I myself heard.

And giveth the lord for a fine. For the signification of this word 'finis' see sections 174, 183, 194, 441.

Of fines due to the lord by the copyholder, some be by the change or alteration of the lord, and some by the change or alteration of the tenant, the change of the lord ought to be by Act of God, otherwise no fine can be due, but by the change of the tenant either by the Act of God or by the act of a party a fine may be due; for if the lord do allege a custom within his manor to have a fine of every of his copyholders of the said manor at the alteration or change of the lord of the manor, be it by alienation, demise, death or otherwise, this is a custom against the law, as to the alteration or change of the lord by the act of the party, for by that means the copyholders may be oppressed by multitude of fines, by the act of the lord. But when the change groweth by the Act of God, there the custom is good, as by the death of the lord. And this, upon a case in the Chancery (g) referred to Sir *John Popham* Chief Justice, and upon conference with *Anderson, Periam, Walmesley,* and all the judges of Serjeants' Inn in *Flee[t]street,* was resolved, and so certified into the Chancery. But upon the change of alteration or the tenant, a fine is due unto the lord.

Of fines taken of copyholders some be certain by custom, and some be incertain, but that fine though it be *incertain,* yet it must be *reasonable.* And that reasonableness shall be discussed by the justices upon the true circumstances of the case appearing unto them, and if the court where the cause dependeth adjudgeth the fine exacted unreasonable, then is not the copyholder compellable to pay it. And so it was adjudged (h), for all excessiveness is abhorred in law. See more concerning fines of copyholders in my Reports (i), which are so plainly there set down as they need not be rehearsed here.

(g) T.39 Eliz. between the copyholders of the manor of Guiltirns in the county of Northumberland and Armestrong, lord of the manor, in Chancery.

(h) Easter 1 Jas in Com. Pleas rot. 1845 between Stallon & Brady.

(i) Bk 4, the cases of copyholds.

Section 75

They have no other evidence. This is to be understood of evidences of alienation, for a release of a right by deed a copyholder (that cometh in by way of admittance) may have, and that is sufficient to extinguish the right of the copyhold which he that maketh the release had.

Section 76

And such tenants shall neither implead nor be impleaded, &c. This is evident and needs no explanation.*

But if they will implead others, ... they shall have, &c. Put the case that the demandant in a plaint in nature of a real action recovereth the land erroneously, what remedy for the party grieved? For he cannot have the King's writ of false judgment in respect of the baseness of the estate and tenure, being in the eye of the law but a tenant at will and the freehold being in another; he shall have a petition to the lord in the nature of a writ of false judgment, and therein assign errors and have remedy according to law.**

Of formedon in the descender at the common law. By the opinion of *Littleton* as there may be an estate tail by custom with the co-operation of the Statute of *Westminster* 2 cap. 1, so may he have a *formedon in descender*, but as the statute without a custom extendeth not to copyholds, so a custom without the statute cannot create an estate tail. Now, it is not a sufficient proof that lands have been granted in tail, for albeit lands have anciently and usually been granted by copy to many men and to the heirs of their bodies, that may be a fee simple conditional as it was at the common law. But if a remainder have been limited over such estates and enjoyed, or if the issues in tail have avoided the alienation of the ancestor, or if they have recovered the same in writs of *formedon* in the descender, these and such like be proofs of an estate tail. (y) But if by custom copyhold may be entailed, the same by like custom, by surrender, may be cut off, and so hath it been adjudged; (z) some hath holden that there was a *formedon* in the descender at the common law.***

* 4 H.4.34 adjudged in Parliament.
** 14 H.4.34, 1 H.5.11. *Old Nat. Brev.* 18. 13 R.2 s.v. False judgment. 7 E.4.19, 21 E.4.80.
*** Bk 3 fo. 8, 9 in Heydon's case. Bk. 4, fo. 22, 23. 15 H.8 Br. entitled tail.
   (y) E.19 Eliz. between Hill & Upcheic. Customs in the manor of Overhall in Essex. 21 Eliz. Dier 366. 23 Eliz. Dier 373.
   (z) 10 E.2 formedon 55. 21 E.3.47 Com. Pleas 240. 4 E.2 formedon 50.

Section 77

For it is said, that if the lord, &c. And here *Littleton* saith truly that is said so, for so it is said in *13 E.3, 13 R.2, 32 H.6 & 7 E.4.19.**

But he setteth not down his own opinion, but rather to the contrary, as hereafter in this chapter appeareth. But now 'Experience the great instructress' hath made this clear and without question, that the lord cannot at his pleasure put out the lawful copyholder without some cause of forfeiture, and if he do the copyholder may have an action of trespass against him, for albeit he is *holding at the will of the lord,* yet it is *according to the custom of the manor.***

(b) And *Britton,* speaking of these kind of tenants, saith thus, *and these are privileged in this way, that they are not to be ousted from such tenements so long as they perform the services that appertain to their tenements, nor can their services be increased or altered so that they shall do any other or greater services.* And herewith agreeth Sir *Robert Danby* Chief Justice of the Court of Common Pleas *M.7 E.4.19* and Sir *Thomas Brian* his successor *M.21 E.4.80,* viz. that the copyholder doing his customs and services, if he be put out by his lord, he shall have an action of trespass against him.

Chapter 10. Section 78

Tenants by the verge. This tenant by the verge* is a mere copyholder, and taketh his name of the ceremony of the verge. Tenure in villenage or by base tenure is thus described by *Britton,* (a) *Villenage is a holding of the demesnes of any lord delivered to be held at his will by villein services for cultivation for the lord's use, and where livery is given by the rod and not by title deed or inheritance, and neither wardship and marriage nor other real services like homage and relief can be demanded of ancient demesnes or of villenages.*

To the steward (seneschal), which we call a steward. *Seneschallus* is derived of *sein* a house or place, and *schalc* an officer or governor; some say that *sen* is an ancient word for justice, so as *seneschal* should signify *the officer of justice*; and some say that steward is derived of *stew*, that is, a place, and *ward*, that signifieth a keeper, warden or governor; and others that it is derived of *stede*, that signifieth a place also and *ward* as it were the keeper or governor of that

---

* 13 E.3 s.v. prescript. 20. 13 R.2 false judgment 7. 32 H.6 s.v. Subpoena 2. 7 E.4.19.

** See sect. 81, 82, 84, 132.

(b) See 42 E.3.25. Britton fol. 165.

* 14 H.4.33.

(a) Britton fol. 165 d. F.N.B. fol. 12 Livery by the verge.

place; but it is a word of many significations. In this place it signifieth an office of justice, viz. a keeper of courts, &c. *Fleta* describeth the office and duty of this officer at large most excellently: ** *Let the lord provide himself with a circumspect and faithful steward, a man provident, discreet and gracious, humble and modest, pacific and temperate, who is versed in the laws and customs of the country and in the office of a steward, one eager to protect his lord's rights in all things, who has the knowledge to correct and instruct the lord's under bailiffs in their errors and doubts, who will spare the needy, but whom neither entreaty nor bribery will swerve from justness or pervert from justice, whose office is to hold the courts of the manor and enquire of withdrawals of customs, services, rents, suits of court, market, mill, and view of frankpledge, and of other liberties belonging to the lord, &c.* The residue pertaining to his office is worth your reading at large. Every steward of courts is either by deed or without deed, for a man may be retained a steward to keep his court baron and leet also belonging to the manor without deed, and that retainer shall continue until he be discharged. The lord of a manor may make admittances out of court and out of the manor also, as at large appeareth in my reports.***

Section 79

To the bailiff. This word 'bailie' as some say cometh of the French word *baylife*, in Latin *balivus*, but in truth bailie is an old Saxon word* and signifieth a safe keeper or protector, and *baile* or *ballium* is safe keeping or protection, and thereupon we say when a man upon surety is delivered out of prison *released on bail*, he is delivered into bail, that is, into their safe keeping or protection from prison; and the sheriff that hath *custody of the county* is called *bailiff* and the county *his bailiwick*.

Reeve is derived of the Saxon word *gerefa* or *gereve*, and by contraction or rather corruption *gereve* or *reve* and is in Latin *præfectus* or *præpositus*. It signifies as much as *appruator*, a disposer or director, as wood-reeve, sheep-reeve, shire-reeve, &c. whereof more shall be said hereafter. See *Fleta bk 2, ch. 67*** where he treateth of the office of the bailiff, and *ch. 69 de officio præpositi,* of the office of the reeve, and what belongeth of duty and right to either of them, which words are too long here to be inserted, only this I will take out of him, *The bailiff of every manor should be true in word, diligent and faithful in his work, and known, vouched for and chosen as a careful and*

** See sect. 92 & 379. Fleta bk 2 ch. 66. See Stat. de extent maner. 14 E.1.
*** See bk 4 cases of copyhold, fo. 26, 27, 30.
* See Lambard, exposition of Saxon words.
** Fleta bk 2, ch. 67.

progressive man, one who has a working knowledge of the law enough to qualify him for a responsible position and is upright enough not to seek out unjust grounds of complaint against the lord's tenants and others under him out of spite and greed, &c. Once chosen as the best manager and cultivator, &c. the reeve should be publicly presented to the lord or his steward and the office should be imposed on him straight away. It follows that he should not be a sleepy or lazy fellow, but one who strives might and main day in and day out to promote the lord's interests, &c. The residue concerning both the offices being worth your reading.

To the bailiff or to the reeve. Littleton intendeth into the hands of the lord by the hands of the bailiff or the reeve.

Or to two honest men of the same lordship. The custom doth guide these surrenders out of court, and the custom must be pursued.

And they shall present all this at the next court, &c. By the surrender out of court the copyhold estate passeth to the lord under a secret condition*** that it be presented at the next court according to the custom of the manor. And therefore if after such a surrender, and before the next court he that made the surrender dieth, yet the surrender standeth good, and if it be presented at the next court, he to whom the use is shall be admitted thereunto; but if it be not presented at the next court according to the custom, then the surrender becometh void, and so it was clearly holden Easter 14 Eliz. in the Court of Common Pleas which I myself heard.

Section 80

There be many and divers customs. This was cautiously set down, for in respect of the variety of the customs in most manors, it is not possible to set down any certainty, only this incident inseparable every custom must have, viz. that it be consonant to reason, for how long soever it hath continued, if it be against reason, it is of no force in law.

Against reason. This is not to be understood of every unlearned man's reason, but of artificial and legal reason warranted by authority of law: Law is the height of reason.

Section 81

They are called tenants by base tenure. Of this sufficient hath been spoken before.

Section 82

Tenant at will according to the custom may have an estate of in-

*** See bk 4, fol. 25, Kite & Quaintin's case.

heritance, &c. Here note that *Littleton* alloweth that, by the custom of the manor, the copyholder hath an inheritance, and consequently the lord cannot put him out without cause.

But if a man, &c. will let such lands or tenements to another, to have and to hold to him and to his heirs at the will of the lessor, these words (to the heirs of the lessee) are void. For in this case if the lessee dieth, and his heir enter, the lessor shall have a good action of trespass against him, &c.* By which it is proved that by the death of the lessee, the lease is absolutely determined, which is proved by this, that if the heir enter the lessor shall have an action of trespass, *wherefore with force and arms* before any entry made by the lessor.

For that the custom of the manor may aid him to bar his lord in an action of trespass, &c. Hereby it appeareth that by the opinion of *Littleton*, the lord against the custom of the manor cannot oust the copyholder.

Section 83

By the custom. For what a copyholder may or ought to do or not do, the custom of the manor (*a*) must direct it, for *the custom of the manor is to be observed* (*b*). But if there be no custom to the contrary, waste either permissive or voluntary of a copyholder is a forfeiture of his copyhold.

Section 84

The one, tenant by the custom, shall do fealty, and the other not. And the doing of fealty by a copyholder* proveth that a copyholder so long as he observes the custom of the manor and payeth his services hath a fixed estate. For tenant at will that may be put out at pleasure shall not do fealty. For to what end should a man swear to be faithful and true to his lord, and should bear faith to him which he claimeth to hold of him, and that lawfully he shall do his customs and services, &c., when he hath no certain estate, but may be put out at the pleasure of the lessor, or he himself may determine it at his pleasure; of these kind of customary tenants, and of many things concerning them, you may read more in the fourth book of my Reports,** fol. 21, 22, 23, &c. Thus much as I have here set down may suffice for the understanding of such cases and opinions as *Littleton* hath expressed.

* 10 E.4.18, 22 E.4.13, 2 R.2 barre 237, 11 H.7.22, 21 H.7.12.
(*a*) Bracton, bk 2, fol. 76.
(*b*) See bk 4, fol. 21, 22 &c. in cases of copyhold.
* See sect. 132.
** Bk 4, fol. 21, 22, 23. &c.

5. FROM Year Books, *De Termino Michaelis Anno vii Edwardi quarti*, sine loco (1515?), fol. 19.

In action of trespass of goods taken by tort, the defendant pleads in bar that the plaintiff said that he himself is the lord of the manor of Kings B. and that he and all those to whom was the estate he had in the said manor have had time out of mind after the death of each tenant holding any parcel of the manor at the will of the lord according to the custom of the manor to use to have the best beast or the best good if he have no beast, as well from those of which the property was to him at the time of death as from the other goods sold to others to his own use in such a way that the occupation be to him at the time of death &c. And saith indeed that one A.B. held parcel of the manor at will according to the custom of the manor and had sold the same goods to one J. to his own use and continually had their occupation until the time of his death &c. and died; after which death the plaintiff as lord of the manor seized the horse as the best beast &c. And it was mooted in this matter if the lord enter and oust his tenant at will according to the custom of the manor, if he hath any remedy against his lord. Danby: it seemeth that he hath, for if the lord oust him he doth to him a tort, for he is as well inheritor to have this land to him and his heirs according to the custom of the manor as any man is of lands at the common law, an he makes fine when he enter &c. Littleton: I saw once a subpoena sued by such a tenant against his lord and it was held by all the justices that he recover nothing by this, for it was held that the entry of the lord was lawful upon him inasmuch as he is tenant at will &c. And, sure, writ of false judgment nor writ of right shall he have either, for no franktenement is in him but the franktenement is in the lord &c. Danby: the judgment on the subpoena was, as I understand it, he was to have recovery of the franktenement because he could not have any other writ for to recover the franktenement &c. but he had good writ of trespass against the lord an he could not justify his entry &c. And, sure, if the king enter on my land, I have no remedy but my petition &c., but the king is bound of right to restore me, in the same sort is the lord bound to restore his tenant at will according to the custom &c. Catesby and Pygot: in your case, if the king enter on land, yet all the same the franktenement is in me and not the king, for he cannot have it without matter of record &c. Danby: I well see, but suppose that he takes the profits, what remedy, &c. Catesby: none, &c.

6. FROM Year Books, *De Termino Hillarii Anno xxi Edwardi quarti*, sine loco (1530?), fol. 96, no 69.
Trespass of breaking house and close.

The defendant saith that the place where &c. is two houses and a certain acre of land, the which was before and at the time of trespass and is now parcel of the house of B., of which one Rouland L. was seised in his demesne as of fee &c. and that the said land was custom land and the two houses and land let to the defendant for term of life, by force of which he was seised &c. as of freehold according to the custom of the same manor, and gave colour to the plaintiff &c. Briggs: it is contrary to his estate to say that he is tenant by copy of court roll and to say that he is seised of freehold. Brian: he has said by force of custom and this he can have well enough; which the court conceded. Briggs: if the lord wish to put him out, he hath no remedy whom he prove that he be but tenant at will. Brian: this was never my opinion and I believe will never be, for then all the copyhold in England would be defeated, for that I understand that so long as the tenant pay the customs and services, if the lord put him out of possession, he shall have action of trespass against him. Catesby: it is settled that the tenant shall prescribe against the lord, but the most that imports to me is, in such place where the land is devisable, that the testator can empower his executors to sell the land notwithstanding that the heir is in by descent, and their sale shall be good, but that is by the custom. Brian: of this sort is the custom of the manor, where they have such estate, as they have alleged. And, if the plaintiff hath such matter, he can show how the tenant has failed in payment of his service of which the plaintiff was seised. And how he, through default of payment, entered and was seised, so that the defendant made the trespass &c. And the plea was held good enough. And on another day the plaintiff waived this plea and demurred to the plea of the defendant, because he could not prescribe to have the land against his lord for that it was contrary to his estate &c.

7. FROM D. Jenkins, *Eight Centuries of Reports, or eight hundred cases adjudged in the Exchequer-Chamber, or upon writs of error*, London 1771, pp. 242-3.

CASE XXVI

The Earl of Arundel being seised in fee of the manor of Haselbury in the county of Dorset (of which manor divers copyholds are parcel) grants one of the copyholds to one Meryfield for life; (and the custom there is, that the widow of such copyholder shall have it for

her life); afterwards the earl conveyed the said manor to A. Earl of
Northumberland and to the heirs male of his body, the remainder
to Henry his brother of the like estate, with a proviso, that if the said
A. or Henry his brother or any heir male of their bodies should alien
or discontinue the said manor, or any part thereof, or otherwise
directly or indirectly to act so that the said manor should not revert
to the said Earl of Arundel, that then the donor and his heirs might
enter, as if the said donees respectively had died without heir male
of their bodies; afterwards the Earl of Northumberland takes wife;
afterwards Meryfield dies and his wife has his estate; and the Earl of
Northumberland grants the said copyhold, which the said widow
holds, to one Langer for life; (the custom there allows such grants
of copyholds in reversion); afterwards the Earl of Northumberland
commits treason and is attainted of it, and dies without issue male;
the wife of Meryfield dies, the earl of Arundel enters; Langer enters
upon him; the earl brings trespass against Langer: judged against
the earl by the judges of both benches, upon a special verdict found
of this case. The special verdict found the said matter, and also the
Statute of 26 H.8, cap. 13, which gives the forfeiture of estates tail
for treason, (but it gives no entry to a stranger who has right), and it
found also the Statute of 33 H.8, cap. 20, which vests in the King
the actual possession of land of persons attainted of treason, without office found, and gives entry to strangers who have right.

Resolved in this case:—1st. That if a manor where there are copyholds be granted to A. upon condition, and A., before or after the
condition broken, grants a copyhold before entry for the condition
broken, that the grantor shall not avoid this copyhold, for the copyholder is in by the lord for the time being, and paramount the grant.

8. FROM R. Keilwey, *Reports D'ascuns Cases (qui ont evenus
aux temps du Roy Henry VII et du Roy Henry VIII ...) seligès
horse des papieres de R.K. par J. Croke,* London 1688, pp. 76–7.

Of Michaelmas Term in the Year 21 Henry 7.

24. Trespass.

Anne Tropnell & W. Twynytho bring a writ of trespass against John
Kyllyk & others de lour close debruse &c. To which the defendants
say that the plaintiffs should not have action, for they say that the
place where &c. is & at the time &c. was 20 acres of land in Nutfield
aforesaid, the which are &c. and time out of mind were parcel of the
manor of Nutfield in the said county, of which manor the plaintiffs
are and before the trespass at all times were seised in their demesne
as of fee. And the defendants say that the said plaintiffs and all those

whose estate they have in the said manor, by their steward for the time being, have time out of mind demised and used to demise all the customary lands and tenements, and not the demesne lands of this same manor, to each and every person who would take them by copy of court roll of the same manor for term of life, of years, or to him and his heirs at the will of the lord according to the custom of the same manor, rendering and paying to the lords of the same manor for the time being the rents and services aforetime due and accustomed, and also to make fine to the lord of the same manor for their entry into the same land according to the custom of the manor, and that within the precincts of the said manor there is and during all the said time has been amongst others a certain custom, namely, that each such tenant at each such demise made by copy of court roll, their heirs and assigns, after making their fine to the lord of the said manor, should have, hold, enjoy and retain all such lands and tenements issuing from these demises at the will of the lord according to the custom of the manor during their estate, term and interest in the same lands and tenements granted, without expulsion or interruption by the lords for the time being, as long as such tenants make and render to the lords of the manor for the time being all due and accustomed services for their said tenements and as long as they do nothing contrary to the reasonably used and approved customs within the said manor. And the aforesaid defendants say that the said 20 acres of land where &c. are and time out of mind have been customary lands, and not in demesne, demisable by copy &c. and that one N. Carew aforetimes &c. was seised of the said manor and of the 20 acres of land parcel &c. in fee, and being so seised, at his court &c. in the year 14 Edward 4 at Nutfield aforesaid, by one H. Marlond then his steward, this same N. did thereupon, of the said manor then by him held, according to the custom of the manor, and for a fine of 13s. 4d. to the aforesaid Nicholas for his entry into the same lands and tenements, demise to the said defendants 20 acres of land, by copy of court roll, to have and to hold to them and their heirs at the will of the lord according to the custom of the manor, rendering yearly &c. the due and accustomed services, by force of which the defendants entered and became seised and possessed according to the custom of the said manor, which estate from the said Nicholas in the said manor the plaintiffs have; and they say that they have performed all services and paid all rents &c. up until the time of the obtaining of the writ and throughout the same time have done nothing contrary to the custom of the said manor, by force of which they entered and held the tenements as well they might &c., and have demanded judgment if an action. And the plaintiffs have demurred in law on the plea and the demurrer entered Rotulet 445. And to Frowike it seemed the prescription is sufficiently good to bind the lord that he may not oust the customary tenants. And it was adjourned until the utas of Hilary to enquire of this matter. Also Michaelmas 22 Henry 7 Palmer, who was for the plaintiffs in the like matter, argued that customary tenants could not prescribe against their lord to hold land against his will, for their estate is but at will, which cannot have continuance in perpetuity, and because of this they could not prescribe to any common against a stranger by reason of their tenure, but there they shall be aided by their lord, for himself and for his tenants at will. Hence, conversely, by prescribing against the lord himself they defeat the thing that should enable them to the prescription, to wit, the interest of the lord in the lordship &c. Kingsmill: I agree that a particular tenant at will cannot prescribe in his sole tenancy, but when the prescription and custom run throughout all the manor, it seems to me that in this way it can well lie in custom, for if the lord can sue them for their fines and rents arising upon the tenure, then it is no less a compelling reason why they should be able to prescribe against him, for their estate has respect to the lordship, because it runs throughout the manor. But I will agree that if they infringe the custom in any point, they have forfeited their estate, to wit, if they make waste, default on payment of their rents, and suchlike. To the which, Fisher conceded, and they said they had conferred with the other justices, who hold the same opinion. And Frowike former chief justice, God rest his soul, was of the same opinion, by which Brudenell, who was for the defendant, made his plea certain. And the plaintiff to have a day to reply, which note. And query &c.

9. FROM E. Coke, *The Reports*, London 1658, book 4, fols. 21–22.
Brown's Case
Michaelmas 23 & 24 Eliz. 1581
In the Common Pleas.

A copyholder dieth leaving a son and a daughter by one venter, and a son by another venter; the premises being in lease for years by licence; the eldest son dieth before admittance; held that the daughter should inherit, not the son. Held also, 1st. That though a copyholder hath, in judgment of law, but an estate at will, yet custom hath so established his estate that it is descendible, and his heirs shall inherit, and so his estate is not merely at the will of the lord, but at the will of the lord according to the custom of the manor. 2nd. That since custom hath created such inheritance, the descent shall be directed according to the rules of common law, as in the case of uses; but it doth not partake of the collateral qualities of descent of other inheritances, not being assets nor subject to dower or courtesy without a special custom, nor tolling entry by descent cast. 3rd. That the heir before admittance may enter and take the profits, and there may be a 'possession of the brother' (*possessio fratis*), and his surrender is good, but without prejudice to the lord's fine.

The lord may enter on his copyholder for non-performance of his services; but if he ousts him without cause, the tenant may have trespass.

Alienation by a copyholder is a disseisin of the lord, and a forfeiture of his estate.

A copyholder cannot have a writ of false judgment on an erroneous judgment against him, but may sue to the lord by petition.

A surrender may be on condition reserving rent.

Grants by copy by bishops bind their successors, and the King, when the temporalities are in his hands, and the grantee may have aid of the King.

The admittance of a particular tenant is the admittance of the remainder-man, but without prejudice to the lord's fine.

An admittance to a copyhold may be pleaded as a grant.

A copyhold in fee is but a particular estate.

Copyholder in fee made a lease for years, the lessee entered; the copyholder having issue a son and a daughter by one venter, and a son by another, died; the eldest son died before admittance; it was adjudged, that the land should descend to the daughter of the whole blood. And in this case three points were resolved by the whole court.

1. Although a copyholder hath in judgment of law but an estate at will, yet custom hath so established and fixed his estate, that by the custom of the manor it is descendible, and his heirs shall inherit it, and therefore his estate is not merely at the will of the lord, but at the will of the lord according to the custom of the manor: so that the custom of the manor is the soul and life of copyhold estates, for without custom or if they break their custom, they are subject to the lord's will; and by custom a copyholder is as well inheritable to have his land according to the custom as he who hath freehold at the common law, for custom is the other law: custom and usage from time whereof &c. may create and consolidate inheritances, for custom overcomes the common law. And copyhold estates are of great antiquity, for Bracton, who wrote in the time of the reign of King Henry 3, writes of them, bk 2, ch. 8, where he says, *If he should wish to transfer from himself to another, let him first restore it to the lord or his servant* (i.e., to the steward of the manor) *if the lord should not be present, and from their hands let the transfer be made to another &c., because he himself hath not the power to transfer, since he hath not a free tenement.* And the same book, folio 76: *And always in this kind of socages, the custom of the place is to be*

observed. In the year 4 Edward 1 (who was the son of Henry 3) by the statute called Extent of manors, there it is said, *It is to be enquired of all freeholders &c. It is to be enquired also of customers, viz. How many there be and much land every of them holdeth, what works and customs he doth, and what the works and customs of every customer be worth yearly, and how much rent of assize he paith yearly besides the works and customs, which of them may be taxed at the will of the lord and which not.* By which it appeareth, that the whole Parliament esteemed of them as of customary tenants. 2. That their rent is accounted parcel of the rent of assize. 3. That some of their customs within some manors are arbitrary at the lord's will, as fines incertain &c., and that within some manors their customs are certain, and all that as custom hath allowed.

42 Edward 3.25 a, b. The lord brought an action of trespass against his copyholder, who pleaded not guilty; the jury gave a special verdict, that the copyholder had not done his services, by which he broke the custom of the manor, for which reason the entry of the lord was adjudged lawful, and that he should have the corn then growing; which proveth that he entered for the forfeiture and could not put him out without cause; so 33 Edward 3, Trespass 254: If a copyholder makes an alienation, it is a disseisin to the lord and a forfeiture of his estate.

13 Richard 2, False Judgment 7. It is there adjudged, that where an heir of a copyholder recovered in a plaint in the nature of an assize of *mort d'ancestor* in the court of the Bishop of London as of his manor of Stepney in Middlesex, the tenant brought a writ of false judgment returnable in Common Pleas, which writ of false judgment did not lie in that case; but there it is said, that he hath no other remedy but to sue to the lord, who hath the freehold, by petition, and he may, if there be cause, reverse the judgment; by which it appeareth, that the heir of a copyholder is inheritable according to the custom and shall recover by plaint in nature of an assize of *mort d'ancestor*; but it is true that Charleton there saith, that he shall not have an assize against his lord as tenant in ancient demesne shall have, because he hath not the freehold, as Bracton saith.

2 Henry 4.12 a. A copyholder brought an action of trespass for breaking his close and cutting his trees, and the defendant pleaded not guilty, the jury found the defendant guilty and assessed damages, and the plaintiff recovered.

1 Henry 5.11,12. A copyholder may surrender to the use of another, reserving rent with condition of re-entry for non-payment, and for default of payment may re-enter. 4 Henry 6.11. 21 Henry 6.37. If a bishop granteth customary lands by copy and dieth, the copyhold is not determined by his death, for he was lord for the time being, and

this grant shall bind the King, and the grantee, (the temporalities being in the King's hands) shall have aid of the King.

7 Edward 4. Danby, Chief Justice, said, that a copyholder is as well inheritable to have his land according to the custom as he who hath a freehold at the common law.

21 Edward 4.80 b. Brian said, that his opinion always had been, and ever should be, that if such tenant by the custom paying his services be ejected by his lord, that he should have an action of trespass.

15 Henry 7.10 a & 27 Henry 8.28 a,b. A bishop granteth lands by copy and dieth, the temporalities come into the King's hands, the copyhold estate standeth, and he shall have aid of the King.

15 Henry 8, Tenant by copy, Brook 24. The heir of a copyholder tenant in tail shall recover in a *formedon* in the descender by all the justices. By which cases it appeareth, that the judges in all successions of ages have allowed copyhold estates to be established and sure by the custom of the manor, and descendible to their heirs as other inheritances are.

10. FROM C. Calthrope, *The Relation betweene the Lord of a Mannor and the Copyholder his Tenant,* London 1635, pp. 4–7.

Master *Fitzherbert* saith, that this term *copyholders* is but a new term, newly found out, and that in old time they were called tenants in villenage or base tenure; and this, saith he, doth appear in the Old Tenures, for no copyholders are there spoken of, although there were at that time such tenants. But then saith, they were called tenants in villenage, and saith, as appeareth 44 Henry 4, if a false judgment be given against them in the lord's court, they shall have no remedy but sue to their lord by petition, because to hold by copy of court roll, which is as he saith base tenure, is to hold in villenage, which said opinion of *Fitzherbert* have been by divers wrested to make no diversity between tenure in villenage and tenure by copy of court roll or base tenure, wherein whatsoever interpretation may be made, Master *Fitzherbert's* meaning is very plain, and the Book of the Old Tenures is to be far otherwise understood, as also, I suppose, all other authorities in our law do make and appoint difference between the said tenures. And first, touching the Book of the Old Tenures, it is plain that the book maketh a plain distinction between tenure in villenage and *tenure* in fee base, which is understood this *tenure* by copyhold and calleth it a fee, although a base fee, and maketh divers distinctions between them, and saith that the *tenants* in *villenage* must do all such things as their lord will command them. But otherwise it is of the *tenants* in base fee. And this it seemeth the said

Book of Old Tenures to be by Master *Fitzherbert* misrecited, which I am the bolder to affirm, saving the due reverence to his learning, because one Mr *Thornton* of *Lincolns* Inn, a man very learned in his late reading thereupon the *Statute* of *Forger de faits*, speaking of *forging court rolls*, did plainly affirm the Book of the Old Tenures to be mistaken by Mr *Fitzherbert* in this point. And besides, for the further credit of *copyholds*, we ought to consider the great authority of Mr *Littleton*, who, amongst the rest of his *Tenures* doth make a divided chapter thereof, differing from the *tenure* in *villenage*, shewing there the suits and plaints of *copyholders*, saying that they have an estate of inheritance according to the custom, and delivereth his own opinion, that if a *copyholder* doing his services be expelled by the lord, he shall have an action of trespass against his lord, and saith that *Danby* and *Brian 21 Edward 4* were of the same mind, according to which is Bracton and the said precedents of *Henry 3* and the writ used in the time of *Richard 2*, besides many other reasons at the common law &c., proving that by use and circumstance things may alter and change their original nature.

As for example, the services of *Socage tenure* was at the beginning, (as Mr *Littleton* saith) to till the lord's land, &c. And yet now by consent of the lord and by continuance of time are turned into money and other services in lieu thereof. Even so may be said of *copyholds*, as long as the *tenants* themselves be free, though their *tenure* were at the beginning never so bond and base, yet by course of time they may gain more liberty and freedom and grow to more estimation and account.

11. FROM E. Coke, *The Compleate Copyholder*, London 1641, pp. 4–7, 12–14.

Section VII

AND in the reservation of these services, the lords had special respect unto the quality of the land; did they transfer their bocklands, that is, freehold lands, they would never reserve villein services; did they transfer their folklands, that is, copyhold lands, they would never reserve free services; but still they suited their services according to the nature of the land. The reason, I gather, was this, in those days none but men of good account and reckoning enjoyed the said bocklands, whereas folklands were in the hands of men of meaner sort and condition, and therefore had not the lords' care been extraordinary in reserving apt service, they should have much wronged their tenants; and thus much *Lambard* verifieth,* saying, *Land by writing was hereditary, free and immune; land truly without writing from officials was*

---

* Lambard in his explication of the Saxon word, Terra exscripta.

L

obliged to servitude in some sort; the former many nobles and gentle-folk, the latter very uncouth rustics and peasants, possessed. Lambard termeth these bocklands, *Free and immune lands, not because they were free and immune from all services, but because the tenants themselves were free and burdened with services only as free men.* But I much wonder, why this bockland doth to this day retain the name of freehold land, since time hath bred such an alteration that in point of service a man can scarce discern any difference between freehold lands and copyhold lands. The favourable hand of time hath so infranchised these copyholders that whereas in the *Saxons'* time their services did consist wholly in feasance, now they consist in render, in user, and in prender, as freeholders' services did in those days. And on the other side, time hath dealt so unfavourably with freeholders, and hath so abridged them of their former freedom, that if you compare the service of the freeholders with the service of the copyholders, *Thou rather sensest here how much that freedom shall be.* How many freeholders are there at this day charged with base services, as many (I doubt not) as there are copyholders? No marvel then that many able men turn copyholders and many peasants turn freeholders; no marvel, I say, that men of all sorts and conditions, promiscuously, both freeholders and copyholders, since there is such small respect had unto the quality of the land in the reservation of our services. Yet observe, I pray, though time hath so infranchised these copyholders that they have in manner shaken off all villein service, yet they retain a badge of their former bondage, for they remain still subject to the lord's will; therefore at this day they are termed tenants at will. But with freeholders otherwise it is, for they are not in that subjection to their lords; peradventure in this respect only bocklands may be termed freehold lands and folkland villein lands; and yet time hath dealt very favourably with copyholders in this point of will, as well as in the point of service.

Section VIII

FOR, as I conjecture, in the *Saxons'* time, sure I am, in the *Normans'* time those copyholders were so far subject to the lords' will, that *seasonably and unseasonably the lords could at will resume and revoke their holdings from them,* as *Bracton* and *Fleta* both speak,* the lords upon the least occasion, sometimes without any colour or reason, only upon discontentment and malice, sometimes again upon some sudden fantastic humour, only to make evident to the world the height of their power and authority, would expel out of house and home their poor copyholders, leaving them helpless and remediless by any course of law and driving them to sue by way of petition.

* Bracton bk 4, treatise 3, ch. 9, no 5. Fleta bk 5, ch. 51.

Section IX

BUT now copyholders stand upon a sure ground, now they weigh not their lord's displeasure, they shake not at every sudden blast of wind, they eat, drink and sleep securely, only having a special care of the mainchance, viz. to perform carefully what duties and services soever their tenure doth exact and custom doth require; then let lord frown, the copyholder cares not, knowing himself safe and not within any danger, for if the lord's anger grow to expulsion, the law hath provided several weapons of remedy, for it is at his election either to sue a subpoena or an action of trespass against the lord. Time hath dealt very favourably with copyholders in divers respects.

Section XIV

THIS opinion of *Bracton* and *Fleta*, both consenting in one, that copyhold land is parcel of the lord's demesnes, wanteth not modern authority to second it, for 15 *Elizabeth* in the *Exchequer* I find it adjudged in the case of a common person, howsoever it is otherwise in the King's case, that if the lord of a manor granteth away *all his demesne lands*, the copyholds parcel of the manors pass by these general words; neither doth this want reason to confirm it, for in the time of *Henry* the 3 and *Edward* 2 when *Bracton* and *Fleta* lived, copyholders were accounted mere tenants at will, and therefore after a sort their lands reputed to continue still in the lord's hands, and now, though custom hath afforded them a surer foundation to build upon, yet the frank tenement at the common law resting in the lord, it can be no strange thing to place their lands under the rank of the lord's demesnes. But to deliver my mind more freely in this point, I think that howsoever according to the strict rules of law these copyholds are parcel of lords' demesnes, yet in propriety of speech (if propriety can be in impropriety) they are more aptly called the copyholders' demesnes, for though the frank tenement be in the lord by the common law, yet by the custom the inheritance abideth in the copyholders; and it is not denied, if a copyholder be impleaded in making title to his copyhold, he may justly plead, that *he is seised in his demesne*, with this addition, *according to the custom of the manor*. Therefore I conclude, that howsoever the common law valueth the title of copyholder, yet he hath such an interest confirmed unto him by custom, that the lord having no power to resume his lands, at your own pleasure they are (though improperly) called (yet peradventure truly accounted) the lord's demesnes, and that in the eye of the world, howsoever it be in the eye of the law, that these lands alone can properly challenge the name of the lord's demesnes (if the lands in the possession of inferior lords may properly challenge that name) which the lord reserveth in his own hands for the maintenance of his own board or table, be it his waste ground, his arable ground, his pasture ground, or his meadow, be it his copyhold which he hath by escheat, by forfeiture, or by purchase, or be it any part of his freehold land, of which I must speak a word by the way, not to prove that it is demesne, for manifest proofs are not wanting, but to shew you in what sense it is taken, and how far it extendeth.

Section XV

A freehold is taken in a double sense; either 'tis named a freehold in respect of the state of the land, or in respect of the state of the law.

Section XVI

IN respect of the state of the land, so copyholders may be freeholders; for any that hath any estate for his life, or any greater estate in any land whatsoever, may in this sense be termed a freeholder.

Section XVII

IN respect of the state of the law, and so it is opposed to copyholders, that what land soever is not copyhold is freehold, and in this sense I take throughout this discourse.

12. Oxfordshire Record Office, Dashwood Collection VIII. 34 Proposals of an Agreement for the Inclosing of the West End of the Town of Duns Tew by Joint Consent, March the 9th, 1651.

Imprimis 1. That there be a survey how much every man's land is in the West End and to be set out into such proportions equally according to the goodness of the land that it may be divided to every man according to lot.

2. That all commoning be divided equally according to yardlands, the Constable's Way and Mole-catching and all other waste grounds divided equally by the yardland.

3. That for all vicarage tithes there be as much meadow and pasture ground allowed as shall be worth twenty and six pounds a year according to the present estimation.

4. That in lieu of the tithe corn for every yardland there must be so much land set out as will arise out of greensward and the third part of the value out of arable.

5. That the fallow for this year is not to be ploughed.

6. That Sir John Reade is to discharge the three quarter of maslin yearly out of the tithe according to ancient custom upon Rogation Monday in the parsonage barn.

7. That on Thursday next Sir John Reade, Mr Coxeter, Thomas

Castle, George Raves, John Castle and William Paine is to go to Mr Halloway of Oxford, a counsellor, to perfect these articles.

13. FROM Bremhill Court Book. (British Museum, Additional Manuscript 37270), fols. 105v., 112, 114.

16th October 20 Elizabeth: ... It is condescended and agreed at this court between Sir Edward Baynton knight lord of the manor aforesaid and his tenants of the same that they shall inclose and make several their lands in the common fields of Foxham and Avon, and also to exchange one with another for the same. And the said tenants that so doth exchange and inclose doth agree to pay yearly to the said Sir Edward and Dame Anne now his wife one bushel of beans for every yardland they have during the lives of the said Sir Edward and Dame Anne and either of them. ...

30th September 21 Elizabeth: ... At this court all the tenants of Foxham are agreed to inclose and make several their lands in the fields of Foxham aforesaid according to the former order. ...

2nd October 21 Elizabeth: ... Item they present as follows, viz., It is ordered and agreed by the assent and consent of the lord of this manor and all the tenants of the same that no tenant shall put into the corn fields and mead at the breach thereof but two rother beasts or horse beasts for every acre, and they that have no land in the fields shall have no common there under penalty for each and every beast or horse put contrary to this order, Forfeit 10s.

And also it is ordered and agreed as follows, viz. That no tenant shall have going upon the lain sand fields but three sheep for every acre that he there hath and two sheep for every acre that he hath in the fallow clay fields, and that none of the lord's tenants wanting sheep of his own to stuff his ground in the fields shall put out his common there to any other than to the lord's tenants under penalty to each of them for each sheep, Forfeit 4d. ...

At this court John Hewes one of the freeholders of this manor is contented and agreed to exchange with the lord's customary tenants of this manor for so many acres as the lord's tenants hath in Cling Hill they shall have so many in number of the said John Hewes in the clay, and that he is licensed to inclose all his said land in Cling Hill as well all that was his own before this agreement as also that which he hath in exchange of the said tenants, upon this condition, that he the said John Hewes shall not challenge, have nor demand any manner of common within the said manor but utterly seclude himself and his heirs of all his common for all manner of cattle in the said manor for ever, and for affirmance hereof he hath to this order and agreement put his hand as appeareth in the old court book &c.

14. Public Record Office, Special Collections, Rentals and Surveys, General Series, portfolio 3, number 11. (*circa* 1546)

ALL and every the King's tenants and other persons having any part or portion by way of allotment in the Heath in this parish of Bedfont take warning in the King's Highness' name so to note, mark with stake, plough or otherwise every such part and portion within the same Heath according to the marking and measuring out thereof by the Book of Allotment as every person may from henceforth by their said marks, stakes or other notes certainly know the same, and that you the King's tenants and other persons for your better understanding and knowledge of your said parts and portions and in what places the same lieth do attend upon the 6 persons or some of them of the said parish that were appointed and sworn for the measuring and laying out of the premises the three several Sundays next ensuing, who having a true copy of the said Book of Allotment delivered unto them shall by the same upon your requests made to them in that behalf the said several days instruct and shew unto every of you your said parts and portions accordingly, and that you and every of you fail not thus to do for the certain and perfect understanding and knowledge of your said parts and portions upon pain of losing of the same.

Dated in London this 5th day of January

George Wright

AFTER hearty commendations, forsomuch as by the advice and counsel of Mr Chancellor and others of the King's commissioners order is taken that a true copy of the Book of Allotment shall be delivered unto you and that you or four of you shall give your attendance in the parish of Bedfont the three several Sundays next ensuing, to the intent by the same book you shall instruct and shew every person his part and portion appointed in the Heath and where the same lieth according to the said book. These shall be therefore to require you in the King's Majesty's name to give your attendance the said three several days accordingly and to go with the said persons that shall require to know where their parts and portions lieth to shew them the same, and further that you do cause this proclamation here inclosed to be read in the parish church of Bedfont every of the said several Sundays in the time of the most audience for the warning of the said persons to give their attendance upon you accordingly, praying you in any wise not to fail to be diligent in the accomplishment hereof as I may report the same unto the King's said commissioners and partly consider your pains to be taken in that behalf. At London this 5th day of January

Your loving friend
George Wright

To:—Henry Draper gentleman, John Townsende, John Kychell, Edward Weland and John Scherbert of the parish of Bedfont and to every of them.

The first Sunday	Richard Kempe	
Henry Draper	John Suyler	
John Townesend	John Sherebard younger	
John Lucas	George Downynge	
John Kechell	Robert Tyle	The 2nd day
Ambrose Frymley	Roger Kempe	Henry Draper gent.*
Robert Andrewe		Ambrose Frymley ⎫
Edward Walond		John Sherebard ⎬ 5d.

Sum of their expenses the said day at the Rose ⎱ 16d.

Roger Kempe
Robert Tyle
Thomas Sacheley
George Downynge
Sum of the exp. 21d.

The book of the heath
BEDFONT

To:—Henry Draper gentleman   John Kychell ⎫
   John Townsende   Edward Weland ⎬ This boke be
                          John Sherbert ⎭ delivered

Hatton Field

John Fraunces for lands in his own occupation	: 1 ac.	1
John Dowell for one house in the occupation of Eleanor Blythe	: 1½ ac.	2
Richard Broune for land in the tenure of John Apulbie	: 2 ac.	3
Richard Broune for land in the occupation of the said Apulbie	: ½ ac.	4
John Wadesberie for lands in his own tenure	: 1 ac. 1 rood	5
Anice Dowell for lands in her own occupation	: 1 rood	6
Richard Annshame for land in the occupation of John Grafton holden by indenture	: 1½ ac.	7
Robert Griffith for one cottage in the occupation of Richard Johnson	: 1 ac. 1 rood	8
Thomas Halfsaker for one house in his own hands	: 1 ac. 1 rood	9

* Manuscript damaged hereabouts.

Robert Griffith for lands in his own occupation	: 4½ ac.	10
Elizabeth Woode for land in the occupation of Henry Draper	: 3 rood	11
John Sherebard for one house in the occupation of Richard Hache	: 1 ac. 1 rood	12
Scherberts Furlong beginning with an acre and half		
The same John for lands in his own occupation	: 5½ ac.	13
Robert Goode for certain lands in common	: ½ rood	14
Henry Draper for lands in the occupation of Robert Andrew	: 1 ac. 3 rood	15
The churchwardens for lands in their own hands	: ½ rood	16
John Saler for lands in common	: ½ rood	17
John Kechall for lands in his own occupation	: 4½ ac.	18
John Sherebard for lands in the occupation of Richard Swallow	: 1½ ac.	19
Thomas Phillippes for lands in the occupation of Ambrose Frymley	: ½ ac.	20
John Lucas for lands in the occupation of John Hall	: 2 ac. 1 rood	21
Percival Brodebelt for the parsonage there	: 1 ac. 1 rood	22
Thomas Halfsaker for land in the occupation of John Gilder	: 1 ac. 1 rood	23
John Townsende for lands in his own tenure	: 3 ac.	24
Henry Tiesdale for land in the occupation of John Wadesbury	: ½ rood	25
John Bechame for lands in his own occupation	: 1 rood	26
Kemps Furlong beginning with half acre		
Richard Kempe for lands in his own occupation	: 3½ ac.	27
Robert Griffith for one cottage in the occupation of William Blancke	: 1 ac. 1 rood	28
Robert Tale for lands in his own occupation holden of Robert Downes	: 1 rood	29
Richard Clerke for land holden of the king by indenture	: ½ ac.	30
Robert Griffith for one house in the occupation of Thomas Katcheley	: 1 ac. 1 rood	31
John Dowell for lands in the occupation of Henry Draper	: 1 ac. 1 rood	32
Phyllis Kinge for lands in the occupation of John Geles	: 1 ac. ½ rood	33
Richard Broune for lands holden of the king by indenture in the tenure of John Apulbie	: 2½ ac.	34
Elizabeth Woode for lands in the occupation of Henry Draper	: 1 rood	35

Robert Downes for lands in the occupation of the said Henry Draper	: 9 ac. 1 rood	36
John Lucas for land in his own tenure	: 1 ac. $\frac{1}{2}$ rood	37
Margaret Tiesdale for land in the occupation of John Wadesburie	: 1 ac. 1 rood	38
Robert Griffith for lands in his own occupation in the right of his wife holden of Robert Downes	: 1 rood	39

The Vicars Furlong

Sir Richard Halyng vicar there for lands in his own tenure	: 3 roods	40
The heirs of John Stephens for one house in the occupation of John Foote	: 1 ac. 1 rood	41
Robert Griffith for one cottage in the occupation of Thomas Fielder	: 1 ac. 1 rood	42
Anice Kempe for lands in the occupation of Roger Kempe	: 1$\frac{1}{2}$ ac.	43
Miles Freyke for lands in the occupation of John Wedesborow	: 1 ac. 1 rood	44
John Kempe for lands in the occupation of Robert Griffith	: 3 ac.	45
Roger Clerke for lands in the tenure of Edward Weland	: 3$\frac{1}{2}$ ac.	46
George Downyng for one cottage holden of Robert Downes	: 1 ac.	47
John Childe for lands in the occupation of John Townsende	: 3 roods	48

77 acres 1 rood

Bromehill Field
which beginneth at the town's end besides the loam pits

John Sherebarde for one tenement in the occupation of Richard Hache	: 1 ac.	1
John Kichell for lands in his own occupation	: 4$\frac{1}{2}$ ac.	2
Thomas Halfsaker for one house in his own hands	: 1 ac.	3
Thomas Phillippes for land in the occupation of Ambrose Frymley	: $\frac{1}{2}$ ac.	4
John Dowell for one house in the occupation of Eleanor Blithe	: 1 ac.	5
The same John for lands in the occupation of Henry Draper	: 1 ac.	6
George Downyng for one cottage in his own hands holden of the said Robert Downes	: 1 ac. 1 rood	7
Margaret Tiesdale for land in the tenure of John Wedesbury	: 1 ac.	8

Elizabeth Woode for lands in the occupation of Henry Draper	: 1 rood	9
Phyllis Kinge for lands in the occupation of John Geles	: 1 ac. ½ rood	10
Anice Kempe for lands in the occupation of Roger Kempe	: 1½ ac.	11
John Fraunces for lands in his own occupation	: 1 ac.	12
Anice Dowell for land in her own occupation	: ½ rood	13
John Kempe for lands in the occupation of Robert Griffith	: 3 ac.	14
Richard Broune for land in the occupation of John Apulby	: 1 rood	15
Richard Clerke for land holden of the king by indenture	: ½ ac.	16
John Townsende for land in his own occupation	: 3 ac.	17
Richard Browne for land in the tenure of Apulbie	: 1 ac.	18
Roger Clerke for land	: 3 ac.	19
Elizabeth Woode for land in the occupation of Henry Draper and by him letten to Robert Andrew	: 2 ac. 1 rood	20
The heirs of John Stephens for one house in the occupation of John Foote	: 1 ac.	21
Robert Downes for land in the occupation of Henry Draper	: 8 ac.	22
Miles Freyke for land in the occupation of John Wedesborow	: 1 ac.	23
John Lucas for lands in the occupation of John Hall holden of Robert Downes	: 1 ac. 1 rood	24
Robert Tile for land in his own tenure holden of the said Robert Downes	: ½ rood	25
Richard Haling vicar there for land in his own tenure	: ½ ac.	26
Richard Anshame for land holden of the king by indenture	: 1 ac.	27
John Lucas for land in his own occupation	: 1 ac. ½ rood	28
Henry Draper for land in the occupation of Robert Andrew	: 1 ac. 3 roods	29
John Bechame for land in his own occupation	: ½ rood	30
John Wedesbury for land in his own occupation	: 1 ac.	31
Robert Griffith for lands in his own occupation holden of Robert Downes	: ½ rood	32
John Sherebarte for lands in the occupation of Richard Swalow	: 1½ ac.	33

Thomas Hassaker for lands in the occupation of
  John Gildes : 1 ac. 1 rood 34
Robert Griffith for lands in his own occupation : 4½ ac. 35
note he hath but 1½ ac. in the Long Furlong and the
residue in the triangle of 3 acres. Sollers triangle
John Soler for one acre and half in common : ½ rood 36
John Sherebart for lands in his own occupation : 4½ ac. 37
Richard Brown for land in the tenure of Apulbye
  holden of the king by indenture : 2 ac. 1 rood 38
Brodbelte Furlong
Percival Brodbelt for the parsonage there : 1 ac. 39
Richard Kempe for lands in his own occupation : 3½ ac. 40
Robert Griffith for one house in the occupation of
  Thomas Shacheley : 1 ac. 41
The same Robert for one cottage in the occupation
  of William Blancke : 1 ac. 42
The said Robert Griffith for one cottage in the
  occupation of Thomas Feilder : 1 ac. 43
The same Robert for one cottage in the occupation
  of Richard Johnson : 1 ac. 44
John Childe for land in the occupation of John
  Townsende : 1 ac. 45

68 acres 3 rood

Poundfurlong Field

John Sherebarde for lands in his own occupation : 4½ ac. 1
Roger Clerke for lands in the tenure of Edward
  Welande : 3 ac. 1 rood 2
Henry Draper for land in the occupation of Robert
  Andrew : 1½ ac. 3
Richard Broune for lands holden of the king by
  indenture : 2½ ac. 4
John Wadesbury for lands in his own hands : 1 ac. 1 rood 5
Elizabeth Woode for lands in the occupation of
  Henry Draper : ½ ac. 6
John Shereberte for land in the occupation of
  Richard Swallow : 1½ ac. 7
Anice Dowell for lands in her own tenure : ½ rood 8
John Childe for land in the occupation of John
  Townsende : 1 ac. 9
John Fraunces for lands in his own tenure : 1 rood 10
Richard Broune for lands in the occupation of John
  Apulbie : 1 rood 11

John Dowell for land in the occupation of Henry
Draper   : 1 ac.   12
Percival Brodbelte for the parsonage there   : 1 ac. 1 rood 13
Robert Goode for lands in common   :   ½ rood 14
Phyllis Kinge for lands in the occupation of John
Geles   : 1 ac.   15
Thomas Phillippes for lands in the occupation of
Ambrose Frymley   : ½ ac.   16
Robert Griffith for lands in his own tenure holden
of Robert Downes   :   ½ rood 17
note half acre left in that furlong for waste
Kemps Furlong
John Kempe for land in the occupation of Robert
Griffith   : 2½ ac.   18
Richard Broune for lands in the tenure of John
Apulbie   : 2½ ac.   19
Robert Griffith for one cottage in the occupation of
Thomas Feilder holden of Robert Downes   : 1 ac. 1 rood 20
Margaret Tiesdale for lands in the tenure of John
Wedesbury   : 1 ac. 1 rood 21
John Lucas for lands in his own occupation   : 1 ac.   22
Thomas Halfsaker for lands in the occupation of
John Geles   : 1 ac.   23
The heirs of John Stephens for one house in the
occupation of John Foote   : 1 ac. 1 rood 24
Anice Kempe for land in the occupation of Roger
Kempe   : 1 ac. 3 roods 25
John Lucas for land in the occupation of John Hall
holden of Robert Downes   : 1 ac.   26
John Sherebarte for one tenement in the occupation
of Richard Hache   : 1 ac. 1 rood 27
Thomas Halfsaker for one house in his own hands : 1 ac. 1 rood 28
Sir Richard Haling vicar there for lands in his own
tenure   :   3 roods 29
Elizabeth Woode for lands in the occupation of
Henry Draper and by him letten to Robert
Andrew   : 2 ac.   30
Robert Griffith for one house in the occupation of
Katcheley   : 1 ac. 1 rood 31
John Bechame for lands in his own occupation   :   ½ rood 32
John Townsende for lands in his own occupation : 4 ac.   33
John Kichell for land in his own occupation   : 3½ ac.   34
Richard Anshame for land holden of the king by
indenture   : 1½ ac.   35

Robert Griffith for one cottage in the occupation of Richard Johnson	: 1 ac. 1 rood	36
The churchwardens for lands in their own hands	: ½ rood	37
Richard Kempe for land in his own occupation	: 3½ ac.	38
John Dowell for one house in the occupation of Eleanor Blythe	: 1 ac.	39
Henry Tiesdale for lands in the occupation of John Wadesbury	: 1 ac. ½ rood	40
Miles Freyke for lands in the occupation of John Wadesbury	: 1 ac.	41
Robert Tile for land in his own occupation holden of Robert Downes:	: ½ rood	42
Robert Downes for land in the occupation of Henry Draper	: 9 ac.	43
George Downyng for one cottage in his own hands holden of the said Downes	: 1 ac. 1 rood	44
Robert Griffith for land in his own occupation in the right of his wife	: 4 ac. 1 rood	45
Richard Clerke for lands holden of the king	: ½ ac.	46
Robert Griffith for one cottage in the occupation of William Plancke in the right of Elizabeth his wife	: 1 ac. 1 rood	47

74 acres

15. Northampton Record Office, Wykes (Yarwell) Collection, no 544.

Copy

Articles of agreement made and agreed upon the 16th day of April 1596, 38th Queen Elizabeth, between Francis Tresham esquire, son and heir apparent of Sir Thomas Tresham knight, for and in the behalf of himself and the said Sir Thomas Tresham on the first part and John Reade esquire on the second part and Laurence Rogers citizen and ——— of London on the third part, William Gilbert on the fourth part, Edward Walpole the younger on the fifth part, Robert Moyer on the sixth part, William Lynnell on the seventh part, Thomas Walpole on the eighth part, Edward Walpole the elder on the ninth part, John Parker on the tenth part, Frances Welch widow and relict of Richard Welch deceased and William Welch their son on the eleventh part.

1.   Imprimis it is agreed that every of the said parties shall have in severalty to them and their several heirs all such lands and grounds in Haselbeech in the county of Northampton as now be set out and appointed to be had by every of them by a true survey of a true surveyor of his particulars with his part ratably of the common.

2.   And all feedings, commons, profits and commodities thereupon to be raised of any part within his own ground, town or field without any manner of molestation of any lord or any person.

3.   And that every of them shall make unto the other of them upon reasonable request such assurance thereof as shall be reasonably devised by both their counsellors at the charges of the lord.

4.   And the said Francis Tresham promiseth to all the said parties except the said Mr Reade that if the parts or portions to them severally allotted do not amount unto or do not contain so much ground as the residue of the grounds which the said parties before this time had in the other parts of the fields of Haselbeech aforesaid, and such portion for their commons as their rate doth amount unto according to their agreement set down in the beginning of the survey of the manor in Meas. Haselbeech aforesaid according to the true meaning thereof, that then the parties which shall lack the same shall have to him and his heirs assured by Mr Tresham double as much as he shall lack upon true and perfect notice of measurement at

any time given to the said Francis, provided always that Edward Waple junior hath two acres given him more than his one yardland.

5. And the said John Reade agreeth that he will sever, divide and fence the portion to him allotted from the residue of the premises, the highways or other freeholders' grounds, with sufficient ditches, quicksets and hedges before the end of two years now next ensuing and at all time hereafter shall maintain the same for a good defence between the grounds allotted to other of the said parties without any manner of timber of the freeholders.

6. And the said Francis Tresham shall and will in like manner sever, divide and fence the grounds allotted to all other of the said parties from the grounds which shall be left to be in the demesnes or occupation of him or the said Sir Thomas with sufficient ditches, hedges and quicksets before the end of the fences two years aforesaid and at all times thereafter shall maintain the same for a good defence between his said grounds and the grounds allotted to the said other parties as well lying upon highways as other freeholders' grounds.

7. And that every of the said parties shall and may hold and keep the premises to them severally allotted without paying any tithes or any other payments for tithes in field or town tithe thereupon to be arising at any time whilst the said Francis, his heirs, executors or administrators or assigns or any of them may have the lease of the parsonage at Haselbeech aforesaid or any sure course that law may advise us by our counsel, every of them to pay therefore such rent as according to the rent of 20s. a yardland yearly amounteth unto, at two several days, our pay-days, St Michael, and the ancient subsidies.

8. And all the said parties shall bear from time to time their equal parts of all such fifteenths or taxes and charges as shall be to be paid equally and indifferently by the inhabitants of tax Haselbeech aforesaid, either for the repair of the church, highways or otherwise, according to their portions being rated in the whole to forty yardlands, the parsonage yardland quarter being excepted, in which rate the aforesaid Mr Reade is to be rated according to his lands in Haselbeech, and every freeholder to have common in the lanes and highways according to his rate of land, and every officer to have authority to strain of the land within the field or town if any the inhabitants shall be behind unpaid. Nevertheless it is agreed if the counsel learned in the law of the said several parties shall like of the

title and tenure and be fully satisfied therein, then this agreement to stand, or else to be void.

Francis Tresham	Edward Waple	John Parker
John Reade	William Lynnyll	Edward Waple
William Gylbert	Robert Moier	

16. Northamptonshire Record Office, Wykes (Yarwell) Collection, no 16(4)

THIS INDENTURE of twelve parts made the twentieth day of August in the one and fortieth year of the reign of our Sovereign Lady Elizabeth by the grace of God of England, France and Ireland Queen Defender of the Faith &c. Between Sir Thomas Tresham of Rushton in the county of Northampton knight on the first part, John Read of Cottesbrook in the said county of Northampton esquire on the second part, William Gilbert of Haselbeech clerk in the said county of Northampton and Bridget his wife on the third part, William Lynnett otherwise called Lynnall of Haselbeech aforesaid yeoman and Agnes his wife on the fourth part, Edward Walpole the elder of Haselbeech aforesaid yeoman on the fifth part, Robert Mowyer of Welford in the county of Northampton aforesaid yeoman on the sixth part, Lawrence Rogers of the City of London yeoman and Beatrice his wife, daughter and heir of George Ward, on the seventh part, Thomas Elboroughe of Brixworth in the county of Northampton aforesaid yeoman and Frances his wife late the wife of Richard Welche and Isabel Welche sole daughter and heir of the said Richard Welche on the eighth part, John Parker of Haselbeech aforesaid yeoman on the ninth part, Thomas Walpole of Haselbeech aforesaid yeoman on the tenth part, Edward Walpole the younger of Haselbeech aforesaid yeoman and Amy his wife on the eleventh part, and Alexander Lovell of Guilsborough in the said county of Northampton yeoman and Agnes his wife, one of the daughters and heirs of Robert Jeneways deceased, on the twelfth part, and between every of them. WHEREAS the said parties to these presents be the day of the date hereof severally and lawfully seised of several estates of inheritance of and in divers lands and tenements and hereditaments within the town and fields of Haselbeech aforesaid amounting very nearly unto the whole content of the same town and fields and be agreed and do intend to make such conveyance that each part to these presents shall have as well the quantity of land which he hath lying dispersed within the said fields of Haselbeech laid together to be holden and enjoyed in severalty without intercommoning for ever hereafter as also divers messuages, closes, lands and parcels of ground in like manner to be holden to them and their heirs according to a description of the said town and fields appearing in a plot indented tripartite, whereof two of the same plots be annexed, the one unto that part of these presents which remaineth with the said Sir Thomas Tresham, and the other one unto one other part of these presents remaining with the said John Read; and the third part of the same plot is under the hands and seals of the said Sir Thomas Tresham, and of the said John Reade, and remaineth amongst and is delivered to go and be for ever to, for and amongst all other the parties to these presents, setting forth by the colours and names of the parties made therein and thereupon and otherwise each mans plot and quantity of ground together with his messuages to him appertaining and to be conveyed by the said agreement, AND WHEREAS the parties to these presents be further agreed as herein hereafter appeareth now to the intent of the same agreement may be effected and each party to these presents, their heirs and assigns and every of them may be assured to hold as well the plot to him assigned in severalty as all other things within the said town and fields according to the true meaning of these presents THEREFORE WITNESSETH this present indenture that it is agreed by and between all and every the parties to these presents for them and their several heirs and assigns that they and every of them at all times hereafter for ever (these presents or any act for further assurance, or any other matter or thing notwithstanding) shall and will do and perform all and every such suit and service as well in respect of residence as of tenure, and pay, bear and satisfy all such their rents and other sums of money as heretofore they or any of them have paid, or should have paid, due each to other if this present agreement or any conveyance thereupon had never been had or made for or in respect of their, or any of their lands, tenements or hereditaments in Haselbeech aforesaid either as service, chief rent, certainty, headsilver, landsilver or otherwise unto our Sovereign Lady the Queen's Majesty that now is, her heirs, successors, assigns, farmers or tenants to the fees called Winchester Fee and Berkhamstead Fee or by any of the parties to these presents to any other of them or to such or those whose estates they have in any manors, lands, tenements or hereditaments in Haselbeech aforesaid; and also pay and be chargeable to pay all and all manner of taxes and assessments for the fifteen provision, soldiers, poor or for any other matter or thing to be levied or assessed upon the inhabitants or landholders of or in Haselbeech aforesaid, according to such rate, proportion and quantity of land, as all and every the parties to these presents had before the making hereof THAT IS TO SAY the said Sir Thomas Tresham, his heirs and assigns after the rate of twenty four yards land and the said John Reade, his heirs

M

and assigns after the rate of seven yards land and an half, the said
William Gilbert and Bridget his wife during their lives and the life
of the longest liver of them and after for one year after the rate of
one yardland and a half, and the said Sir Thomas, his heirs and
assigns after their deceases and after the end of the said one year
for the said one yardland and an half or more than the said twenty four
yards land, and the said William Lynnell, his heirs and assigns after
the rate of one yardland and an half, and the said John Parker, his
heirs and assigns after the rate of three quarters of one yardland,
and the said Edward Walpole the younger, his heirs and assigns after
the rate of one yardland, and the said Robert Mowyer, his heirs
and assigns after the rate of one yardland, and the said Lawrence
Rogers and Beatrice his wife and the heirs and assigns of the said
Beatrice after the rate of one yardland, and the said Thomas
Elborough and Frances his wife and the said Isabel Welche, her
heirs and assigns after the rate of one yardland, and the said Thomas
Walpole, his heirs and assigns after the rate of one quarter of one
yardland, and the said Edward Walpole the elder, his heirs and
assigns after the rate of one quarter of one yardland, and the said
Alexander Lovell, his heirs and assigns after the rate of one yardland
and a quarter AND FURTHERMORE it is mutually agreed by and
between all the parties to these presents, their heirs and assigns that
the herbage of one way in the fields of Haselbeech aforesaid commonly called Naseby Way and of the passage of one way in the fields
of Haselbeech called Harborough Way from the town to the watering
place called Hallyewell or coming from Hallywell Spring appearing
in the said plot or description hereunto annexed as is afore said shall
be had, taken, used and enjoyed by all and every the parties to these
presents, their heirs and assigns according to the quantity of their
lands aforesaid, and the same way and all the other common and
highways in Haselbeech aforesaid be repaired and amended, and the
parties hereunto, their heirs and assigns for ever hereafter charged
and chargeable therewith according to their aforesaid quantity of their
land in Haselbeech aforesaid, other than such ways as be now open and
hereafter shall be made lanes, in which lanes every owner and occupier
of any land making any lane of any of the said now open ways shall
be charged with the repair of the same ways within the same lanes
AND THAT one spring in the fields of Haselbeech aforesaid called
or known by the name of Chawdwell Spring appearing in the said
description shall be kept open for ever to be used by all the inhabitants and landholders in Haselbeech aforesaid for watering of
their cattle and other necessary uses as heretofore it hath been And
that it shall and may be lawful to and for all and every the parties
to these presents their heirs and assigns, farmers and tenants of any

lands, tenements or hereditaments within the town and fields of Haselbeech aforesaid to dig for ever hereafter at all times seasonable and convenient and to have, take and carry away between Saint George's Day and Michaelmas Day yearly for ever hereafter for their necessary repair or new building of their or any of their houses, tenements or fence walls in Haselbeech aforesaid or any other necessary uses there stone and sand in the open stone pit and sand pit within the fields of Haselbeech aforesaid not breaking above one acre of ground about either of the said stone pit or sand pit and following the vein of stone and sand now opened until the same sand pit and stone pit or either of them shall be decayed, and then for their like use to break or dig in or near unto the same sand pit or stone pit and to have and take the same for their like uses as afore said for ever hereafter as is also afore said, and to have free passage as usually heretofore hath been accustomed and as in the same plot appeareth to and from the said stone pit it lying upon one furlong in Haselbeech aforesaid called Stone Pit Furlong and to and from the said sand pit lying in or near one way there called Harborough Way both appearing with the passages to and from the same in the said description hereunto annexed as is afore said. FOR THE TRUE performance and sure holding of the which agreement and all and every the parts, clauses, articles and contents thereof all and every the parties to these presents for each of them severally and for their own several heirs and assigns only do by these presents covenant each with other, their heirs and assigns IN WITNESS whereof the parties to these presents have hereunto interchangeably put their hands and seals the day and year first abovewritten.

Thomas Tresham   John Read   William Gilbert [seven marks] Sealed and subscribed by the within named Sir Thomas Tresham in the presence of Edward Read, George Vavasor, Robert Greene, George Bagshaw, George Levens.

This indenture delivered unto Lawrence Rogers by George Levens the 10th of January 1599 according to a letter of attorney hereunto annexed in the presence of, by me, John Flamested, George Bagshaw. This indenture sealed, subscribed and delivered unto the within-named Lawrence Rogers the 10th of January 1599 by the within-named William Gilbert, William Lynnell, Robert Mowyer, John Parker, Edward Walpole the elder, Edward Walpole the younger, Thomas Walpole and Alexander Lovell and Agnes his wife, also by Bridget wife to William Gilbert, Amy wife to Edward Walpole the younger and Agnes wife to William Lynnell, likewise sealed, subscribed and delivered by me John Read in the presence of John Flamested, George Levens, George Bagshaw.

17. Northamptonshire Record Office, Wykes (Yarwell) Collection, no 16(2).

TO ALL CHRISTIAN people to whom these present writings shall come Sir Thomas Tresham of Rushton in the county of Northampton knight sendeth greetings WHEREAS the said Sir Thomas Tresham for and in part of performance of an agreement specified and appearing in one deed indented of twelve parts bearing date the twentieth day of August last past, whereunto the said Sir Thomas Tresham and Lawrence Rogers of the city of London yeoman and Beatrice his wife daughter and heir of George Warde be two of the parts, and in one plot or description indented tripartite of the town and fields of Haselbeech in the said county of Northampton, two parts whereof be annexed unto the parts of the said deed indented of twelve parts, which remain with the said Sir Thomas Tresham and John Reade of Cottesbrook in the said county of Northampton esquire, Hath by his poll deed of feoffment bearing date with these presents and for the considerations therein appearing granted, enfeoffed and confirmed unto the said Lawrence Rogers and Beatrice his wife and unto the heirs of the said Beatrice divers messuages, lands, tenements and hereditaments within the town and fields of Haselbeech as by the same several deeds whereunto for further certainty relation be had may amongst other things therein contained more at large appear. NOW THIS present writing witnesseth and the said Sir Thomas Tresham for, and in further part of performance on his part of the said agreement in the said indenture of twelve parts specified, doth covenant and grant for him, his heirs, executors and assigns to and with the said Lawrence Rogers and Beatrice his wife, their heirs and assigns by these presents in manner and form following THAT IS TO SAY that he the said Lawrence Rogers and Beatrice his wife, their heirs and assigns, shall or may at all times hereafter lawfully, quietly and peaceably have, hold, occupy and enjoy the said messuages, lands, tenements and hereditaments to them the said Lawrence Rogers and Beatrice his wife and to the heirs of the said Beatrice by the said deed poll granted, enfeoffed and confirmed by the said Sir Thomas Tresham according to the true intent and meaning of the same deed indented of twelve parts without any lawful let, trouble, eviction or disturbance of or by the said Sir Thomas Tresham or his heirs or assigns or of or by any other person or persons which do, can or shall lawfully have or claim any estate, right, title, interest, use, charge or demand of, in or to the said messuages, lands, tenements and hereditaments whatsoever or any of them from, by or under the said Sir Thomas Tresham or his estate therein AND that the same premises may now be acquitted and discharged or otherwise from time to time at all times convenient after reasonable request shall be well and sufficiently saved and kept harmless of and from all bargains, grants, tithes, charges, troubles and encumbrances whatsoever heretofore had, made, committed, done or wittingly and willingly suffered by the said Sir Thomas Tresham or by his assent, consent, means or procurement (the rents, customs, duties, and services therefore to be due hereafter to the lord or lords of the fee or fees thereof only excepted and foreprised) AND further the said Sir Thomas Tresham doth further covenant and grant for him, his heirs, executors and administrators to and with the said Lawrence Rogers and Beatrice his wife, their heirs and assigns by these presents that he the said Sir Thomas Tresham and Dame Merill his wife and the heirs and assigns of the said Thomas Tresham and all and every other person and persons which do or shall lawfully claim or have any estate, right, title, use, interest or demand by, from or under the said Sir Thomas Tresham of, in, to or out of the said premises before mentioned to be granted and enfeoffed unto the said Lawrence Rogers and Beatrice his wife and the heirs of the said Beatrice except before excepted shall and will at all times hereafter for and during the space of ten years next ensuing the day of the date of these presents at the costs and charges in the law of the said Lawrence and Beatrice his wife, their heirs or assigns and within convenient time after reasonable request for that purpose to be made, make, do and execute and suffer to be made and executed all and every such further acts and devices in the law for the further and better assurance of the said premises unto the said Lawrence Rogers and Beatrice his wife and the heirs of the said Beatrice according to the true meaning of the aforementioned deed indented of twelve parts and of the said poll deed of feoffment and of these presents as by the said Lawrence Rogers or Beatrice his wife, their heirs or assigns, his, their or any of their counsel learned in the laws shall be reasonably devised or advised and required not extending to any bonds or covenants or comprehending therein any further warranty of the said premises than against the said Sir Thomas Tresham, his heirs and assigns and all others which do or shall claim by, from or under him. AND SO THAT the said Sir Thomas Tresham nor his heirs be not compelled thereby to travel for the making, suffering or executing of any of the said acts or devices above four miles from Rushton aforesaid if he or they be not restrained by superior authority to travel so far, which if there be then any such restraint then not to travel from the place whereunto he or they shall be restrained, anything before mentioned to the contrary notwithstanding. IN WITNESS whereof the said Sir Thomas Tresham unto these presents hath put his hand and seal. DATED the twelfth day of

November in the one and fortieth year of the reign of our Sovereign Lady Elizabeth by the grace of God of England, France and Ireland Queen Defender of the Faith &c.

Thomas Tresham

Sealed and subscribed by the within-named Sir Thomas Tresham in the presence of Edward Reade, George Vavasor, Robert Greene, George Levens, George Bagshaw.

Memorandum, that this deed was delivered by George Levens unto the within-named Lawrence Rogers by virtue of the letter attorney hereunto annexed in the presence of John Flamested, George Levens, George Bagshaw.

18. Northamptonshire Record Office, Wykes (Yarwell) Collection, no 16(3).

TO ALL CHRISTIAN people to whom this present writing shall come Sir Thomas Tresham of Rushton in the county of Northampton knight sendeth greeting. KNOW ye that the said Sir Thomas Tresham for and in part of the accomplishment of performance of an agreement specified and appearing in one deed indented of twelve parts whereunto the said Sir Thomas Tresham and Lawrence Rogers of the city of London yeoman and Beatrice his wife daughter and heir of George Warde be two of the parties, and in one plot or description indented tripartite of the town and fields of Haselbeech in the said county of Northampton, two parts whereof be annexed unto such parts of the said deed indented of twelve parts as do remain with the said Sir Thomas Tresham and John Reade of Cottesbrook in the said county of Northampton esquire, Hath granted, enfeoffed and confirmed and by these presents doth grant, enfeoff and confirm unto the said Lawrence Rogers and Beatrice his wife and to the heirs and assigns of the said Beatrice all the messuages, houses, lands, tenements and hereditaments which the said Sir Thomas Tresham hath or of right ought to have in Haselbeech aforesaid within the several plots or parcels of ground or otherwise appearing by the said plot or description or the table or any other thing appearing to appertain and belong or to be set out, assigned, allotted or allowed within the town or fields of Haselbeech aforesaid unto or for the said Lawrence Rogers TO HAVE AND TO HOLD all the said messuages, houses, lands, tenements and hereditaments so by the said plot appearing to appertain to the said Lawrence Rogers with all their and every of their appurtenances unto the said Lawrence Rogers and the said Beatrice his wife and the heirs of the said Beatrice for ever to the only proper use and behoof of the said Lawrence Rogers and of the said Beatrice his wife and the heirs of the said Beatrice for ever. AND THE SAID Sir Thomas Tresham and his heirs all and singular the said messuages, lands, tenements and hereditaments of the said Sir Thomas Tresham's in or by the said plots appearing to belong unto the said Lawrence Rogers and the said Beatrice his wife and unto the heirs of the said Beatrice against the said Sir Thomas Tresham, his heirs and assigns shall warrant and defend by these presents for evermore. IN WITNESS whereof the said Sir Thomas Tresham hath to these presents put his hand and seal DATED the twelfth day of November in the one and fortieth year of the reign of our Sovereign Lady Elizabeth by the grace of God of England, France and Ireland Queen Defender of the Faith &c.

Thomas Tresham

Memorandum, that seisin and possession was delivered the 10th of January in the year 1599 by George Levens attorney authorised by virtue of a letter of attorney unto him made from Sir Thomas Tresham knight of and in one half acre within the plot of the within named Lawrence Rogers and Beatrice his wife in Haselbeech of the lands of the said Sir Thomas in the name of all the lands of the same Sir Thomas within that plot contained allotted to the said Lawrence and Beatrice, which possession and seisin was so delivered after by the said attorney after he had by virtue aforesaid entered and taken possession himself in the presence of

George Bagshaw
William Gilbert

Sealed and subscribed in the presence of Edward Reade, George Vavasor, George Levens, Robert Greene, George Bagshaw.

19. Northamptonshire Record Office, Wykes (Yarwell) Collection, no 16(1).

BE IT KNOWN unto all men by these presents That I Sir Thomas Tresham of Rushton in the county of Northampton knight have constituted, ordained and appointed my well-beloved servant George Levens my true lawful attorney for me and in my stead and name and as by my deeds to deliver unto Lawrence Rogers of the city of London yeoman and Beatrice his wife daughter and heir of George Ward the three several writings hereunto annexed being all three of them by me sealed and subscribed and into the messuages, lands, tenements and hereditaments whereof the said Lawrence and Beatrice are by the purport of one of the said three writings hereunto annexed to be enfeoffed by me the said Sir Thomas Tresham for and in my stead and name or into any part or parcel of them or any of them in the name of the whole to enter and take possession and after such entry made or possession taken thereof or of any part or parcel thereof in the name of the whole full and peaceable possession and seisin thereof or of any part or parcel thereof in the name of the whole to give and deliver unto the said Lawrence and Beatrice or to their certain attorney in that behalf according to the form, force and effect of the said writing of feoffment ratifying, approving and allowing whatsoever my said attorney shall do for me concerning the premises or any of them as if I myself had done the same. IN witness whereof I the said Sir Thomas Tresham have hereunto put my hand and seal dated the twentieth and sixth day of November in the two and fortieth year of the reign of our Sovereign Lady Elizabeth by the grace of God Queen of England, France and Ireland Defender of the Faith &c.

Thomas Tresham

Sealed, subscribed and delivered in the presence of Edward Read, George Bagshaw, Robert Greene, George Vavasor.

20. FROM J. Aubrey, *Wiltshire. The Topographical Collections of John Aubrey, F.R.S., A.D. 1659–70*, ed. by J. E. Jackson, Devizes, 1862, p. 310.

To Robert Flower and John Lewes, These, at Rowde.

Whereas there hath been a general agreement by yourselves and all the tenants freeholders of the manor of Rowde, as likewise the parson there, for the inclosing of your common field, whereunto my Lord of Rutland by his steward and Mr Pewe his officer, and myself in the behalf of my son, have given our assent, since which time as well yourselves as the rest of the inhabitants there whom this concerneth have submitted yourselves to the judgment of four persons equally named to see that every one in this partition might respectively have what of right pertains unto him, who being now willing to do their best endeavour to this purpose, it is said that you two only, contrary to your former assents, do now intend to interrupt this work, the which if you shall persevere to do I presume you will be enforced to make good your former agreement, with your charge and trouble. I do therefore wish you for the avoiding of both, quickly to join with your neighbours in this work, the rather that I conceive you shall reap benefit by this inclosure as well as others. And I recommend you to God. From Stock this 20th of January 1619,

Your loving friend,
Anthony Hungerford

21. FROM J. Ritchie, *Reports of Cases decided by Francis Bacon in the High Court of Chancery (1617–1621)*, London 1932, pp. 183–7.

Cartwright *v.* Drope and others

Verulam, L.C.

1619

Tothill 110

At the date of the agreement next hereinafter mentioned Shackerley Marmion esquire was seised in fee of two third parts of the lordship of the manor of Aynho in the county of Northampton and Sir Paul Tracy knight of the other third part thereof. The demesnes of the manor consisted of about one hundred acres of inclosed land and 300 acres of uninclosed land in the west or lower part of the manor. The lords, copyholders, freeholders and tenants of the manor had common for their horses and cattle in the unenclosed land in both the lower and upper parts thereof. Among the freehold tenants of the manor was the corporation of Magdalen College, Oxford, which had let its land to one Edward Love. In 1611 the said S. Marmion, having occasion to raise money for the payment of his debts and redemption of rent-charges on his interest in the manor in favour of his younger brothers, sold parts of his demesnes to Thomas Drope, the parson of Aynho, and others. Thereupon an agreement under seal was entered into between the said S. Marmion, T. Drope and the other purchasers of parts of the demesnes, and several free-holders including the said college, by which it was agreed that, if it should be thought fit to inclose any part of the uninclosed land of the manor, then all the parties should assent thereto and should exchange their lands so that the lands of each of them might lie together and be held in severalty.

In 1615 Richard Cartwright esquire purchased from S. Marmion esquire and Sir P. Tracy knight their respective parts of the manor and thus became the lord thereof. The said R. Cartwright finding that he and the said purchasers and the other tenants were suffering great loss through injury to their cattle by reason of their all inter-commoning in the uninclosed fields of the manor, offered that, if according to the said agreement he might take into severalty and inclose his demesne pieces of the said fields, he would give up all common in these fields, and he suggested that the others owning parts of the said fields should do likewise. In July 1618 the new lord and the said purchasers, freeholders and tenants chose four persons to consider the convenience of the proposed inclosures and they reported in favour thereof.

A further agreement dated January 12, 1618, was then entered into between the said lord and the freeholders and tenants that all their lands in the west or lower fields of the manor should be forthwith surveyed and admeasured by two surveyors, and that then such proportionable parts of the said land should be allotted and set out to each of the parties to be held in severalty and inclosed as by the two surveyors and the four persons aforesaid or the greater part of these six persons should be thought fit.

These six persons allotted and set out to each of the parties one or more plots of land in the west or lower fields as being answerable in quantity and quality to his lands which before lay dispersedly therein. T. Drope, R. Love the administrator of E. Love now deceased, and R. Staunton, another tenant, refused to accept the plots set out to them, or to assent to the acceptance by R. Cartwright esquire of the plots allotted to him, and they persuaded other freeholders and tenants also to refuse to do so.

On May 11, 1618, R. Cartwright esquire accordingly exhibited his bill in Chancery against T. Drope and the other freeholders and tenants of the manor for the performance of the said agreements.

On June 22, 1619, Verulam, L.C., in accordance with an offer made by the plaintiff ordered that a commission should be awarded to the aforesaid six persons and two other persons to be named by the Master of the Rolls to reconcile all differences concerning the plots if they could, or otherwise to certify their opinion as to the inclosure to the Court.

On October 19, 1619, the matter again came before his Lordship, when it appeared from the certificate of the commissioners and the book of plots subscribed by them that they in substance approved the plots previously set out, but that the parson objected that if the inclosure should stand his yearly living would be diminished, and the college objected that the land laid out for them was not of equal value to their present lands; and his Lordship then referred the matter to Masters Moore and Rich to consider and report. The Masters reported that the parson was well recompensed by the allotment of the commissioners for the plaintiff's own tithes of his demesnes, they having allotted him £48 in lieu thereof, whereas before the plaintiff's tithes amounted to only £28 a year; and that the college and Love their tenant would receive good recompense, £30 a year being assured for the plots allotted to them in lieu of their own land which was not worth above £12 a year.

On November 9, 1619, the cause again came before his Lordship who, besides ordering and decreeing that the plaintiff should pay to the parson and his successors over and above the said £48, the sum of £12 to make up in the whole £60 a year for all manner of tithes of the said demesnes.

Ordered and *Decreed* that from thenceforth all the plots as they were then set out by the commissioners and appearing particularly by the book of plots subscribed by them should stand and be enjoyed in severalty for each accordingly by the plaintiff, his heirs and assigns, by the college and their successors, by the parson and his successors, and by every of the other defendants according to their several estates respectively as was intended by the commissioners' certificate and book of plots both which were to stand and be performed in all parts by all the parties according to the true intent and meaning thereof; and that the book of plots should be inrolled in the Court to remain upon record together with the decree.

Tirwhitt *v.* Pharrow and others
Bacon, L.K.
1617
Tothill 110

The lord and freehold tenants of a manor entered into an agreement for mutual exchanges of portions of their lands and for the inclosure of their several lands. It appeared that the carrying out of the agreement would greatly increase the value of the lands and would benefit not only the parties but the whole neighbourhood. On the faith of the agreement the lord sold the manor for an enhanced price, took a lease thereof from the purchaser at an enhanced rent, bound himself by covenants and bonds to the purchaser to cause the agreement to be carried out, and incurred expenses in plotting and inclosing the lands. The tenants refused to perform the agreement and interfered with the work of inclosure. In a suit by the lord against the tenants for relief: *Held*, that the defendants should suffer the plaintiff to inclose the manor according to the agreement without disturbance, and that he and they should severally have and enjoy the lands allotted to them.

Westminster (Dean) and others *v.* Eldridge and others
Verulam, L.C.
1617–1620
Tothill 110

An agreement between the lord of a manor and certain of the freehold and copyhold tenants, for the inclosure and enjoyment in severalty by the respective parties of portions of the common pasture and wood grounds of the manor, was confirmed by the Court and enforced against the other tenants and occupants on its appearing that it was for the general benefit of all the inhabitants of the manor.

22. Birmingham Library Manuscript no 505454.

Hampton Lovett

This bill indented made the 23rd day of September in the 3rd year of the reign of our Sovereign Lord King Edward the 6th &c.

We do present that Henry Jones of the said parish hath there inclosed about 2 acres of land out of the common which hath been common out of mind. Further we inclose every one of us somewhat to our discommodity both of poor and rich and no man discontent therewith and further we have not to present to you.

Henry Jones, William Pooler, George Tylor, Thomas Poler, Thomas Parsons and John Saunders constable.

The Parish of Saint Andrew in Droitwich

The presentment of John Alynson, Henry Cole, John Paynter and William Smythe.

Imprimis we do present upon our oaths that one Gilbert Wheeler gentleman enclosed a leasow called the Hide containing 20 acres which was common about 10 years past with the fields there.

Item one Edward Newporte gentleman enclosed a certain leasow containing 6 acres called Standie Croft about 30 years past which was common as before.

Item one William Dethyke gentleman enclosed a certain leasow containing 9 acres called Casses Croft about 40 years past which was common as before.

Item William Dethike and Gilbert Dethyk gentlemen inclosed a certain lane shooting down to Baners Moor about one year past, was wont to be common time out of mind.

Item John Trymnel inclosed a certain leasow containing 2 acres in Suckenell about 10 years past which was common as before.

Item William Penie inclosed a lane called Leadsmith Lane about 2 years past, was common time out of mind.

Item one Thomas Barrett inclosed a certain parcel of the King's highway about one year past to enlarge his garden ground which was common as before.

Item John Butler the younger gentleman and Roger Mole inclosed a certain highway leading to Broad Meadow about 14 years past which was wont to be common time out of mind.

The Parish of Saint Peter's in Droitwich

The presentment of Simon Dawks, George Harries, Thomas Caswell, Laurence Olyver and Walter Willes.

Imprimis we present upon our oaths that one John Whythe gentleman hath inclosed a certain highway containing 3 acres leading about the farm there called the farm of Saint Peter's about 10 years last past which was wont to be common time out of mind.

Item one William Byrt keepeth a leasow several about 10 years past which was wont to be common every third year from Michaelmas to Candlemas.

Item one Roger Jeffreys hath taken in a common and set pales about the same to the great annoyance of the inhabitants there which has been common time out of mind.

Item Roger Smythe hath inclosed a certain parcel of the highway leading to the Seales there which was wont to be common time out of mind.

Item Thomas Barrett a certain parcel of highway which leadeth to Worcester which was common time out of mind.

Item they say that the said John Withe hath inclosed a certain parcel of ground containing one acre about 20 years past which was wont to be common time out of mind.

The Parish of Doverhill

The presentment of John Baillie, John Hill, William Hancoke, Thomas Hemyng and William Parkes. First we do present that the tenants of Wychbold lordship have inclosed by their whole agreement among themselves and with the lord's assent every man for his portion 5 or 6 acres of land which should be common always after harvest and thus they do for the only maintenance of their cattle and better increase of their husbandry.

Item we do present that within the said lordship there is one cottage decayed about 27 years past by one Walter Hayford to the which belonged 3 acres of land and acre and a half of meadow, the rent thereof 13s. 4d., which land is now Elizabeth Hayford's widow and now in the tenure of William Hancoke.

Item we do present that Mr Wall, lord of Inmey hath inclosed one whole 'oodde marke' in Inmey and also taken away 40 acres of land and meadow from a tenement that one Thomas Shreve now dwelleth in and converteth the same to his own use.

Item we do present that in Inmey township is one tenement called Thorbonds with a ploughland belonging to the same is decayed about a year since by the said Mr Wall and no man dwelleth therein and hath the same in his own hands and also another tenement late in the tenure of Thomas Leks with 5 acres thereunto belonging is decayed by the said Mr Wall.

23. Shakespeare's Birthplace, Manorial Documents and Court Rolls, Great Alne. (*circa* 1552)

A Declaration of all the Inclosures made within the lordship of Raunde Alne what time and by whom and upon what considerations they were taken in and inclosed, exhibited by Richard Smythe, Roger Grene, John Smythe, George Jenks, Thomas Grene, John Hemmyng, John Parker, John Mace, Richard Mace, William Grene.

First we say and affirm that about forty years past or more the whole lordship of Alne did lie open and none enclosure made within the said lordship, at which time all the tenants and inhabitants thereof were neither able to breed any cattle nor to maintain their teams for lack of some severalty, by reason whereof they were for the most part poor and needy persons, scant able to pay their rents, whereupon they all made suit to the abbot of Winchcombe being then lord thereof that every tenant might inclose certain land out of common fields according to their quantity, who at the next court following condescended that sundry enclosures should be made as hereafter ensueth.

Imprimis the farmer by the abbot's licence and consent of all the tenants did enclose of the lord's demesnes these parcels following: a piece of ground called the Lenche, another called Apulton, a piece called the Cleif and another called Newland and Stocking, all which hath been kept several and so enjoyed ever since, in recompense whereof every tenant had licence to enclose certain acres according to the quantity of his land which they took, and the parson 2 closes, and in further recompense thereof the said abbot licensed all the said tenants with the parson for their only benefit and commodity to enclose and keep several a parcel of ground called Broad Yard, which they have enjoyed ever since and yet do, the lord and his farmer clearly exempted.

Item Sir Robert Throkmorton knight about the same time by the abbot's licence and consent of all the tenants did enclose a parcel of ground called the Gowars, all which was the lord's demesnes except 3 acres, for which he agreed with the tenant thereof who at this present is contented therewith and ever hath been since the enclosure.

Item a parcel of ground called Ruddyngs and another parcel called Welcome were enclosed about 40 years past by the abbot's licence and consent of all the tenants, in recompense whereof the tenant thereof forsook his common in all the other fields.

And further we say that Sir George Throkmorton knight since he was farmer of the said lordship, upon a composition and agreement between him and all the tenants and inhabitants within the said lordship made by divers honest and substantial men in these parties, to his no little cost and charge did enclose and set with quickset hedge and ditch the whole lordship with all arable land, meadow, pasture and commons to the same belonging from all other towns and fields thereunto adjoining, to the great profit, commodity and advantage of all the tenants and inhabitants thereof, in consideration whereof and in recompense of all his common within all the fields and commons of the said lordship for four hundred sheep and three score cattle which the farmer had kept and might keep within the said fields and commons, hath withdrawn from us and other the tenants and inhabitants aforesaid the common in certain parcels of ground called Rottam, Alysam, the Moors, and Briars Furlong, which were enclosed within one hedge in the abbot's time, and ever hath kept several from Candlemas to Lammas. And for further recompense the said Sir George did enclose a parcel of the demesnes called Hoke Furlong and Broke Meadow containing by estimation 18 or 19 acres, the meadow whereof was yearly destroyed before the said inclosures and never common but from Lammas to Candlemas. Also the said Sir George in consideration and for recompense of his charges and common aforesaid upon the said agreement did enclose 2 pieces of common, the one called Ashbarrow, whereupon he hath made a warren of conies and builded a lodge, and the other is called the Nether Wood, which lieth open and common as before.

Item a parcel of ground called the Breach containing 3 acres was appointed by the consent of all the tenants to Richard Smythe, one of the tenants, notwithstanding it lieth open and common as before.

And whereas certain parcels of ground lying at the Woodhouse called Hasdeyns, Standhyll and Newland be supposed to be Lammas common, they have been enclosed time out of mind and never common, as we have heard reported by our forefathers.

And where three ploughs are supposed to be decayed within the said lordship, one at the farm and 2 at the Woodhouse, the farmer keepeth at this present 12 oxen and tilleth as much as for his commodity and benefit he thinketh meet. And the land at the Woodhouse is divided into five parts, notwithstanding 3 yardland is still in tillage, which is as much as ever was tilled, so that neither house nor plough is decayed but divers newly builded and all the tenants as well or better able to live as before the enclosures and the lordship enriched since in old.

24. FROM I. S. Leadam, *The Domesday of Inclosures* (2 vols.), London 1897, vol. ii, pp. 485–9. Earl Spencer's Manuscripts (1519?)

In most humble wise sheweth unto your grace your daily orator John Spencer of Wormleighton in the county of Warwick, that where one Sir Simon Mountford knight was seised of the manor of Wormleighton aforesaid, and so seised was attainted for treason done against the noble prince King Henry VII by reason whereof the said manor with all other lands and tenements which were the said Simon's were forfeit to his grace, and he being thereof seised by his letters patents granted the said manor of Wormleighton to one William Cope then being cofferer to his grace to have to him, his heirs and assigns for ever paying yearly therefore to the king and to his heirs yearly 20 marks, which was then but of the value of £8, and so the rent was increased to the king by the said William when he inclosed the said manor to 20 marks a year, and so duly paid yearly, and the same William Cope afore the time of inclosure purchased of the mesne lords within the same lordship all the rest of the lands and tenements within the said lordship. And so the said William Cope inclosed the same lordship of Wormleighton long time before the said John Spencer bought the said lordship of the said William Cope to his great cost and charge which hath cost him to the said William and his executors 20 hundred pounds, whereupon he made him a dwelling place where he had none to inhabit himself in his country where he was born, for at Hodnell where he dwelt before he had it no longer but during the nonage of his uncle's son which now there dwelleth and hath done these 3 years, and so this 3 years the said John Spencer hath been building in Wormleighton to his great cost and charge.

And first in building and maintaining of the church and bought all ornaments, as cross, books, cope, vestments, chalices and censors, for all the church gear that was within the church at the time when husbandmen were there inhabited was not worth £6, for they had never service by note, for they were so poor and lived so poorly that they had no books to sing service on in the church. And where they never had but one priest, I have had and intend to have 2 or 3. And also he hath builded and inhabited 4 houses, and men, women and children dwelling in them. And so, what with his own house and the other 4 houses, there is within 20 persons as much people as was in the town before. And where there is no wood nor timber growing within 12 or 14 miles of the same lordship, the said John Spencer hath there set trees and sown acorns for timber and wood, and double diked and set with all manner of wood both in the hedgerows and also betwixt the hedges adjoining to the old hedges that William Cope made before in the said lordship, whereupon now groweth much wood which is already grown to the profit of all them that should dwell in the said lordship as also to the country adjoining thereunto, for in those parts there is no wood, so that the poor men of the country are fain to burn the straw that their cattle should live by, therefore it were a great loss to destroy those hedges, for it is a greater commodity than either corn or grass in those parts, for they were set to the most increase of wood that might be devised at the great cost and charge of the said John Spencer, as first in purchasing, building, hedging and ditching of the same, which hath been to him a marvellous charge above all men and most loss shall have if ye be not good and gracious lord to him in the same, for he hath none other pasture left him now in his country but the same, which if now should be put in tillage and none of that reserved that were tillage for pasture several reserved for his cattle, it should be to his utter undoing, for his living is and hath been by the breed of cattle in his pastures, for he is neither buyer nor seller in common markets as other graziers be, but liveth by his own breed of the same pastures and sold it when fat to the city of London and other places yearly as good cheap in all these 5 or 6 years past as he did in other years when they were best cheap within 2s. in a beast and 2d. in a sheep, and he hath bred and fed within the said lordship, which was never good for corn, as the country will testify, more cattle this 6 years than was bred in the lordship when the town was inhabit in 20 years afore or shall be in 20 years after it shall be inhabited.

(1522?)

In most humble wise sheweth unto your grace John Spencer of Wormleighton in the county of Warwick, beseecheth your grace in the way of charity, that he put not his land all in tillage in so short space as your grace have given injunction, which is by Candlemas next, and also to put down his hedges and ditches by the same day, which he cannot do in so short space to follow the injunction but to his undoing, for he shall destroy all his cattle that is going on the same ground for lack of meat, for if he should sell his cattle now in the dead time of winter, he should lose and sell it for half the money that it is worth, for he hath no manner of fat cattle now left him at this time but his breed. And to put down his hedges that be now ready grown, which be now 20 years old, which be now grown full of all manner of wood, to great profit and one of the greatest commodity in that country, above corn or grass, and also to the great profit of the tenants that shall inhabit within the said lordship, for there is very little wood growing within 14 mile of the same. And for that

N

wood is one of the greatest commodities in those parts, the said John
Spencer did set and double ditched and double hedged and set it
with wood as well betwixt the ditches as also in the hedges to his
great cost and charge, which if now should be thrown down, should
not be only a great loss to the said John Spencer, but also to the
country and also to the tenants that shall inhabit the same, for there
is none other intercommoners within the said lordship, but only the
lord and the tenants of the same. And if the hedges were thrown
down, it should cause much variance betwixt the tenants of the same
lordship and towns adjoining thereunto which have no right of common there. Therefore the said John Spencer beseecheth your grace
that the hedges may stand unto such time as your grace may have
due proof whether it be to a more commodity and common weal for
the country there that the said hedges to stand or to be thrown
down, and also to have a reasonable time to put the land in tillage,
that is, the one half betwixt this and Easter, and to make the one half
of the housing betwixt this and Michaelmas, and the other half of
the land to be put in tillage by Easter come twelve month. And to all
as afore said the said John Spencer is content to follow and perform
as your grace shall appoint him, trusting that your grace will consider
him above all other insomuch as he never inclosed it, and bought it
of a high price as William Cope improved it, and also hath been
at great cost with the church, which he found greatly in decay, and
also builded him a manor place where was none before but a sorry
thatched house, to his great cost and charge, wherein he now dwelleth
with little lack of 60 persons, and that the land be not all put in
tillage, but some to be reserved for certain cattle for the maintenance of
his house, and he shall daily pray for the preservation of your noble
grace.

25. Public Record Office, Star Chamber, James, bundle 16, no
13, membrane 2.

Sworn 8 February in the fifth year of King James—William Mills.

The answer of Sir Thomas Humfrey knight defendant to the Information of Sir Henry Hobart his Majesty's attorney-general.

The advantage of exceptions to the incertainties and insufficiencies
of the said Information to this defendant now and at all times hereafter
saved to so much thereof as toucheth and concerneth this defendant
and is material to him to make answer unto and for the better satis-
faction of this honourable court herein this defendant saith, that he
at the time of the exhibiting of the said Information was and yet is
lawfully seised of an estate of inheritance as he taketh it of and in

the said manor of Swepstone and Nethercote in the said county of Leicester in the Information mentioned and so hath been thereof seised for these seven and twenty years now last past or thereabouts and this defendant saith, that he minding to make his mansion house and dwelling in and upon the premises being his only means of livelihood and having no house wherein to dwell did above six and twenty years last past take into his own hands and occupation two tenements and eighty acres of land or thereabouts to the said tenements belonging in the town of Swepstone, the one of which then was in the possession of one William Dudley and the other of one Arnold Kerk being tenants at sufferance to this defendant of the said tenements and lands and did of the said tenements make himself a dwelling-house and kept the same lands in his hands for the maintenance of the said house and hath ever since dwelled in the same house as his only place of habitation and thereupon hath kept hospitality for the maintenance of thirty people continually or thereabouts, being a far greater number than ever was maintained thereupon by the said Kerk and Dudley during their holding the same, and howbeit the said Dudley and Kerk had no estate at all in the said tenements but at the will of this defendant, yet this defendant did allow the said Dudley eight pounds the year so long as he lived, being a sole man and living with his own son being this defendant's tenant of another tenement in Swepstone aforesaid, and did allow the said Kerk another house and lands in the said town of Swepstone worth twelve pounds the year during the life of the wife of the said Kerk who was tenant there before marriage and upon her death gave him thirty pounds, the said Kerk then intending to dwell upon a freehold of his own worth five hundred pound. And this defendant further saith, that about the same time one Henry Gillatt being tenant at sufferance of one tenement and six and twenty acres or thereabouts thereunto belonging in Swepstone aforesaid, being old and impotent and diseased and not able to manure the said land, did give up the possession thereof to this defendant, who did occupy it together with the said eighty acres as a demesne to his said dwelling-house, which this defendant ever since hath used for hospitality and toward the maintenance of his house and did suffer the said Gillatt to dwell in the said house during his life rent free and to hold and enjoy a close of this defendant's in Swepstone aforesaid worth four pounds ten shillings the year rent free during his life. And this defendant saith, that about the same time one James Heys being tenant at sufferance to this defendant of another tenement and about six and twenty acres in Swepstone aforesaid, at the desire of the said James this defendant placed him in another better living in the said town and did let the said house wherein the said James formerly dwelt and all buildings thereto

belonging with lands to the value of twenty nobles the year to one
Thomas Bickley who keeps an inn in the said house to the great commodity and convenience of those that travel those parts and for the
good and benefit of those that come to the coalmines within one mile
thereof and doth keep up the said housing in good reparation and
maintain a greater number of people in his said house than were before. And this defendant further saith, that one Robert Fenton being
tenant at sufferance to this defendant of another tenement and about
six and twenty acres of land thereunto belonging in Swepstone aforesaid, he this defendant about the time aforesaid did at the request of
the said Robert, being unable to manure the said land, remove him
from the said tenement to a cottage in the said town of Swepstone
which had no land lying unto it and did lay thereunto so much land
in Swepstone aforesaid as is yearly worth to be let seven pound the
year, for which this defendant hath only ten shillings rent, and to
the said tenement from which he so removed the said Robert Fenton
at his own desire as is afore said, this defendant did lay fourteen acres
of land and did demise the same to one Thomas Borrowes who
dwelleth thereon and liveth very well in the same. And for and concerning the depopulations, decays and ruins of farms, tenements and
houses of husbandry by the said informations supposed to be done
by this defendant in the town of Nethercote in the Information mentioned, this defendant saith, that he at the time of the Information
exhibited was and yet is seised of an estate of inheritance of and
in the said manor of Nethercote and so has been seised for the space
of seven and twenty years last past, since which time one tenement
only has been severed from the land therewith used being about the
quantity of six and thirty acres, which tenement is the manor house
of the said manor of Nethercote and has been and is kept up in fit
and due reparations and is now inhabited by one Henry Biddle that
lives very well therein and has land laid unto it worth twenty nobles
the year being now occupied therewith. As for the other tenement
in Nethercote aforesaid by the said Information supposed to be ruin-
ated, depopulated and decayed having about six and thirty acres of
land thereunto belonging, this defendant saith, that the said tenement
was void and not inhabited at the time this defendant came to the said
land, which tenement is now also kept up in fit and due reparations
and is now in lease for divers years yet to come to one Henry
Flambstone that lives well and in good sort thereon, having twenty
acres of ground or thereabouts laid unto it. And this defendant saith,
that since his coming to the said towns and above twenty years past
he hath erected one farm anew in Swepstone and has laid thereunto
one hundred and twenty acres of land or thereabouts which were in
the hands of the said Gillatt, Hays and Fenton in small quantities not

able to maintain several families and has made thereof a good and tenantable farm which this defendant demised to one Roger Ortone. And this defendant added to another tenement in the said town that had under twenty acres belonging thereunto the quantity of fifty acres lying in the said towns wherein the said James Heys now dwelleth and occupieth the said land and hath also lately laid to three tenements in Swepstone aforesaid from which the land was taken away an hundred acres of land in Swepstone aforesaid. And this defendant further saith, that whereas at his first coming to the said town of Nethercote none of the tenants or inhabitants there had an estate in their lands they then occupied, this defendant hath demised all the said lands in the said town to divers tenants being seven in number for the rent of eight pounds the year or thereabouts during the lives of the tenants thereof, the said lands being worth two hundred mark the year at the least. And this defendant saith, that at his coming to the said towns there were in the said towns only two inhabitants rated in the King's Book, the one at twenty shillings land, the other at three pounds goods, whereas now there are in the said towns six inhabitants every one twenty shillings the year in land and one at three pounds in goods, and this defendant at twenty pounds land. And saith further that there be more families now in the said towns than there were when this defendant came to the said towns and more people maintained by three score at the least than there were then and in good sort and quality and more sufficient for the service of the common wealth. And for and concerning any conversion of arable land into pasture by this defendant in the said town of Swepstone this defendant saith, that he hath converted from pasture to tillage within the said town of Swepstone as much pasture ground as he hath there converted from tillage to pasture, which he hath done for the better husbanding of the said ground according to the course of husbandry of the said country, other than so much as he hath lawfully done as he thinketh for the provision of his house, and doth not decay the number of acres of arable and tillage in the said town but upholdeth the quantity of arable land yearly according as hath been long time used in the said town. And as for and concerning any conversion by him supposed to be made in the said town of Nethercote this defendant saith, that he never had any of the said lands in his hands this sixteen years but hath demised them to tenants for lives as aforesaid who use the same in tillage at this day as usually heretofore they were. And this defendant for further full plain and direct answer to the said Information saith, that to all other the supposed depopulations, pullings down and letting to decay of houses, farms, tenements, buildings, conversions of arable land into pasture, stopping up of highways, and other offences and misdemeanours wherewith this defendant is in any way by the said Information charged and which are and be examinable in this honourable court that he is not thereof guilty in such manner and form as in the said Information they are and be alleged against him, all which this defendant is ready to aver and prove as this honourable court shall award and doth in all humbleness submit himself to the censure of this honourable court and hath endeavoured to rectify anything that was amiss and is willing to do what shall stand with the pleasure of this honourable court to which he submitteth himself and craveth the benefit and allowance of the general pardon in Parliament made since the said supposed offence and doth aver that the said matters in the said Information mentioned are none of the offences nor this defendant any of the persons excepted in the said pardon, and humbly prayeth to be dismissed out of this honourable court with his reasonable cost and charge in this behalf by him sustained.

James Whitelocke

26. Public Record Office, State Papers, Domestic, Charles I, vol. 499, no 10.

Depopulation—Mr Hungerford and Mr Southby

THAT upon the commission of enquiry after depopulation, the Lord Archbishop of Canterbury and other the commissioners, at the solicitation of Thomas Hussey gentleman, did direct a letter in nature of a commission to certain persons within the county of Wiltshire to certify what number of acres in South Marston in the parish of Highworth were converted from arable to pasture and what number of ploughs were laid down &c.

Whereupon the Archdeacon with two others did return certificate to the Lord Archbishop &c.

Upon this certificate, Mr Anthony Hungerford, Mr Southby with 15 others were convented before his Grace and the other commissioners at the Council board, where, being charged with conversion, Mr Anthony Hungerford and Mr Southby, with some others, did aver that they had made no conversion other than they had when they came to be owners thereof.

His Grace said that they were to look no further than to the owners, and certificate was returned that so many acres were converted and so may ploughs let down.

They alleged that this certificate was false and made without their privity, and therefore Mr Hungerford in the behalf of the rest did desire that they might not be judged upon that certificate, but that they might have the like favour as Mr Hussey had, to have letters of the same nature directed to other commissioners, or a commission if it might be granted, to examine upon oath, whereby the truth might better appear.

His Grace replied to Mr Hungerford, 'Since you desire it and are so earnest for it, you shall not have it.'

They did offer to make proof that since the conversion there were more habitations of men of ability and fewer poor, and that whereas the King had before 4 or 5 soldiers of the trained band, he now had 9 there; that the impropriation was much better to be let.

His Grace said to the rest of the lords, 'We must deal with these gentlemen as with those of Tedbury, to take £150 fine and to lay open the inclosures'.

Which they refusing to do, they were threatened with an information to be brought against them in the Star Chamber, and accordingly were within a short time after by the said Mr Hussey served with subpoenas at Mr Attorney his suit in the Star Chamber, and this, as Mr Hussey told Mr Hungerford, was done by my Lord Archbishop his command.

27. British Museum, Cottonian Manuscripts, Titus F. iv, ff 322–3 July 5, 1607. *A Consideration of the Cause in Question before the Lords touching Depopulation.*

In redress of these offences. Inclosure, converting of arable.

Depopulation made the pretended cause of this last tumult. 2 things may fall into consideration

1. Whether the time be fit to give remedy, when such encouragement may move the people to seek redress by the like outrage, and therefore in Edward the sixth his time the remedy was not pursued until two years after the rebellion of Kett.

2. Whether these pretended be truly inconvenient and therefore fit to consider what just reason may be alleged for

I. *Inclosures* which are

1. *Security of state from*
   i Foreign invaders who cannot so easily march, spoil and foray in an enclosed country as a champion.
   ii *Domestic commotions* which will be prevented when their false pretences (inclosures) which they use to stir up the mob are taken away.

2. *Increase of wealth and people proved*
   i By the contrary: the nurseries of beggars are commons as appeareth by fens and forests, of wealthy people the enclosed countries, as *Essex, Somerset, Devon &c.* Fuel which they want in the champion is supplied by inclosures. And labourers increased as are their employments by hedging and ditching.

   ii By comparison: as *Northamptonshire and Somerset*, the one most champion, more ground, little waste, the other all enclosed but inferior in *quantity* and *quality*, yet by advantage of severalty and choice of employment exceeding far in

People for the musters of:

Horses		
Northants.	20 lances	80 light horse
Soms.	50 lances	250 light horse
		60 petronels

Foot		
Northants.	600 trained	600 untrained
Soms.	4000 trained	12000 untrained

Profit or wealth by the:

		£	s.	d.
Subsidy	Northants.	976	1	4
	Soms.	3832	12	10
Fifteenth	Northants.	963	0	0
	Soms.	1138	0	0
Tenths	Northants.	217	0	0
clergy	Soms.	651	0	0

II. Leaving the employment of the ground to discretion of the occupants, so all the houses and land may be maintained in several tenantries, ingrossing being truly the disease and not converting, which may be justified for

1. *Equality*, for the Law of tillage having left *Essex* and many other shires to their choice, and thereby no inconvenience in the state found, and that all arguments alleged for those counties will infer as much for the inland shires of *Northampton*, *Leicester &c.*; and because their situation so remote from any port or navigable river (whereby the charge of carriage far exceeding the full worth of the corn they sell) leaveth to them a disadvantage only, it were more just to give the free employing of their ground to such husbandry as will reduce them to an equality of benefit with the *navigable* shires, which is by grazing (to which their soil is more fit than other counties) whereby the vent of such *their commodities shall be more easy* being by drift *and not by carriage*.

2. For the true balancing of our best commodities, wool and corn (wherein the overweight will appear in the last), for in Henry VIII his time wool was the tod 7d. and 8d., barley (the greatest grain of the inland shires) 6d. and 8d. the bushel. The one is now usually 24d. the tod, the other 18d. and 2od. the strike. So wool risen above two thirds holdeth almost a proportion, with all other commodities treble improved by the increase of moneys, and corn little more than double, is the reason of converting arable; to reduce the profits equal to the husbandman, for keeping the land in divided tenantry. The good individual is the good general, for corn being dearer than cloth or meat comparatively, the husbandman will plough, since his only end is profit; if equal or under, no reason to constrain him, for that law which divideth labour from profit (as the Act of Tillage) is what causeth the great difference of the wealths and abilities of several shires as they are oppressed with that *Statute*.

III. *Depopulation*, which (as all other engrossment) admitteth no defence, doth justly move a course of remedy, which must be for

o

1. Redress of what is already done, either by

    i A new law (for the old is defective and will hardly support an information). And to reach to all is most just, since by no reason *Antiquity* ought to turn mischief into conveniency, when it were more fit that he that by longest offending hath done the most prejudice and received the best benefit, should in the punishment undergo the greatest censure. And therefore it were convenient to tie by Statute all men to hold as their demesne not above the 4th part of any manor, the other 3 to be divided into tenements and no one to exceed 100 acres. And that no man in the same parish should keep two such tenements in his occupation or

or   ii By the authority of Council, as about the 9th of Henry 7, 22 Henry 8, and 4 or 5 of Ed. 6, when the offenders were called up and were by order enjoined to re-edify half as many in every manor as they had decayed and became bound by recognizance, as appeareth in the *Exchequer* in the case of *Andrews of Winwick* and others, from time to time to maintain so many and so much land to them as they were ordered by the Lords to do.

2. Prevention of that to come. And that may best be to cause through the champion countries or the whole kingdom such a survey to be made by commission as was 7th of Edward the First returned into Chancery and at this day called the Hundred Rolls, expressing what land is the lord's demesne and the particular number of all the houses and quantity of land belonging to them in every parish in the kingdom. That done, to enjoin in every parish by a new law that number to be maintained, and the *judges* in their circuits usually to enquire of all defaults therein. And that upon every decay or unpeopling of any of those houses recorded, and no other within the space of one year builded within the same manor or near thereunto with a like quantity of ground annexed to it, it shall be lawful for the Lord Treasurer and the Barons of the *Exchequer* to lease it for 21 years only as a mortmain and demise it for that term to the King's use, and return it in charge into the *Exchequer*.

By redressing the fault of *Depopulation* and leaving enclosing and converting arbitrable as in other shires, the poor man shall be satisfied in his end—habitation, and the gentleman not hindered in his desire—improvement. But as there is now a labour to suit out dwellings for as much stock of people as the common wealth will bear, it must likewise be fit, as good husbands do with their grounds, to provide that you do not overburthen it, but as they do with their increase, remove them to other places, so must the state, either by transferring to the wars or deducing of *colonies*, vent the daily increase that else will surcharge the state, for if in London, a place more contagious than the country, the number of christenings doth weekly by 40 exceed the burials, and that the countries proportionally doth equal if not outgo that rate, it cannot be but that in this state, as in a full body, there must break out yearly tumours and impostures as did of late.

SUGGESTIONS FOR FURTHER READING

THE READER will probably want to turn to R. H. Tawney, *The Agrarian Problem in the Sixteenth Century*, London 1912, and perhaps to C. M. Gray, *Copyhold, Equity and the Common Law*, Cambridge, Mass. 1963. He will find E. C. K. Gonner's *Common Land and Inclosure*, London 1912, much the best book on that subject. The farming background is dealt with in E. Kerridge, *The Agricultural Revolution*, London 1967.

Glossary of Legal Terms

fieri facias: fi. fa. for short: a writ wherein the sheriff is commanded that he cause to be made out of the goods and chattels of the defendant the sum for which judgment was given.

formedon: a writ of right used for claiming entailed property, in 3 forms:—(i) in the descender—brought by issue in tail claiming by descent, (ii) in the reverter—brought by reversioner after estate tail is spent, (iii) in the remainder—brought by remainderman after the determination of the estate tail.

habendum: that part of a deed or grant beginning in law Latin *habendum et tenendum* and in English 'to have and to hold'.

in forma pauperis: in the form or guise of a poor person exempt from liability to pay the costs of an action.

modus: short for *modus decimandi:* money payment in lieu of tithe.

mort d'ancestor: assize brought by the rightful heir against one who wrongfully took possession of his inheritance on the death of his ancestor.

novel disseisin: action at law for recovery of seisin of land by one who had himself been recently dispossessed.

par terme d'auter vie(s):   for term of life of another (others).

pendente lite: pending litigation, with lawsuit pending.

quare ejecit infra terminum: action by which a termor could recover the term of years from anyone else claiming title through the lessor.

qui tam: a qui tam action is one brought on a penal statute by an informer who sues for the penalty as well on his own behalf as on that of the Crown.

scire facias: sci. fa. for short: judicial writ requiring the sheriff to make known to the party concerned that he should come before the court to show cause why execution should not be made against him.

summage: toll payable for packhorses.

supersedeas: writ commanding the stay of legal proceedings which ought otherwise to have proceeded, in 2 forms:—(i) supersedes pendente—pendente lite, q.v., and therefore temporary, (ii) supersedeas omnino—altogether and for ever, the proceedings no longer having any foundation.

trespass: breach of law or duty, any actionable wrong, a tort, in 3 main forms:—(i) trespass to person, (ii) trespass to goods, (iii) trespass to land, which consists in wrongful entry in some manner or form, for which the legal remedy is one of the following writs:—(a) trespass quare clausum fregit (de close debruse)—a trespass consisting in, without legal justification, 1. entering upon land in the possession of the plaintiff, or 2. remaining upon such land, or 3. placing or throwing any material object upon it; (b) trespass de ejectione firmae—action of trespass with writ of ejectment whereby a person ousted or amoved from an estate for years might recover damages, and, from 1499, possession thereof; in later forms called writ of ejectment. The above actions were for damages &c. immediate upon the unlawful act. Trespass *on the case* was a form of action in which the damage complained of was not immediate but consequential upon an unlawful act.

INDEX OF PLACES

INDEX OF PERSONS

INDEX OF SUBJECTS